THE SIX

RMS *Titanic.*
(HFX Studios – Alex Moeller and Tom Lynskey, model by Vasilije Ristović)

THE SIX

THE UNTOLD STORY OF THE TITANIC'S CHINESE SURVIVORS

STEVEN SCHWANKERT

PEGASUS BOOKS
NEW YORK LONDON

Pegasus Books, Ltd.
148 West 37th Street, 13th Floor
New York, NY 10018

First Pegasus Books cloth edition April 2025

Cover images:
RMS *Titanic.* (HFX Studios – Alex Moeller and
Tom Lynskey, model by Vasilije Ristović)

Headshots left to right:
A CR10 seaman's identity card for Lam Choi, believed to be the *Titanic* survivor
Ah Lam. (The National Archives 356009)
A possible image of *Titanic* survivor Lee Bing, reproduced from a glass plate, *c.* 1920.
(Courtesy of the Cambridge City Archives, Cambridge, Ontario)
A photo of Fong Wing Sun, believed to be *Titanic* survivor Fang Lang, *c* 1920.
(Courtesy of the Fong Family)
A CR10 seaman's identity card for Yum Hee or Yum Hui,
believed to be the *Titanic* survivor Ling Hee.
(The National Archives 261023)

ISBN: 978-1-63936-867-9

10 9 8 7 6 5 4 3 2 1

Printed in the United States of America
Distributed by Simon & Schuster
www.pegasusbooks.com

CONTENTS

For QX

FOREWORD

When I made my film *Titanic* and told the story of fictional Third-Class passenger Jack Dawson, there was another storyline I filmed and wanted to include. And that was the real-life rescue of a Third-Class passenger, a Chinese man found floating on a piece of wreckage. That man's grit and determination to survive and my admiration for him inspired the now-famous Jack and Rose ending to *Titanic*.

Steven Schwankert and the researchers behind the award-winning documentary *The Six* have brought a little-known aspect of *Titanic* history and the Chinese experience overseas vividly to life. A historian who has spent the last quarter-century exploring China's lakes, rivers and seas, and plunging into the country's rich maritime history, Schwankert and his team solved what was an enduring mystery – the identity and fate of *Titanic*'s six Chinese survivors.

In the more than twenty-five years since *Titanic* was released, we've learned much more about the great ship, its remains and, especially, its passengers. *The Six* is an important story, especially now. It shows us the suffering and perseverance of a group of men who ended up on history's most famous ship. It takes us beyond that fateful night and demonstrates that for the determined and courageous – like these six Chinese men – even a great shipwreck didn't drown their dreams or sink their ambition.

James Cameron
New Zealand, January 2025

NOTES ON MEASUREMENTS AND ROMANISATION

Doing a proper deep dive into *Titanic* history is not unlike biblical archaeology. To produce original research based on fact, rather than a remixed regurgitation of legend and myth, one must put on cotton gloves; get out a pair of tongs; and, word by word, line by line, extract what is factual from any number of suspect eyewitness statements, newspaper interviews, media conjecture and outright lies.

The hulk of the *Titanic* story as we currently know it is encrusted in the rust and barnacles of hearsay and history. As such, we must chisel away numerous layers of impacted half-truths and nonsense to expose the bare metal that is the facts of *Titanic*'s sinking and the survival of the Chinese passengers aboard it.

To do this, I begin with the premise that the testimony given at both official inquiries into the sinking – the United States Senate Inquiry and the British Wreck Commissioner's Inquiry – forms the bedrock of the factual case regarding *Titanic*'s loss. We know that this testimony is, in places, flawed or inaccurate and that will be addressed or considered on an individual basis. It is also, of course, incomplete, because several main figures in the *Titanic* story, including Captain Edward Smith, Chief Officer Henry Wilde and First Officer William Murdoch, went down with the ship. However, it does form the official record and, as such, it gives us the ability to consider the primary question regarding each person's testimony or account: could the person have been chronologically and physically present to witness the circumstances he or she is describing?

Beyond the testimony, there are statements that individuals made to the press, either close to the time of the sinking or later in life, perhaps in personal letters. The same standard applies: could the individual have seen what they claim to have seen, or are they merely repeating things they heard or read elsewhere?

Some researchers take every person's statement at face value: where they were, when they were there and what they saw. That is at minimum naïve and at worst borders on reckless disregard for the truth in a story strewn with conjecture and genuine misinformation. The approach chosen for this book is to place known and verifiable facts at its centre so that accurate conclusions may be drawn from new and existing research.

Chinese Names

For the historian and storyteller, China from 1912 and throughout the twentieth century is a rich canvas upon which to work, with plenty of conflict, revolution and upheaval to twist the lives of that country's people, leaving their stories for us to untangle today. This early-century chaos has left us with two established Romanisation systems for Mandarin Chinese words rendered in English, and a whole lot of approximations of other dialects, including Cantonese and Toisan, handed down to us without enforced standardisation. At the heart of this story are the names of eight Chinese passengers who sailed aboard *Titanic*, and even after years of research, we still don't know exactly the origin of those Romanised names.

To minimise the confusion the contemporary reader (and this writer) will encounter, all place names are rendered as they would be pronounced today in Mandarin (except Hong Kong, which shall remain as is), using the Hanyu Pinyin system, which gives us spellings including Beijing and Taishan. 'Toisan' will be used to refer to the dialect spoken in Taishan and Taishan will refer to that area of Guangdong province. All given names will be rendered as they appear on official documents at the time, including immigration forms, shipping records and White Star Line tickets. This choice is made only for simplification of the text – it implies no political allegiance or fondness.

Chinese characters used in the text are traditional. The Chinese *Titanic* passengers would have used traditional characters, and so again it is an editorial choice for consistency.

As is Chinese custom, a person's surname appears first, with any given names appearing after that. For example, Lee Bing's family name is Lee, not Bing. He would be Mr Lee.

Measurements and weights will be presented in both the metric and imperial systems unless quoting from documents that specify only one.

INTRODUCTION

Finding the story of eight Chinese passengers of the RMS *Titanic* was akin to panning for gold, only to find a river of diamonds. I never expected there were any major new stories of the world's most heavily researched maritime disaster to be found.

My own journey began with a completely different maritime disaster. In 2013, I began researching a Chinese ship that sank in 1948, claiming more than 2,000 lives. Originally, the intent was to tell the tale of China's biggest maritime disaster, which had been almost completely forgotten, despite happening in the middle of the twentieth century. Its massive loss of life and the mysterious circumstances surrounding its sinking made it a story that I felt needed to be told. In preparing to present that story for the first time to an English-language audience and seeking the best way to contextualise the scale of that disaster for an audience outside China, I thought that the only comparable circumstance that readers would readily understand would be *Titanic*.

My research and interviews with survivors of the Chinese shipwreck progressed. I went back to my shelf of *Titanic* books, including classics such as Walter Lord's *A Night to Remember*, checking the countless pages of voluminous research now available online – and that's when the work suddenly shifted course.

I knew there had been Chinese passengers aboard *Titanic*; it's the kind of detail that I noticed after spending almost my entire working life – more than twenty years – in China. But there was scant detail on the eight men, six of whom survived, and I wasn't working on anything *Titanic*-related at the time. Besides, what more could be discovered about *Titanic*? The wreck was found more than thirty years ago, all the survivors are now dead and James Cameron's film has set the story in cinematic stone. I bookmarked a page referencing the Chinese passengers and continued with my research.

As someone who lies in bed, stares at the ceiling and ponders questions about shipwrecks, I found my contemplations shift from pondering the unsolved mystery of a Chinese ship, and instead I started to obsess about the Chinese passengers. Who were they? Why were they on *Titanic*? Why did such a high percentage of the group survive? What happened to them after they reached New York?

I got to work on this project – this book and a documentary, also called *The Six* – with my creative partner Arthur Jones, a British documentary filmmaker based in Shanghai. As our research progressed, we began to think of the group of Chinese passengers as characters akin to Rosencrantz and Guildenstern in Shakespeare's *Hamlet*. Third-Class passengers and workers who went on to live largely successful lives overseas, they may have been minor characters in the history of the twentieth century, but their respective stories would surface at opportune moments of major significance and shine an important light on both the major players and the wider story.

The story of *The Six* brings to the fore various factors that determined the course of the Chinese experience in the late nineteenth and early twentieth centuries: the waves of migrant labourers coming primarily from southern China; the overthrow of the imperial system in China with the Xinhai Revolution, shortly before *Titanic*'s launch and loss, and its resulting street-level social impact; the US Chinese Exclusion Act and similar anti-Chinese immigration laws in Canada and the United Kingdom; and the integration of Chinese immigrants into communities around the world by both the survivors of the shipwreck and their descendants.

This book seeks to answer many questions and raise many more. Were they heroes? Were they cowards? Or were they just lucky? What happened to the six survivors after they reached New York? Why did they seemingly disappear from history? And could one of the two Chinese passengers who perished at sea be buried in a *Titanic* cemetery in Halifax, Nova Scotia?

For the first time, *The Six* allows the Chinese passengers' part of *Titanic*'s story to be told meaningfully. Until now, they have languished in infamy, have been derided as stowaways and were largely airbrushed out of the famous shipwreck's story. Now, these men may finally gain their rightful place in *Titanic* history, more than a century after that memorable night.

Steven Schwankert
New Jersey, June 2024

SECTION I

I

A PIECE OF WOOD

The man took a deep breath and pushed off as the ground disappeared below him. By stepping into the water, he was attempting to save his own life. Instead, he felt like he was choosing a certain death.

Frigid water punched him in the stomach and forced almost all the carefully drawn breath out of him. On his hands and neck, the salty liquid felt like it was stabbing him with thousands of tiny needles, each trying to burrow and draw out any heat remaining in his body. Slowly, it seeped through the layers of cotton and wool that had protected him for hours on the cold night. The shirts, jacket and coat worked in the air, but against water they were almost powerless.

The screams of the dying surrounded him. There were female voices and male voices. Not long before, some of these gentlemen had gallantly put their families in boats and stepped back, seemingly accepting their fate. Now the same men cried out for anyone to save them, their evening clothes not protecting them against the cold. Women wailed for someone to save their children. The new-moon night covered them in darkness from the moment the ship's lights went out for the last time. In the lifeboats nearby, the ones who had benefited from the gentlemen's acts of selflessness kept their distance, afraid that the unfortunates in the water would swamp them if they returned to assist.

He remembered when he had first swum off the island where he grew up, a forgotten refuge for the survivors of a dynasty that Kublai

Khan had crushed 800 years before. There, the water was clear and warm. Now he swam through black and cold water, looking for a lifeboat, looking for something – anything.

In just a few minutes, he had gone mostly numb, feeling the temperature only on his neck and shoulders, where the air made the water feel even colder. The man did his best to keep his head above the surface, but as each minute passed, his mouth and nose went under more and more. The life jacket helped to counter the weight of his saturated clothes, but the drag made every stroke more difficult.

He didn't know where the others were. Did they get off? Were they in the water too? He thought some of them had made it into a lifeboat, but wasn't sure, distracted by his predicament. He had waited on deck for a boat, but the crew could not get it ready in time. The water came up before the boat could launch, so he chose to swim rather than sink. It will pull me under, he thought, but the rush of air he heard behind never became the suction he feared. Despite years of working as a sailor, this was his first shipwreck. For the moment, at least, he was alive.

Many were already incapacitated or dead. The man swam among them, each body providing a morbid moment of added buoyancy. He wondered whether he should just grab onto one and use the dead to save his own life, but he moved on. Keep swimming, he thought. Keep swimming, or you'll end up like them.

But it was becoming a struggle. The ocean was barely above freezing, the air only slightly warmer. Somewhere out there was a mountain of frozen water, a black island in the middle of the Atlantic that had ripped the ship open and begun its slow but inevitable death.

The noise around him began to subside. The cold had claimed some; others just gave up. Most audible was his gurgling and spouting that accompanied every breath. He had to push himself up to breathe on almost every stroke now. He could not hear or see any boats nearby.

Suddenly, his hand hit something solid. It did not disappear under the water when he pushed on it. He slapped at it. It was big and thick. He raised his other hand to touch it. It felt like a door or maybe a table. The man pulled himself on top of it and pushed the object underneath him. He could just barely get out of the water. He almost toppled back in as it shifted, but he balanced himself. There were no waves to jostle him but to make sure he didn't slide off, the man undid his belt and lashed himself to the object as best he could. The cold had made him feel drunk, commands emerging from his brain but travelling too slowly to his arms and fingers.

It was quiet now. The ocean made no noise, and those in the water were still. There was no light except the stars – so many of them, but so dim. The air was cold, but not like the water had been, at least, it didn't feel that way. The ship didn't get me and the water didn't get me, but I will die here anyway tonight, he thought.

Then there was a flash, not a bright one, but a light from somewhere. It flashed again. The light was moving back and forth, and it seemed to be getting slowly closer. Someone was yelling out in English. The man tried to say, 'Here! Here!' in English, but he could not. He could barely move.

The light was on a boat with a few men aboard it. It was coming closer.

'Here! Here!'

The men on the boat could not hear him but they were approaching him. The light fell upon him, and the man moved, tried to reach out to them, but could not lift his arm.

'Here! Here!'

The officer on the boat shouted and pointed the light toward the man floating on a piece of wood. The officer and mate reached down and lifted the man out of the water, almost a dead weight, wrapped in cold, soaked clothes. The rescued man – who appeared to the officer to be Chinese, or maybe Filipino – thanked the seamen again and again, although he wasn't sure if he was forming the words.

The boat continued searching, the officer calling out and shining the light, but no one else was found alive. Two others had been rescued before the man was pulled from the water. One of them, a portly First-Class passenger, had died.

A few hours later, as dawn broke, a big ship began to approach the constellation of lifeboats spread out across the surface of the water. Slowly, the boats made their way alongside the larger vessel, the man catching sight of its name – Carpathia. Still cold, still exhausted, at least now his limbs functioned properly when he had to reach up and grab the rope net that served as a ladder onto the rescue ship.

Aboard *Carpathia*, he found his compatriots. But not all of them were there.

Years later, in a letter home to family, he recalled the night in a poem:

The sky is high, the waves come rolling by
A piece of wood saves my life
I see my brothers, three or four
The tears roll down as I laugh[1]

2

THE WORLD IN 1912

In 1912, humankind was on the move, building bigger machines and pushing them to the horizon. Many people – mostly men – were searching for work for the first time, not just over the hill but across oceans, farther from their homes than they had ever imagined.

When workers in Northern Ireland hammered the first rivet into place on the steel hulk that would become RMS *Titanic*, railways and steamships had already existed for decades, but as the new century began, people began demanding superlatives in their travel: bigger, further, faster. At the start of the twentieth century, humans were finally reaching the furthest points on the globe. In 1909, American Robert Peary and his team became the first known humans to stand on the geographic North Pole, while Norwegian explorer Roald Amundsen and his expedition arrived at the South Pole in December 1911. Although climbers had reached the top of the highest mountains in Africa and South America at the end of the nineteenth century, summiting the world's highest peaks in the Himalayas and the Karakorum were decades away. Slowly, surely, the world was becoming a smaller, or at least more accessible, place.

In the air, as early as 1875, Count Ferdinand von Zeppelin had been fooling around with designs for airships that combined a giant balloon filled with hydrogen and a gondola that could be attached to carry pilots and a navigation assembly, along with cargo, passengers and weapons. On 24 April 1912, the Imperial German Navy ordered its first Zeppelin for military use. But airships remained in their nascent stage and the idea of using them for a transatlantic passenger service was no closer than space travel.

Two brothers in the United States, Orville and Wilbur Wright, made their first successful aeroplane flights in 1903. But almost a decade later, humans were not measurably closer to flying in them from one continent to another. Like airships, militaries eyed aeroplanes for use in reconnaissance or aerial bombardment, but not for the large-scale transport of people or machines.

Wealthy people began to buy automobiles for recreation and local transportation but, although their popularity was growing, the Ford Motor Co. didn't open its first assembly line to build cars until 1913. However, the slow adoption of the automobile initiated a transformation that would last throughout the rest of the century.

Although no country was even close to being 50 per cent connected, electrification was altering the landscape in large cities around the world and starting to creep out toward more rural areas. Cities like London, New York and Shanghai all had electric streetlights before 1900, but delivering power to dense urban populations was easier and less expensive than stretching kilometres of new power lines to serve fewer customers. The construction of new improved roads suitable for automobiles also paved the way for power lines to be installed alongside them.

In the first years of the twentieth century, coal powered the world. It heated homes, powered factories and provided the fuel that pushed trains down the track and great ships across the oceans. They may have been called steamships, but coal fires generated all the necessary steam. When the White Star Line's passenger ship *Olympic* made its maiden voyage from Southampton, England, to New York in 1910, it used about 3,500 tons of the black stuff, averaging a speed of 21.7 knots (about 40kmh/25mph). Oil as a potential fuel source was discovered in quantity in 1875 but remained a decade or so away from widespread exploitation and use.

With aircraft and automobiles not yet viable, to cover significant distances by land, one boarded a train. Massive rail networks already stretched across North America, parts of Europe, India and from Moscow to Manchuria. If a person wanted to cross an ocean in

1912, one bought a ticket on a regularly scheduled voyage, preferably aboard the swiftest ship one could afford.

The tallest building in the world, the Woolworth Building at 233 Broadway in New York, was in the final stages of completion, reaching 792ft (241.4m). It would hold that title for eighteen years.

Mass communications and media came mostly from the printed word, namely books and large-circulation newspapers. The year's bestsellers show English-language readers' interest in their wider world – or at least, fanciful, fictionalised versions of it. Arthur Conan Doyle, best known as the creator of Sherlock Holmes, sold bushels of *The Lost World*, about an expedition to the Amazon that discovers prehistoric animals, including dinosaurs – a Jurassic Park before there was *Jurassic Park*. Swinging out of the trees came Edgar Rice Burroughs' *Tarzan of the Apes*, a human raised by non-human primates in an African jungle.

Silent films were becoming popular. Films at the time were fifteen to twenty minutes in length, with title cards instead of recorded dialogue, and were often accompanied by a live organist or orchestra in the cinema. Directors like D.W. Griffith and Mack Sennett directed multiple films per year, and early performers like brothers John and Lionel Barrymore, sisters Lillian and Dorothy Gish, and Mary Pickford became known to the public.

The technology to record and play music existed, but a phonograph or early Victrola player was still out of the financial reach of the average person. People enjoyed playing music at home. Live music and theatrical performances were well established and popular, especially in cities, along with touring musicians and circuses that would visit more far-flung areas.

Sports leagues in Europe and North America were starting to take shape. In the United States, sixteen teams, all in cities east of the Mississippi River, opened the Major League Baseball season. The Boston Red Sox began 1912 on the road against the New York Highlanders. The visitors looked forward to inaugurating their new home stadium, Fenway Park, on 20 April. Later that year, American university teams would play the first season of modern college football, with new rules, including four downs, or attempts to gain 10 yards, awarding 6 points for a touchdown score instead of 5 and shortening the field to 100 yards in length – rules that remain in force today, both in college and professional American football.

In the United Kingdom, Blackburn Rovers won their first English Football League title. Then, as now, twenty teams in the top division played thirty-eight matches, with Blackburn finishing above their nearest rival, Everton. Preston North End and Bury were relegated. In cricket, England retained the Ashes and won the sole instalment of a competition called the Triangular Tournament on home ground, defeating the only other two test nations at the time – Ashes rival Australia and third opponent South Africa.

Stockholm, Sweden, hosted the 1912 Summer Olympics from 6–22 July, with twenty-eight nations, almost all from North America and Europe, along with Australasia (a combined Australia and New Zealand team); Chile; Egypt; South Africa; Turkey; and, in the first Olympic appearance by an Asian nation, Japan. Native American athlete Jim Thorpe won the gold medal in the modern pentathlon and the decathlon, two of the United States' twenty-six golds, the most won by any single country. Hosts Sweden led the total medal count with sixty-five.

Europe and Africa

As of April 1912, the United Kingdom already had its third monarch of the new century. King George V, a grandson of Queen Victoria, had been on the throne for fewer than two years, following the death of his father, King Edward VII. Only a few months earlier, George V became the first and only British monarch to attend his imperial durbar in India. Herbert Henry Asquith of the Liberal Party served as His Majesty's Prime Minister. Britain remained the world's greatest power, ruling from the world's largest city, London, with the sun always shining upon the Union Jack somewhere.

Europe was enjoying an extended period of peace, but the undercurrents of revolution and war were already coursing through the continent. In Vienna, an aspiring artist named Adolf Hitler made a living as a day labourer and on the side, sold his watercolour paintings of city landmarks – paintings that seldom included any depictions of his fellow Viennese, or any other people, for that matter. In between making mediocre art and other odd jobs, he first began to consume antisemitic literature and form his diabolical ideas about the Jews and where he thought they belonged in European society.

An established Russian political revolutionary, Vladimir Lenin, had taken up residence in Paris and seized upon the works of dead German economist and philosopher Karl Marx. In January 1912, Lenin and his followers broke away from other Russian socialists and formed an organisation that would later become colloquially known as the Bolsheviks.

In South Africa, an Indian lawyer and activist named Mohandas Gandhi had begun advocating non-violent resistance to racist policies there, founding a utopian community called Tolstoy Farm near Johannesburg.

North America

The increasing wealth, industrial output and military might of the United States had grown during the nineteenth century, and waves of immigration there continued. The year began with forty-six states and ended with forty-eight. New Mexico became the forty-seventh state on 6 January, with Arizona finally joining on 14 February to realise Manifest Destiny, a political and military philosophy that expanded the growing country from the Atlantic Ocean to the Pacific. That year, the Governor of New Jersey, Democrat Woodrow Wilson, and incumbent Republican President William Howard Taft campaigned against each other in the election for US President. Former President Theodore Roosevelt would join the race later in the year, after failing to win the Republican Party's nomination.

One of the world's wealthiest people, and one of its most famous in 1912, was an American. John Jacob Astor IV was his family's youngest child and only son, born in 1864 in New York. On his way to greater renown and riches, Astor found success writing a science fiction novel, *A Journey in Other Worlds*, before financing and serving in his own unit during the Spanish-American War in 1898. Eventually, he began investing in real estate and built the Astoria Hotel, abutting a similar building that had been constructed by a rival cousin, William Waldorf Astor, called the Waldorf Hotel.

Astor was an avid sailor and enjoyed taking his yacht *Nourmahal* along the American coast and to the Caribbean. He lent the boat to the US Navy during the Spanish-American War. Despite his apparent love for the sea, Astor did not have much luck while on it. A mishap in September 1893 led to him beaching the yacht on a bank of the Hudson River and made the front page of *The New York Times*.[1]

In a separate incident, Astor set sail aboard *Nourmahal* on 5 November 1909 from Port Antonio, on Jamaica's north-east coast, but then went missing for more than two weeks. The captain of a cargo ship, SS *Annetta*, claimed he spotted the 250ft (76.2m) yacht on about 14 November, near the island of San Salvador. A hurricane swept through the area and the disappearance led many in the press and New York society to fear the worst.

Astor eventually arrived in San Juan, Puerto Rico, on 21 November, unaffected by the storm. Ultimately, the facts disproved *Annetta*'s sighting: to be in San Salvador on 14 November would have put Astor's yacht about 250 miles (400km) off course, more than the distance between Port Antonio and San Juan.

Asia

In Thailand, Vajiravudh, also known as King Rama VI, survived an attempted coup to retain absolute rule. In Japan, Emperor Mutsuhito, later known as Emperor Meiji, was nearing the end of his reign and the period of reform he championed. Following his death in July, Emperor Taisho assumed the throne. At the time, Japan controlled large parts of China, including the Liaodong Peninsula (now mostly Liaoning Province) and the island of Taiwan. Japan had officially colonised Korea in 1910 and remained in control of the Korean Peninsula.

During the second half of 1911, Outer Mongolia seized upon the crumbling authority of China's Qing Dynasty and shook off Chinese rule, with tacit approval from Russia, forming the Bogd Khanate of Mongolia.

No country in the world saw more turmoil in 1912 than China. In October 1911, the Xinhai Revolution began as a military uprising in the central city of Wuhan, then caught fire across the country, ending millennia of imperial rule and declaring the brittle Republic of China (ROC) on 1 January. For the first time in 5,000 years, China's people would be ruled by someone other than an emperor – and by a government that was not absolute. The Qing Dynasty had failed to fend off foreign incursions and interference from all directions, and the nation's people had suffered from internal rebellions and natural disasters that made their lives unbearable. While China attempted to move away from its imperial past, events and economic conditions that had been initiated decades earlier continued to influence the hundreds of thousands of Chinese who had already begun to leave the country to find work elsewhere.

3

FROM THE FOUR
COUNTIES
TO THE WORLD

We know little about the early life of a man who travelled across the
world, took on many names, worked a variety of jobs, spent thirty-
five years in the United States as an undocumented migrant, and
survived the world's most famous shipwreck along the way. But we
know that Fong Wing Sun (方榮山) could swim, and we imagine
that as a boy he paddled through the warm, clear water of the South
China Sea that surrounded his island home.[1] Perhaps he thought for a
moment that he was swimming like one of the ducks that his family
raised in a nearby pond. Maybe we can bring the ducks down here to
the saltwater next time and we can swim together, he thought. He
turned and swam back to where his father was standing, knowing it
was time to go home.

Xiachuan Island was probably not where the remaining members
of the Southern Song Dynasty court (1127–1279) expected they
would end up. Most likely, they had never even heard of it until their
wet feet first stepped upon its sands. But it seemed like the perfect
hiding place for people fleeing the armies of Kublai Khan: it was a

beyond-the-horizon island that was out of sight, and hopefully out of the minds, of people who wanted to kill them.

Xiachuan was far from unknown. Mariners used it as a navigational landmark, turning south from there to head toward South East Asia. Not all were so lucky; hundreds of shipwrecks fill the waters around it and its larger neighbouring Shangchuan Island, including the South China Sea No. 1 treasure ship, which was discovered in 1983. But it probably wasn't any better known to the Yuan Dynasty (1279–1368) than it was to the former Song leaders. They found safety there.

Centuries later, the island's long-time inhabitants still see themselves as the Song survivors. The Chinese they speak is mutually unintelligible with today's standard Mandarin – they are more likely to find someone in New York or Vancouver's Chinatown who will understand them than they are in Beijing.

A few years into the twentieth century, several dozen kilometres from that island and back on the mainland, a teenager knew that his time at what he called home would soon be coming to an end. Growing up in Hengtang village (橫糖村), Lee Bing (李炳) faced the same pressures that other young men in Taishan faced: no path to the family's property and few, if any, employment opportunities locally. Like so many other men from the Taishan (台山) region before him, Lee Bing's future likely lay elsewhere. The year 1912 had seen massive political upheaval in China as the revolution threw off thousands of years of imperial system, but economic forces at work in southern China and elsewhere were already narrowing the future choices for men born in Taishan at the end of the nineteenth century.

For the Chinese men who would later travel on *Titanic*, at least two, Fong Wing Sun and Lee Bing, were known to be from different parts of Taishan, and it is likely that more – or perhaps even all eight – came from there. The families they loved and sought to support would benefit from their labour without the pleasure of their company. Regular remittances would make life for those who stayed behind easier. In some cases, the overseas sons even built houses in their home villages.

While still under the guise of a temporary departure, at least half of these men left Taishan permanently. They carried their language and customs across the world with them, the way that all expatriates do, but many of them never returned.

*

The boy walked down the main street carrying his books. It wasn't far from school to his home, only a few minutes away – a round trip he made twice a day. School in the morning, back home for lunch, return to school, then home at the end of the day. Sometimes, when it rained hard, his mother made a small lunch for him to eat and he stayed at school for the whole day. Trees shaded much of the walk, which was a relief during the hot months of the year. The school had been built by Christian missionaries, but his teachers were all from their village.

Little Fong Wing Sun liked studying, and particularly he liked writing, both in Chinese and the little bit of English that he was learning. His letters were boxy – all straight lines and right-angle turns, no curves.

The Fong family's village was on some of the best land on Xiachuan Island. Away from both the coast and the island's high hills, they were protected from flooding and landslides. The Fong house was a simple one, with two and a half rooms: one for sleeping, one for general living and food preparation and then a small kitchen area for cooking. His father kept talking about adding some space on top of the house, but it hadn't happened yet.

When he came home from school, Wing Sun put down his books and swept the floor as he was told to do every day. He then tried to finish any school assignments he had before it got too dark to read outside. Working by candlelight was hard on his eyes and it made him tired. Every night his father told him and his brothers and sister to go to sleep, and if Wing Sun was lucky, his father's snoring didn't wake him up.

Wing Sun wondered about the future. Even with his schooling, what would he be able to do? Be a farmer like his father? He read about China's great ancient armies, but to him, his island was China, was the world. Could he travel to Guangzhou someday, even to Beijing where the emperor lived?

The next day, as he walked to school, Wing Sun couldn't stop thinking about the rest of the world. Did it really exist, or was it just a story, like the other stories in his books? Would he ever get to see any of it?

Taishan Today

If you visit Taishan today, you could be forgiven for failing to recognise it as one of the epicentres of the Chinese diaspora. Called '*Toisan*' or '*Hoisan*' in the local dialect, and not to be confused with the sacred mountain in Shandong Province of the same name and Romanised spelling, the area in central southern Guangdong Province includes what is referred to as the '*si yi*' in Mandarin or '*sei yap*' locally, both meaning 'the four counties', namely Enping (locally pronounced *Yanping*), Kaiping (*Hoiping*), Taishan (*Toisan*) and Xinhui (*Sunwui*). Politically, the area was subsumed into Jiangmen Prefecture in 1951.

Taishan natives are quick to point out that this relatively recent reorganisation used to be the other way around. Given this realignment, the area may now also be referred to as the Five Counties. In 2022, Jiangmen Prefecture had a population of about 4.8 million and a size of almost 9,500 square km (3,668 square miles), with Jiangmen as its largest city.[2]

Kaiping remains a popular tourist destination today, thanks to the presence of the distinctive *diaolou*, several fortified structures built at the end of the nineteenth century to provide families with protection against armed bandits that occasionally raided the area. The city of Taishan features several pedestrian streets containing homes and storefronts, all built with money provided by those who had emigrated overseas and wanted to demonstrate their gratitude for the support and well-being of relatives back home.

As of 2021, the population of the Four Counties stands at about 1 million, with most of those residents still classified as rural. Notably, no airport serves Taishan directly; visitors from parts of China or overseas usually fly into Zhuhai, just north of Macau, then proceed by bus or car for about ninety minutes to two hours. The smaller Guangdong city of Foshan also has an airport 55km from Jiangmen, which is more often used by domestic travellers. A regional rail service takes passengers to and from Guangzhou or Zhanjiang on the coast. The area is also accessible via a series of highways.

Enjoying a subtropical climate, today the area looks fertile and prosperous, although not as much as other parts of Guangdong further east, specifically the cities part of the Pearl River Delta that form a halo around Hong Kong. Including late-twentieth-century boomtowns like Guangzhou, Shenzhen and Dongguan, it is those cities that became the heart of China's initial economic growth engine after reform and opening in 1979. Although far from impoverished, central Taishan can't compare to its eastern neighbours for neon and pure economic firepower; its average income is about half that of the residents of the Pearl River Delta cities.

Taishan became the initial centre for Chinese labour immigration because of both success and misfortune and also political geography. The Guangdong coastal area in general developed beyond a strictly agrarian economy more quickly than surrounding provinces. This saw the rise not only of increased agricultural productivity and the planting of cash crops, but also basic manufacturing of goods that required labour, included the growing of tobacco, the making of textiles and some mining. This kind of success is good for the economy, landlords and manufacturers, but not necessarily for large families – at least, not the younger sons of large families, who are reliant upon inheritance for their own future subsistence.

The Taishan area's ports never developed as fully or quickly as those that were first used and later colonised by European imperial powers. Hong Kong and Macau already existed as major points for trade, and even today, the port of Taishan is dwarfed by those elsewhere in Hong Kong and Shenzhen. As such, the region never received the investment that flowed into neighbouring coastal cities, and its population did not move away from agriculture as a primary economic activity as quickly. Still, the foreign trade that developed along the coast began to act as a magnet for labour and had an impact on the economy of the rest of the province.

In the first half of the 1800s, despite a good climate and a plethora of arable land, a trio of plagues descended upon the area, each exacerbating the other. The first came in the form of military conflict with Western powers, namely France and the United Kingdom, known colloquially as the Opium Wars. Flaring up sporadically between 1839 and 1842, this series of engagements resulted in the ceding of Hong Kong Island to the UK, and the later ninety-nine-year leasing of the surrounding area, which is still referred to as the New Territories. It also opened Guangzhou as a port to foreign trade.

This conflict was the first in a series of disruptions afflicting Taishan. It might never have become an early source for emigrant labour from China, but combined with local Confucian tradition that saw the raising of large families as a duty and a sign of prosperity, a reduction in the amount of usable farmland meant that even a stable population was more than that area could support. Able-bodied sons are an asset when working tracts of land but when sons outnumbered acreage, a big family became a liability.

In 1843, Hong Xiuquan (洪秀全), a would-be civil servant originally from Guangdong, had a fever dream that led him to the conclusion that he was the brother of Jesus Christ and that his brother had commanded him to overthrow the 'devils' of the ruling Qing Dynasty. The Qing, who were ethnically Manchu from north-eastern China, were despised by many of the majority Han Chinese. That ethnic disparity provided fervour even for Taiping troops, who may not have shared Hong's Christian faith.

Hong co-founded a quasi-Christian sect, the Society of God Worshippers,[3] which was as much anti-Manchu as it was Christian. When some of Hong's followers were arrested in Guangxi in 1850, it became an armed conflict and began a rebellion against the Qing Dynasty that would last for the next fourteen years. During this period, Hong and his followers, who took their name from the Taiping Heavenly Kingdom that they sought to establish, assembled a force of as many as 2 million troops, both infantry and cavalry, and killed an estimated 20–30 million soldiers and civilians – mostly the latter.

During this period, Qing Dynasty government services, such as they were at the time, were disrupted, and young men were sought for conscription into the Qing army. Additional taxes were levied on landowners to finance the war against the Taipings. While Guangdong itself was not a major battleground during the rebellion, the Qing government actively persecuted members of the Hakka, or 'guest people', minority there. Although ethnically Han Chinese, the Hakka are linguistically distinct, tracing their history to central China, from which point they migrated or were pushed south, perhaps as part of a political persecution dating back as far as 200 BC. Hong, the Taiping leader, was himself Hakka, and the Qing Dynasty viewed other Hakka as being in league with him, although support for the Taipings among the group was far from universal.

A separate violent struggle took place, on and off, around the same time. The Red Turban Rebellion had the similar intent of restoring the Ming Dynasty, but instead of being sparked by religious fervour, the initiators were the Heaven and Earth Society, whose members at the time wore red headdresses that led their uprising to be named the Red Turban Rebellion by Western observers. This, in turn, reignited conflict in the Four Counties area between existing Han Chinese residents of Guangdong and Hakka settlers, which may have ultimately resulted in 1 million deaths.

With an excess of labour and a shortage of land, a rebel army and the imperial backlash against it, as well as regular clashes with menacing foreign powers, Taishan seemed suddenly unappealing to young men who were not in line to inherit land. The combination of economic need and opportunity elsewhere led to the beginnings of a migrant labour force that would continue for the next eighty years.

*

However, smack in the middle of the nineteenth century, alongside smouldering domestic conflicts affecting the area, one event changed the course of Taishan's history. Gold was discovered thousands of kilometres away, first in California in 1848 and then in Australia in 1851.

Although migrant labour had always existed in some form, there had been little need or opportunity for large numbers of Chinese workers outside of China. Since the Ming Dynasty it had been officially for a Chinese person to leave Chinese territory, as the emperor liked to keep all his subjects nearby. That said, no local official would bother to prosecute a Chinese person returning from overseas, although he might tax the person some of his earnings. Few, if any, Chinese lived in Europe, North America or even elsewhere in Asia, despite the first known Chinatown having existed in Manila, Philippines, since 1590. The so-called China trade was largely conducted in Chinese cities by foreign buyers dealing with Chinese merchants, although Chinese sailors also participated. Those same buyers may also have brought and sold foreign goods, even if demand for foreign goods in China was generally weak.

This demand for Chinese workers does not include the so-called 'coolie' labour trade in the first half of the nineteenth century, when Chinese labourers were sent to Latin America and South East Asia as indentured servants, exchanging a fixed period of work, usually seven years, for the promise of a plot of land upon completion. Many died either during the journey or the agreed period of labour and some ended up as virtual slaves, unable to pay off the agreed debt they had promised to work.

When gold was discovered, California was an American-controlled territory but not yet a state, having been won from Mexico in the Mexican–American War of 1846–48. While it quickly became the most populous of the United States, at the time it was also considered an unwelcoming frontier. Getting there from both the rest of the United States and the rest of the world required an arduous, overland journey or a long and similarly treacherous sea voyage.

The discovery of gold changed that immediately. The first gold strike came closer to what is now Nevada than the coast and occurred only days before the United States assumed formal control over the California territory. Gold had arguably fuelled the exploration and settling of the Western Hemisphere, so the precious metal's ability to spur great change and irrational action was nothing new. But for the first time individuals, rather than governments and national commercial concerns, would be the initial direct beneficiaries of this find. Suddenly, the race was on to get to California and dig out as much gold as possible before it was gone.

For Chinese workers, especially the young men of Taishan, this was an entirely new proposition. Besides a dangerous trip across the Pacific Ocean, finding the money required to make the journey and the inherent risks of travelling overland in the mid-nineteenth century, there were no particular barriers to Chinese wanting to stake their claim. No identity documents were necessary to leave China and none were needed to land in California. Of course, a Chinese miner or camp worker could find himself – and at this time, it was always men – assaulted, bullied or killed by other miners. But that treatment was not reserved for the Chinese: Black miners, Native Americans and even those of other European descent could also be victims of violence in the lawless lands of the gold fields. While some Chinese miners did work independently, most hired themselves out as workers to larger mining operations.

The would-be miners did not intend to immigrate. They planned to go to California, work until they made their fortune and then return to China. Immigration issues did not arise at that time because there was no such plan. Starved for labour in a suddenly booming territory that needed all the strong backs and strong hands they could recruit, California immigration policy was not particularly picky – not for the time being, at least.

*

One day, close to his twelfth birthday, Wing Sun's father met him on the way home from school. This was out of the ordinary; he normally only saw his father at night. 'Wing Sun, this year you will finish school. It's time for you to start working.'

The boy was shocked, but even with his gaping mouth, he said, 'Yes, Father.' There was no other answer – no negotiation and no chance for a different outcome. He turned and looked in the direction of his school, trying to turn away from his future instead.

He shouldn't have been surprised. His schooling would end in a couple of years anyway; it was only a primary school. Many of the boys in the village and on the island had left to go to work. His brothers had stayed, but his father needed them. It seemed like they could handle the family's work without him. The others were finding jobs away from the island in other countries, like the United Kingdom and the United States. He didn't really understand what that meant, why they had to go so far.

Wing Sun's father said that a man he knew would arrange something for him. First, he would travel to Hong Kong, and once there, the man would help him find a job. Wing Sun didn't ask the questions that came to mind: How will I come home from Europe or the United States to celebrate Spring Festival every year? How will I speak to foreigners when they don't speak Chinese and I don't speak … whatever they speak?

On the last day of school, Wing Sun thanked his teacher and said he would not be returning for the next term, that he would go to find work. 'Keep reading, Wing Sun. You are smart. Keep reading,' the teacher said.

A few days after the term ended, Wing Sun's father told him he would be leaving on Thursday. On Wednesday night, his mother prepared a special meal, with braised chicken, pork, even some local oysters. Wing Sun, his father and brothers even drank a bit of liquor that his father had made, wishing him a safe journey. He packed his things in a cloth bag.

His mother had made him a couple of new shirts and a pair of pants. Along with those, he added a blanket, a small cooking pot, a bowl, a pair of chopsticks and a spoon. It's hard to pack for a trip when you don't really know how long you'll be gone or where you will be going.

The Migration Begins

The news about gold in California travelled quickly, and the first Chinese miners arrived before the end of 1848. The first few years of the Gold Rush saw hundreds of Chinese miners arrive, but that number quickly swelled to 20,000 in 1852. The rapid surge in numbers and the intense competition for gold led to negative and sometimes violent opposition from European miners. Still, that did not deter a further 20,000 Chinese from going to California by the end of the decade, unconcerned about threats and diminishing returns on gold strikes.

A small economy developed to support the Chinese miners and their needs. Entrepreneurs realised that a good living could be made by opening restaurants, selling mining equipment and providing other services, including money transfers and even prostitution. Although some merchants brought their wives to California, prostitution was sadly one of the few sources of work for inbound Chinese female immigrants at the time.

As more Chinese arrived, social institutions transplanted from China began to take hold. *Sze Yup* associations formed to help new arrivals adjust to their new environment. Vestiges of those organisations still exist in San Francisco and other parts of the United States.

California became part of the United States in 1850, with the US Government keen to ensure that the territory would be under federal control. With a state government subsequently formed and then with full representation in the federal government, more formal opposition to the influx of Chinese immigration began. However, after California achieved statehood, and with the United States spreading across the North American continent in its so-called 'Manifest Destiny', the growing nation needed to unify its west with its east. To solidify political control, spur settlement of the Midwest and boost trade, the United States began the construction of transcontinental railroads.

During the Gold Rush, Chinese workers had proven their willingness to work hard for little money. These were just the kind of labourers that railroad construction needed. A new wave of Chinese immigrant workers began to arrive in the 1860s specifically for this purpose.

There was another reason Chinese workers were in such high demand: more than 600,000 men were killed during the American Civil War, fought from 1861–65. Although mostly white, that number also included Black soldiers, Native Americans and perhaps Asians. Taking on the crushing labour that would be required to build massive national railways would mean importing workers, at least temporarily.

In the end, despite mistreatment and lower wages than non-Chinese workers, the Chinese railroad builders were the best on the line. Overall, they were healthier because they drank boiled water, both by itself and as tea, preventing waterborne diseases like dysentery. An almost entirely Chinese team also set the single-day record for most track laid: 10 miles and 56ft (16.11km).

Chinese workers would later be used in other railway projects, including through California's Sierra Nevada Mountains. When the Pacific Railroad was completed at Promontory Summit, Utah, in May 1869, Chinese workers were excluded from the famous photograph marking the event. Fewer than fifteen years after the railroad's completion, Chinese workers would be legally prohibited from entering the United States.

Hong Kong and Beyond

Regardless of legal restrictions on immigration, there was no slowing in demand for men who would do difficult and dirty work in a world that was desperately in need of difficult and dirty work. In the early years of the twentieth century, Chinese workers coming out of Taishan were no longer people with little or nothing to lose, as their predecessors the gold miners and the railroad workers may have been. Looking for work overseas was now an economic choice. As previously stated, if a man were going to work a long, hard day, he may as well do it for as much money as he could earn.

By that time, heading overseas was a well-worn path. 'With a number of their kinsmen already in the United States and returning as lenders to China, job seekers from [the Four Counties] had a better chance of obtaining loans through the credit-ticket system than men from other parts of Guangdong,' one scholar wrote.[4] Indeed, when Fong Wing Sun, Lee Bing and the others began their work on ships, so many Chinese workers, especially those from the Four Counties, had gone before them that the United States had enacted laws to keep them out. Along the way, those forerunners had put various systems in place, including foreign remittance, recruiting agents and mutual aid societies, restaurants, boarding houses and Chinese grocery stores. The work wasn't necessarily easier but getting there wasn't as difficult as it had been.

At this point, Taishan men preparing to go overseas were not uneducated. Almost all would have had some education and were basically literate. Of the eight Chinese men that later boarded *Titanic*, only one, Cheong Foo, could not write his own name. Fong Wing Sun had received several years of instruction at a local school, possibly run by missionaries. Still, many began their working lives in their teens, leaving them at the bottom of the totem pole during their early years. This basic skillset gave them a slightly wider and better selection of job opportunities. Instead of working only on ships as cooks or stokers, they would undertake bit of mechanical work as they gained experience and seniority, at least among other Chinese crew members.

The first destination for any of these men was Hong Kong. Southern China's major international port maintained the strongest links with the region and the world, and as such, became the recruitment post for anyone seeking work outside China. From Taishan, it would have taken one to three days by land or boat to reach. No identity papers were required to enter Hong Kong, and even if they were, the Qing Dynasty government at the end turn of the twentieth century had no mechanism to issue them.

Upon arrival in Hong Kong, Taishan men found their way to the western end of Hong Kong Island, along Des Voeux Road West. Here they found a series of boarding houses, employment agencies and remittance offices catering for them. Men just in from the sea or some other assignment mixed on the street with the new arrivals. Some would visit shops to restock, then go to a restaurant for a decent meal before their next ship set sail. An employment agent could get a young man a job on a ship for a fee (the agent also collected a fee from the ship for recruiting each new mariner). Given the vast number of ships moving in and out of Hong Kong, someone wanting a job on a ship need not wait long to find employment.

British ships began using Chinese crewmen in the early part of the nineteenth century, if not before. The Chinese proved themselves to be hard workers and, unlike their British counterparts, they didn't drink as much. As the British trading presence expanded throughout Asia, ship owners and captains hired more Chinese sailors for regional shipping routes. With the presence of Chinese sailors becoming a regular sight aboard British ships, these men simply continued their employment wherever their employer sent them or wherever they could find work.

The Bristol Archives in Bristol, England, contain shipping records teeming with crew lists that are filled with the names of Chinese sailors going all over the world: Melbourne, Australia; New York, USA; Calcutta (Kolkata), India. There were enough Chinese workers to satisfy the increasing demands of global trade. They accepted their difficult working conditions with little complaint and they didn't cost a lot of money.

Chinese sailors and a few entrepreneurial merchants began to establish the first Chinatowns, which were originally little more than a series of boarding houses, shops, and restaurants in less-developed areas where the men could stay in between shipping voyages. The Chinese sailors caused trouble in only one area: food. Unhappy with the already low-quality grub served to European sailors, Chinese crews over time got their own cooks and their own stores. Being a Chinese cook was a good job, although almost constant work from morning until night. It was less dirty and strenuous than shovelling coal all day and it gave the cook a bit of power, as he had some control over the quality and quantity of food that he and the other sailors received.

Ships, especially cargo ships, hired sailors per voyage. The ship would leave from a designated port, in this case Hong Kong, and travel to one or more other ports carrying freight and perhaps passengers, then likely returning to the original port. Voyages usually took months, sometimes a year or more. Sailors were paid wages based on their assigned task and experience, and provided with meals and whatever accommodation they could find on board. Some ships paid wages only at the end of the voyage; others paid them monthly or upon stops at specific ports.

When the trip was over, the sailors would depart the ship, although those on board could sign up for the next trip if one was already scheduled. Sailors who distinguished themselves through good or hard work might be requested to stay by ship's officer; likewise, unruly sailors would be told not to return. Occasionally, sailors that caused trouble or became ill would be left along the way. Some sailors also signed up for particular voyages because they intended to leave the ship at a certain destination. Desertion was a breach of contract and a serious offence.

On board British ships, the captains and officers were always British, even if the crew were entirely Chinese. On early sailing ships, men slept in dark, crowded, cold areas. Conditions on steamships were marginally better, with the men sleeping in hammocks and eventually simple bunks.

The Chinese Exclusion Act

In 1882, the US Government enacted legislation to prevent entry into the country by the vast majority of Chinese, especially workers. Signed into law by President Chester A. Arthur on 6 May 1882, this legislation marked the first time the United States banned immigration based specifically on race and national origin. The act prohibited the immigration of Chinese labourers for a period of ten years and denied naturalisation rights to Chinese immigrants already in the country.[5]

Anti-Chinese sentiment had intensified as economic conditions in California deteriorated throughout the 1870s. Politicians and labour leaders there capitalised on these tensions, arguing that Chinese immigrants were taking jobs from American workers and were unable to assimilate into American culture. This rhetoric gained traction, leading to violent attacks on Chinese communities and calls for restrictive immigration policies.

The Chinese Exclusion Act was preceded by the Page Act of 1875, which effectively banned Chinese women from entering the United States. However, the 1882 Act went much further, prohibiting the entry of Chinese labourers, both skilled and unskilled, and those employed in mining. The law allowed exceptions for merchants, teachers, students, travellers and diplomats, though these individuals faced significant hurdles in proving their exempt status.

The restrictions violated the provisions for free immigration by citizens of both China and the United States that were mutually granted in the Burlingame–Seward Treaty of 1868.[6] Ultimately a trade agreement, China did not seek its cancellation even after the Exclusion Act was enacted, despite protests over the new restrictions on China's citizens.

The Act drastically reduced Chinese immigration to the United States and separated families, as those who left the country in the early years of its enforcement were often barred from re-entry. The Chinese population in the USA declined sharply in the decades following the Act's passage. Moreover, the law set a precedent for future discriminatory immigration policies and reinforced negative stereotypes about Asian immigrants.

Initially intended to last for ten years, the Act was extended indefinitely in 1902 through the Geary Act.[7] It remained in effect until 1943, when it was finally repealed by the Magnuson Act, largely as a goodwill gesture towards China, a US ally during the Second World War. However, the repeal initially set a quota of just 105 Chinese immigrants per year and maintained restrictions on property ownership and other rights.[8] Non-native-born Chinese in the United States did not become eligible for citizenship until the 1950s.

After 1882 and the Chinese Exclusion Act, European shipping, especially British, became the primary source of Chinese mariner employment. Britain was still the world's leading power, in part because of its naval strength and extensive maritime trade network. The way out of Taishan was Hong Kong, and the way out of Hong Kong was aboard a ship, likely a British one.

*

The young man's father had accompanied him to the pier. The older man offered many times to carry his bag, but Fong Wing Sun refused. He tried to conceal how heavy it felt, the same way his mother attempted to hide her tears. His sister had cried openly. They had always got along well and he knew he would miss her. Wing Sun's mother gave him some food to take on the boat. 'Try to eat it while it's still hot,' she said.

He looked around the bay. It was high tide, the best time to sail. The greenish water contrasted with the leaves of the trees that traced where the land ended and the beach began. The hills in the background were always the same colour palette. Fishing boats dotted the surface of the water, with men who had filled their nets early and come in to sell their catch. On the dock, some of the other faces preparing to board looked familiar: a couple of boys from the same school and one or two others he had seen on market days.

The captain barked out to those waiting on the pier, 'Come on, come on, before the wind shifts!'

Fong Wing Sun turned to his father, who placed a few coins in his hand. 'Don't lose those,' he said. 'Be careful, son. Eat properly. Take care of your health. Write to your mother.'

'Goodbye, father,' Wing Sun said, bowing slightly. He turned away and walked to the boat. Before stepping down onto the gunwale, he waved to his father, who raised his hand and returned the farewell.

Wing Sun boarded the boat and was almost hit by a bag of dried fish being thrown aboard next to him. He stood at the rail as the boat untied and began to drift away. The boatmen raised the sail, and the boat's slow drift gained speed. He stared at the figure of his father, who seemed to stare back. Wing Sun took one more sweeping look around the bay – this water where he had learned to swim. The hills faded and the trees shrank, and soon he could not see his father any longer. The sun beat down on the passengers in the exposed boat, but the breeze at least made it feel cooler. He found a place for his bag and sat down next to it, pulling the collar of his cotton jacket up over his head to protect it.

Wing Sun watched the boatmen go about their work, tying lines and adjusting the sail. I don't want to be a sailor, he thought. He thought of men he had seen who had succeeded in America, wearing the suits that the Western men wore. That was clean work. He liked that idea. One day, when I succeed, Wing Sun thought, I'll wear a suit and a tie.

Lee Bing had left the area much earlier, seeking his fortune, or at least some basic work, on ships. Their paths would cross years later, on a ship much larger than either of them had ever imagined.

4

THE WHITE STAR LINE

In the early part of the twentieth century, transportation between continents was done by sea. It was a time of transition; while ships, especially those carrying cargo, still moved with sails, increasingly, larger, faster ships driven by steam and powered by coal were leading the trade, especially for passengers between Europe and North America.

Major shipping lines, namely those operated by British, French and German companies, competed based on two criteria: luxury and speed. Although it is difficult for the twenty-first-century traveller to imagine anyone caring whether they crossed the Atlantic in eight days or six days and a few hours, to the businessperson 100 years ago, the choice was as clear as choosing a non-stop flight would be now.

The telegraph was in regular use at this point but was generally used only for important, almost urgent communication. Wealthy people had telephones in their homes, but again, the idea of the tele-conference or conducting business via telephone was uncommon. One might send a telegram or use the telephone to arrange a business meeting, but an important meeting itself would be conducted in person – even if that meant a transatlantic voyage.

Crossing oceans in ships was nothing uncommon in the early twentieth century. From Chinese Admiral Zheng He's legendary Ming Dynasty (1368–1644) ships to the European explorers who visited the Western Hemisphere, vessels built of wood and powered only by wind had circled the planet for centuries. Even steamships were not particularly new. A hybrid sailing and steam-powered ship, SS *Savannah*, had made it across the Atlantic almost 100 years before, and two pure steamships had first made the crossing in 1838. Steamships enabled and fuelled the waves of immigration that brought millions of people, first from Europe and later from Asia, to North America throughout the nineteenth century.

The major difference by 1912 was scale. Shipyards on both sides of the Atlantic were now able to build ships weighing tens of thousands of tons, capable of carrying thousands of passengers and reaching the other side of the Atlantic in about a week. By 1875, there was regularly scheduled, steam-powered passenger travel between ports around the British Isles, including Liverpool and Southampton in England and Queenstown (now Cobh) in Ireland, and North American destinations including Halifax, a major port in Canada's Nova Scotia, Boston and New York in the United States.

Transatlantic passenger traffic was dominated by European lines. England, France and Germany all had shipping companies that offered regular sailings between their home countries and North American ports, along with other destinations in Europe and sometimes the Middle East or Asia. Germany had the Hamburg America Line (HAPAG); France had the Compagnie Générale Transatlantique (CGT); and in England were the Cunard and White Star Lines, bitter rivals that chose opposite strategies to attract their passengers.

Cunard Versus White Star

Samuel Cunard got his start as a shipping magnate when his company won the first British transatlantic steamship mail contract in 1839.[1] The company eventually began carrying passengers and in 1879 it renamed itself the Cunard Steamship Company Ltd. In 1841, the first ships bearing the designation 'Royal Mail Ship', abbreviated to RMS, went into service. This was more than an official title. Carrying the Royal Mail, which refers to all letters and other parcels, was lucrative, especially when combined with revenue from cargo and passengers.

Compared to Cunard, the White Star Line was a latecomer to the Atlantic. In 1869, a shipowner and director of the National Line named Thomas Henry Ismay purchased a bankrupt shipping company called the White Star Line, which had run aground financially after a series of ship disasters and poor management. The company had pioneered passenger and freight shipping from the United Kingdom to Australia, but this longer route was far riskier, with a fast journey still requiring more than two months to complete one way. White Star cost Ismay £1,000 (over £100,000 today), not an insignificant investment at the time, but it was a move that could expand National Line's reach across the globe.

The following year, Ismay was joined by William Imrie Jr, who merged his family's Imrie & Tomlinson holdings[2] with Ismay's to form a company briefly called Ismay, Imrie and Co. The Imries and Ismays were well known to each other: William's father, William Sr, had taken on Thomas Ismay as an apprentice at the start of his career. The elder and junior Ismays and Imries had co-operated for decades. When William Sr died in 1870, a permanent union between the two families' companies seemed obvious; Thomas's ambition was growing but William Jr didn't have his father or his father's friend's enthusiasm for the business.

Despite the number of competitors on the routes, Ismay was keen to use the respective experience he had developed in transatlantic shipping and jump into the race. One history of the White Star Line noted:

> Many sailing packet passengers had been disgruntled at the inefficiency, danger, and primitive conditions encountered when traveling on the sailing packets and emigrant ships, and turned to the steamships, with their properly trained crews, better living quarters and food, and sailing schedules. These passengers were even more willing to pay for the privilege.[3]

Ismay incorporated the new combined venture and rechristened it using the White Star Line name and emblem he had acquired. This was a strange choice considering its chequered history, but it went forward nonetheless.

Competition between Cunard and White Star simmered for decades. Cunard was the most frequent holder of the Blue Riband, an unofficial award for the fastest average speed across the Atlantic (frequently and incorrectly referred to as the Blue Ribbon), but occasionally, it was overtaken by White Star or the Inman Line, another transatlantic passenger shipping company.

Harland & Wolff

In 1871, White Star rolled out *Oceanic*, a ship that could be powered entirely by steam, entirely by wind, or both, with a single funnel and four full-sized masts. It was the first vessel that Ismay's company ordered from a Belfast shipyard called Harland & Wolff. That yard then raised every White Star ship from then on. Their relationship was unique: all ships built for White Star were constructed on a cost-plus-profit basis, with Harland & Wolff earning a 7 per cent premium over each vessel's total expenditure.[4] White Star built its expanding fleet to its own specifications at a consistent and predictable price, and Harland & Wolff's margins were guaranteed by having a partner in an expanding market segment.

Oceanic's maiden voyage was plagued with problems, but Ismay and Imrie stuck to their guns and continued to launch new ships. In 1871, White Star's *Adriatic* took the Blue Riband from speed demons Cunard, establishing its owners as major players on the Atlantic.

Despite Ismay and Imrie's experience and best-laid plans, success in the Atlantic market was not automatic. Although regularised with scheduled sailings and improved on-board accommodation, those improvements did not make crossing the Atlantic any safer. Coastal hazards, mechanical problems, fires on board and inclement weather still posed significant risks to any ship from any line making the journey with any cargo.

The Sinking of RMS *Atlantic*

Ismay's White Star got its first taste of disaster in 1873. On 20 March, RMS *Atlantic* departed Liverpool bound for New York with 950 people on board (ultimately, there were 952, as two children were born during the voyage). However, poor weather dogged *Atlantic* during its crossing, slowing its progress. 'Considered the risk too great to push on, as we might find ourselves in the event of a gale short, out from any port of supply, and so decided to bear up for Halifax,' said Captain James A. Williams in a later official statement.[5]

However, *Atlantic* encountered a storm upon its approach to the Canadian port and Williams, never having sailed to Halifax before, failed to spot Sambro Lighthouse, a critical landmark and navigational aid. *Atlantic* struck rocks at about 3.15 a.m. on 1 April, about 500m from shore in Terrence Bay.

Strangely, every single woman and child aboard, including the two newborns, perished, except for one 12-year-old boy, but 131 of the crew and officers survived, including Captain Williams; only ten crew members died. None of this reflected well on Williams specifically, or White Star in general. A Canadian Government Inquiry found, 'The conduct of Captain Williams in the management of his ship during the 12 or 14 hours preceding the disaster was so gravely at variance with what ought to have been the conduct of a man placed in his responsible position.'[6]

Atlantic's sinking was the worst-known maritime disaster of the nineteenth century – at least in the Atlantic Ocean – claiming 562 lives. Despite the loss of life and magnitude of the disaster, the event was quickly forgotten. Survivors and victims' families were compensated, along with local people who participated in the rescue. A memorial was not erected until 1905, partly with White Star funding.

Joseph Bruce Ismay

In 1862, Thomas Ismay and his wife, Margaret (née Bruce), had a son, whom they named Joseph Bruce Ismay. He was known during his life either by his full name in business and formal circumstances, or Bruce to closer relatives and associates.

The younger Ismay attended Elstree School in Woolhampton, Berkshire, followed by the prestigious Harrow School in Greater London. Bruce was an accomplished football player and was part of the first Liverpool Ramblers amateur team in 1882.[7] After school, he was apprenticed to Ismay, Imrie and Co. to begin learning the family business.

Thomas and Bruce were good business partners, but their personal relationship was tense. There were other Ismay sons, Jason and Bower, but Bruce was the eldest and, whether Thomas liked it or not, had a good head for business. Ismay biographer Frances Wilson wrote:

> The problem for Thomas was that Bruce was the same as him and different, and he feared both aspects of his character. He wanted his eldest son to be his mirror image but not to occupy the same space. Thomas provided him with palatial homes, fleets of servants and an upper-class education, but then resented him for having it easy. Bruce grew up knowing that he was not himself but a failed version of someone else; he was never to forget that he was an inferior model, an imperfect copy.[8]

Eventually, Bruce was designated the company's representative in New York City and moved there in 1887. It was there he met and later married Julia Florence Schieffelin, the daughter of George Richard Schieffelin and Julia Matilda Delaplaine. George Schieffelin, a noted New York attorney, was one of the first people to begin spending summers in Southampton on nearby Long Island, now a popular destination for affluent New Yorkers.

In 1891, Bruce, Julia and the first of their five children returned to the UK, where Bruce took up a position as partner in his father's firm. The North Atlantic Run, as the passenger routes had come to be called, had become the company's focus and White Star continued to enjoy success with two newer ships, *Teutonic* and *Majestic*.

The Riches of Steerage

For passenger lines seeking to capture the Atlantic trade, their marketing was a bit of misdirection. Ships were usually divided into three levels of accommodation and service: First, Second and Third Class. In class-conscious twentieth-century Western society, choosing a level of travel was simple: one travelled in the class one could afford. While a First-Class passenger might wander down to Third Class just to see what was going on and perhaps feel good about their own station in life, Third-Class passengers were not even allowed into Second Class. Quarantine rules prohibited the mixing of classes – at least from lower to upper.

The main British-operated lines, Cunard and White Star, sought to attract the most famous and richest passengers. Although these passengers were the frequent travellers of their time and paid what today would be tens of thousands of dollars for their passage, it wasn't from the well-heeled that the shipping companies made their money. Instead, the lines hoped that Third-Class passengers, mostly immigrants leaving Europe for new lives in Canada or the United States, would want to travel in the lower decks of the same ships and fill the multi-person staterooms below. Commonly and derisively referred to as 'steerage' (after the equipment used to steer the ship with which these passengers shared their space) it was filling the areas closer to the waterline with goods, mail and people that made a voyage profitable.

A New Era

Thomas Ismay continued to lead the White Star Line throughout the 1890s, although his somewhat ambitious son Bruce's role increased steadily. During White Star's primary period in the 1870s and '80s, Ismay continued contracting the construction of ships to Harland & Wolff. However, Thomas cleverly hedged against the risks of operating a passenger line by chartering from other shipping lines many of the vessels used for most White Star departures. That way, in the event of a disaster at sea, Ismay's line's responsibility and liability would be limited.

Still, Ismay didn't want White Star to be known just for operating transport on other lines' ships. In 1897, Thomas planted a final flag for the company, ordering from Harland & Wolff a new ship to be christened RMS *Oceanic*, the same name as White Star's earlier ship. At the time, it was the longest, although not the heaviest, ship ever built, at 704ft (215m) and was a remarkable work of marine architecture. Operating under a similar deal as one Cunard had arranged with the British Admiralty (the Royal Navy's command), White Star received a partial subsidy in exchange for several design modifications in case the Royal Navy needed the ship in wartime.

Oceanic would not have been mistaken for a naval workhorse. It featured 2,000 electric lights and a First-Class dining room that could seat 400 – almost every single First-Class passenger if the ship was sailing at capacity. It was also optimised for profit: along with room for 410 First-Class passengers and 300 in Second Class, there was space for 1,000 Third-Class passengers. For White Star, it was the best of all worlds, and it reasserted its position as the standard bearer for transatlantic luxury.

Thomas's timing was uncanny. *Oceanic*'s maiden voyage began on 6 September 1899. Already suffering from heart trouble, he then had a heart attack on 14 September. The elder Ismay never recovered entirely and he died on 23 November, having seen his final masterpiece go to sea, and dying just before the close of a century in which he had been a major player in shaping its primary mode of trade and transportation. So well regarded was Thomas in Liverpool that flags throughout the city flew at half-mast on the day of his funeral.

With his father's passing, the reins of control of the White Star Line passed into the hands of J. Bruce Ismay, who had his own ideas about how to make his firm's name and reputation – and his own – even more colossal.

Mergers and Millionaires

White Star was successful in positioning itself as the luxury transport provider of choice for the North Atlantic's millionaire class, in particular, John Pierpont 'J.P.' Morgan, the most influential American financier of the late nineteenth century. That his name remains part of one of the United States' largest investment banks more than 100 years after his death demonstrates his legacy in American finance.

Having done well in multiple railroad projects across the United States, Morgan was a bit of a latecomer to investments in shipping. However, with his leverage and resources, he neither needed nor intended to get in on the ground floor. To seize as much of a death grip as possible on his targeted industry, he sought to aggregate several existing shipping firms and then splice those with his railroad interests to offer end-to-end transport options and control as much of that trade as he could. Morgan's interest fell upon one particular company of which he had been a regular customer: the Liverpool-based White Star Line.

Morgan's timing was excellent, at least to attract the attention of White Star's new boss. The American simply made the shipping company's shareholders an offer that they could not refuse – ten times a good year's revenue. However, Ismay shrewdly figured that Morgan was keen and had the money to do better, and the final sale price for White Star was US$35 million (about $1.2 billion in 2024). Knowing that he would remain as managing director, the junior Ismay seems to have had little hesitation in letting go of the ownership stake in the firm that his father had spent more than thirty years building.

Now firmly at the helm and flush with Morgan's cash, Bruce wanted to make his own mark upon White Star, with even bigger and more luxurious vessels. His opening salvo was to direct Harland & Wolff to build the 'Big Four' – *Adriatic*, *Baltic*, *Cedric* and *Celtic*. Except for *Adriatic*, which went to sea as the last of the four, each was designed to become the largest, by tonnage, ship in the world at the time they began service. Each weighed over 20,000 tons, launching between 1901 and 1906. Three of the Big Four served White Star and other lines into the early to mid-1930s; the fourth, *Cedric*, foundered on rocks off Ireland in 1928.

Along with maintaining a White Star standard of building bigger, more luxurious and modern ships, the line also began a trend of almost every one of its ships becoming the largest moving object ever built, with the launch of *Cedric* in February 1903. The age of skyscrapers was still a few years away; at the turn of the twentieth century, major human construction was horizontal and mobile. Upon completion, the Big Four were almost twice as long as the world's tallest structure, New York City's Park Row Building, which opened in 1899 standing at a puny 391ft (119m).

The transatlantic race continued later in the decade of the 1900s. Cunard launched first RMS *Lusitania* in June 1906, followed three months later by the slightly longer and swifter RMS *Mauretania* in September 1906. *Mauretania*, which cruised at an average of 23.69 knots (43.87kmh or 27.26mph), first took the Blue Riband for eastbound travel, which was generally faster due to the push of the Gulf Stream and favourable weather conditions, then the westbound leg later in 1909. The ship held that title until 1929. That was the last time White Star competed for speed on the Atlantic.

However, in the two decades in between, Europe's major shipyards had developed the capability and capacity to build even larger ships – double the weight of the Big Four. For Bruce Ismay, for whom bigger always meant better, it allowed him to conceive of and plan for ships that his father never could have imagined. As early as 1907, Ismay and Harland & Wolff chairman William James Pirrie (Lord Pirrie) began discussing a trio of new ships, each designed to be the largest moving object ever built at launch – the giant rocket boosters of their day. Each would tower over Belfast, where they would be built – each an advancement of human engineering and ingenuity – and the launch and christening of them would be a public spectacle that would require the labour of thousands, and thousands more who would attend and observe. Ismay wanted White Star's pennant to rule the North Atlantic.

RMS *Republic*: All the Wrong Lessons

Harland & Wolff was White Star's exclusive shipyard, but it also served other clients within the International Mercantile Marine Corporation, J.P. Morgan's US-based shipping conglomerate. In 1903, it built a 15,000-ton ship christened *Columbus* for IMM's Dominion Line. The ship was later transferred to White Star, which brought the ship into line after upgrading its standards for on-board luxury. It was rechristened *Republic* and returned to service.

In January 1909, *Republic* was sailing from Boston to the Mediterranean Sea, a route that White Star had pioneered. It was a two-pronged strategy: it created a leisure travel route for Americans wanting to reach holiday destinations in Spain and Italy and it gave Italian immigrants an opportunity to transit directly to the United States. On this particular voyage, the ship may have carried from US$250,000 to US$3 million in its cargo holds – possibly payments for officers, crew and supplies for a large US naval fleet on an around-the-world mission.[9]

Heading east with 742 passengers and crew, *Republic* encountered heavy fog. It enacted standard White Star protocols for the situation – namely, reducing speed and sounding its foghorn. At the same time and nearby, SS *Florida*, a passenger liner of the Anglo-Italian Lloyd-Italiano Line, was bound for New York and similarly hampered by low visibility. It too used its horn to signal its presence to nearby ships.

Just before dawn, *Republic*'s Captain Inman Shelby heard *Florida*'s alert and ordered his ship's engines to full reverse and hard turn to port. Using his ship's whistle, Shelby signalled the unseen ship to do the same.

It would have been difficult for the two ships to get it more precisely wrong. *Florida* sliced into *Republic* amidships at an almost 90-degree angle. It was an early twentieth-century ship's captain's worst nightmare – a collision in the open ocean. Suddenly, more than 1,600 were in peril.

Florida, although damaged, was not in immediate danger of sinking, but *Republic* was. However, the White Star ship had a new device on board that, like a prayer, could call into the great beyond, begging for rescue: a Marconi wireless set. A quick-thinking *Republic* broadcast the world's first radio distress signal – 'CQD', a general call with an added 'D' for 'Danger' – into the void. A US Coast Guard cutter, *Gresham*, received the signal and responded promptly.

Except for a handful of people who were killed in the initial collision, all of *Republic*'s passengers and crew were evacuated to *Florida* and *Gresham*, averting a then-unimaginable calamity at sea. *Florida* sailed for New York and *Gresham* transferred the passengers it had taken aboard to ships that arrived at the accident site later. Despite efforts by *Gresham* to tow *Republic*, the liner was too badly damaged, and on 24 January it sank, 50 miles (80km) south-south-east of Nantucket Island, off Massachusetts, taking its cargo with it – which at today's valuations may have been worth more than US$1 billion. Over a century later, and less than 330ft (100m) below the surface, it remains one of the world's greatest unsalvaged sunken treasures. At the time of the accident, *Republic* was the largest ship ever to sink.

White Star learned all the wrong lessons from the *Republic* incident. The greatest danger at sea was believed to be collision with another ship, specifically a perpendicular crash that would destroy one or more watertight bulkheads, as had occurred in *Republic*'s case. With a Marconi set, a stricken ship could summon help and Atlantic sea lanes were so busy with traffic that there would be many other vessels that could rush to a sinking ship's aid – or so the thinking went. Lifeboats wouldn't save passengers; the vessel itself was the lifeboat. It was more important for a ship to stay afloat long enough for survivors to be transferred to rescue craft.

As White Star prepared to lay the keels of its largest ships ever – each incrementally exceeding its sister ship in length and weight – it took the flawed lessons learned from an averted disaster to heart and designed them into the building of the new ships.

Olympic, Titanic and Britannic

Bruce hoped to dwarf his father's accomplishments with his next upgrade to the White Star fleet. Continuing his company's co-operation with Harland & Wolff, Ismay, encouraged by Morgan, planned for three massive ships. Although they would be fast, challenging Cunard's speed demons was never a consideration – this would be stem to stern luxury. Even Third-Class passengers would marvel at the service and surroundings offered to them.

With the first two named for Mount Olympus and a race of giants called the Titans respectively, both from Greek mythology, the ships' names were meant to convey heft, mass and size. Each would feature a triple-screw propulsion system, using three propellers for stability and efficient speed.

Upon completion, the first ship, *Olympic*, measured 882.75ft (269.1m) long; 92.75ft (28.3m) across the ship, or beam; 175ft (53.4m) from the bottom of the ship's keel to the top of its four funnels; and it weighed more than 40,000 metric tons. The ship was visible during construction from various points around Belfast. Harland & Wolff constructed special bays in which to build it. Construction began in late 1908 and finished in October 1910.

Work on the next ship, *Titanic*, commenced in March 1909. *Titanic* was barely longer than *Olympic*, slightly slimmer and a bit heavier, with modifications being made following the completion of *Olympic*'s construction and entrance into service. It was still the biggest moving object built by humankind when it launched as planned.

Olympic, Titanic and later *Britannic*, not wanting to look slower or smaller than Cunard's speedsters, all sported four smokestacks – even though only three were used. The fourth was merely for face, to maintain the same profile as Cunard's ships.

The *Hawke* Mishap

Although *Olympic*'s maiden voyage and subsequent early crossings went without incident, during its fifth sailing in September 1911, the massive new ship ran into trouble in the form of Royal Navy warship HMS *Hawke*. White Star's Captain Edward Smith was at the helm of *Olympic*. Both were moving through the Solent, a body of water separating the Isle of Wight from the main island of the UK, that includes the area around the port of Southampton.

Olympic, which was far larger than *Hawke*, made an unexpected turn and *Hawke* was unable to avoid it, stabbing into the bigger ship with its bow. No one was seriously injured, but two of *Olympic*'s watertight compartments flooded. Both ships made their way back to port and required significant repairs.

Smith was indirectly blamed for the accident when *Olympic* was found to be at fault, but White Star did not reprimand the captain publicly, despite the embarrassment and cost of repairs and lost revenue. When their newest ship, *Titanic*, was ready to go to sea six months later, Smith was duly named its captain.[10]

With *Titanic* being built in the neighbouring bay, repair work on *Olympic* was accelerated by diverting parts and workers away from *Titanic*. That decision led to *Titanic*'s launch being delayed to 10 April from its original March date.

Incidentally, *Olympic*'s collision with *Hawke* gave rise to a ridiculous conspiracy that claims it was that ship, not *Titanic*, that struck the iceberg and sank. In its twisted logic, the conspiracy alleges that, following the *Olympic* accident, Ismay and White Star wanted to claim the full insurance value of the ship, but the only way to do that would be if it sank. Some repainting and other maritime skullduggery was employed and in April 1912, *Olympic*, masquerading as the new ship *Titanic*, went to sea with plans for a one-way voyage.

Ironically, the real *Olympic* was the only one of her three sisters to survive long enough to be scrapped in 1935. Along with *Titanic* sinking on its maiden voyage, *Britannic* was requisitioned by the Royal Navy during the First World War. She struck a mine in November 1916 and sank off Greece, going down in under an hour. Underwater explorer Jacques Cousteau discovered the wreck in 1975.

*

Following this ship collision, White Star once again learned the wrong lessons. The threat at sea, the company concluded, was not an unseen hazard, floating in a giant ocean. The greatest risk was a collision with another ship. The danger was met with a human solution: a ship large enough that it could survive an accident and remain afloat.

Another White Star ship had been struck by a vessel, and again it had survived, thanks to state-of-the-art watertight construction. Within three years, more than 2,000 passengers had now been involved in two accidents, but only a handful had been lost, and these had been killed by impact, not sinking or drowning. The company clearly did not consider the massive loss of life in a worst-case scenario – that two collisions in three years could have claimed thousands of lives, and likely ruined White Star in the process. To the White Star Line, there was no better lifeboat than a large, solidly built ship.

Britain's Board of Trade, which governed safety aboard ships, had not issued new regulations for lifeboats or other related rescue procedures, despite the size of liners now sailing across the Atlantic Ocean becoming many times larger than when its standards had last been updated. Manufacturing ships to withstand collisions was safe and smart, and White Star certainly believed so.

5

RMS *TITANIC*

Director James Cameron's 1997 film *Titanic* changed our understanding of the ship and its history forever. The story that was already encrusted with the barnacles of legend and myth became wrapped in a new fictional story, and Cameron's painstaking efforts to present *Titanic* accurately, in the way it looked, sank and who was on board. The film not only revived the history of *Titanic* for another generation but rewrote the public's understanding of an event already blurred by bias and sensationalism.

Titanic was a real ship, as this work has already explained at length. However, fans of the film will be sad to learn that Jack Dawson and Rose DeWitt Bukater, however, were not actual passengers. A 'J. Dawson' sailed, and died, on *Titanic*. He is buried in Fairview Lawn Cemetery in Halifax, Nova Scotia. And while there is a good chance that he died from exposure to near-freezing water, like his onscreen counterpart, the 'J' stands for Joseph, not Jack, and Jack is a nickname for John anyway. Rose wasn't the last person rescued from the water. That person was male – and likely Chinese.

In April 1912, *Titanic* was the largest and most luxurious ship in the world. The wealthy of Europe and North America were among the few who could travel on her. Although many of those wealthy families owned yachts, those were pleasure craft – cruise ships were considered far safer for crossing the Atlantic Ocean because of their size and professional crew. Today, people of similar status would fly in their own private planes or at least in the First-Class cabins of commercial jets.

Treasures were lost aboard *Titanic*, but nothing like the Heart of the Ocean sapphire that appears in the film. Rumours continue to circulate that bags of diamonds and other valuables were locked in safes on the ship, but none of the passengers or relatives of victims ever filed insurance claims for such items. Those files give us significant insight into the other items that were brought on board and subsequently lost, including William Carter's automobile and some works of art being shipped as cargo. Third-Class passengers may have lost more common items, like clothing and linens, but relatively, these things were far more valuable – in some cases, it was all those passengers owned.

Cameron could not have created his spectacular movie if *Titanic*'s factual story was not already fabled. Love stories did end tragically that night, fortunes were lost, reputations destroyed and some survived or died because of a last-minute decision or occurrence. The tale of *Titanic* is still regularly repeated more than a century later, specifically because the truth about it is so captivating.

The Real *Titanic* Sets Sail

In the spring of 1912, shipping in and out of the UK was brought almost to a standstill by one of the first large-scale strike actions, a national coal strike that sought to establish a minimum wage for miners.[1] The strike started in late February, and by the time the eight Chinese men boarded a train for Southampton to sail on *Titanic*, it was over. But its effects would be felt for weeks. With no coal to run the boilers upon which the ships relied, many vessels remained stuck in port.

The White Star Line must have felt its luck was running out. *Olympic*'s collision with *Hawke* removed it from service for months, leaving the line without a marquee vessel. *Olympic*'s repairs caused *Titanic*'s launch to be delayed from 20 March until 10 April. The coal strike threatened to delay it again.

Because of *Titanic*'s size, White Star had placed its order for the liner's coal early. When the strike was called, to make sure the supply was sufficient the line cancelled all of its other scheduled westbound departures and transferred the passengers and coal from those ships onto *Titanic*, which was not fully booked for its first voyage.

Normally, the second in a series of three ships would not garner as much attention as the launch of RMS *Titanic* did. As planned, it was larger, barely, than *Olympic*, which had first gone to sea in June 1911. But after the *Olympic* incident and the embarrassment it had caused, *Titanic*'s launch gave White Star the chance to regain the spotlight in transatlantic shipping.

Titanic embodied White Star's concept of safety – it was a ship that could survive a collision with another ship at sea and remain afloat. Four of its sixteen watertight compartments could flood and the ship would still not sink.[2] The danger was that such a crash would demolish the wall between two compartments, allowing both to flood at the same time, but *Olympic*, *Titanic* and later *Britannic* were all built to withstand that kind of accident. A lengthwise impact with rocks or other objects near the ship's waterline did not pose a significant risk, White Star Line believed.

Because of White Star's confidence that its biggest ships would not sink quickly (or at all), supplying *Olympic* and *Titanic* with lifeboats was not a priority. Britain's Board of Trade, which regulated shipping by British-flagged vessels, required that ships weighing over 10,000 tons (*Titanic* weighed more than 45,000 tons) must have sixteen lifeboats with a capacity of 160 cubic metres each. *Titanic* exceeded the number of lifeboats required: the ship was equipped with fourteen full-sized wooden lifeboats that were each capable of carrying sixty-five adults. Two smaller emergency boats, called cutters, also made of wood, had a capacity of forty people each. They could be launched quickly in the event of a crew member or passenger going overboard. It also carried another four collapsible lifeboats that could hold forty-seven people each, with cork bottoms, a wooden deck, bench seats and canvas sides that could be raised. Two of those collapsible boats, C and D, were stored flat beneath the emergency boats, one on each side of the ship. Two more collapsible boats were kept on top of *Titanic*'s wheelhouse, where the bridge was.

Titanic's collapsible lifeboats were designed by the Engelhardt Boat Co. and built by McAlister & Son of Scotland based on Engelhardt's design. Packed flat, like contemporary IKEA furniture, the canvas gunwales folded down almost completely, with the cork bottom only rising about 1.25in (38cm) from the deck. Photos show the assembled boats with sides rising to 2.7in (81cm).

Despite being optimised for storage, the collapsibles had one major drawback: each weighed about 1,000lb (450kg), requiring several men to assemble and place them in the lifeboat davits for loading and lowering. Collapsibles C and D, both stored on deck, required less movement and therefore were available more readily than A and B, which had to be brought down from atop the wheelhouse.

In total, *Titanic* only had lifeboat capacity for 1,178 people. By the time it left for New York after making its final stop in Ireland, more than 2,200 passengers, officers and crew were on board.

Titanic's Chinese Passengers

By 1912, while mass immigration to the United States continued, the peak had already passed about five years earlier.[3] Ships crossing the Atlantic from west to east still carried a variety of nationalities, but by this point, the majority of passengers in any class were from the British Isles: England, Scotland and Ireland (Ireland was still entirely ruled by the United Kingdom at this point). But on this voyage in April 1912, among the melange of thirty-three nationalities travelling on *Titanic* were several uncommon names, at least for White Star's Atlantic sailings. Asian travellers were almost unknown on cruises from Europe to North America, especially Chinese passengers, whose admission to the United States was almost entirely prohibited. And yet, here were eight, fare-paying Chinese men taking the maiden voyage of the world's largest and most luxurious ship.

The passenger manifest listed them together. Where these names came from remains unknown – whether they were provided by the men themselves or their employer, the Donald Steam Ship Line of Bristol, England, and New York, USA, is not clear. For the early twentieth century, the list seems strange: all eight display only two names, although most Chinese names in 1912 would usually have had three characters: a family name, a generational name and then a personal name. What appears on the list were nicknames or working names that the men used – shorter names that their non-Chinese-speaking bosses on board ship could use.

All eight had their occupation listed as 'seaman' and all were identified as being from Hong Kong. Their ages followed their names:

Ah Lam, 38
Fang Lang, 26
Len Lam, 23
Cheong Foo, 32
Chang Chip, 32
Ling Hee, 24
Lee Bing, 32
Lee Ling, 28

Ticket No. 1601, which covered all eight men, cost just under £60; today, that same ticket would cost more than £8,588 ($11,014). That was as significant an investment as it would be today to send eight men across the Atlantic. For many of the immigrants sailing on *Titanic*, the move was all or nothing. Many passengers on *Titanic* had sold property in Europe to finance their trip and packed up all their belongings to travel to North America. There was no going back, and nothing to go back to if they changed their minds or failed.

For the Chinese men, the move was much easier. They owned only what they carried in their steamer trunks and the decision to go to North America was made for them.

Why these men were heading to work on the Donald Steam Ship Company's North American lines is not known. It is unclear whether they were seconded there or if they paid their own way, knowing that the Donald Line would continue to employ them. Paying their own fare would have cost almost several months' wages but it seems a reasonable investment if they knew they could find continued shipping work. However, due to the Chinese Exclusion Act, they would not be free to enter US ports, leaving them to find work only in places like Cuba and Jamaica. Most likely, they were sent there to work, because undertaking a trip by themselves would have been too difficult financially and politically.

These men, who grew up near the shores of the South China Sea, travelled across the Indian Ocean and the Mediterranean Sea to reach northern Europe, and would soon add the Atlantic Ocean and Caribbean Sea to the bodies of water they had crossed. In New York, they would meet SS *Annetta*, a Donald Line fruit boat or cargo ship that mostly carried foodstuffs that was leased to the Atlantic Fruit Company. Upon arrival in New York, *Titanic* was due to stop at the Ellis Island Immigration Station, where customs and immigration officials would register and inspect Third-Class passengers. The Chinese would receive particular scrutiny; although few Chinese passed through Ellis Island, it was still a major US port of entry and they would be required to prove their travel status and undergo a medical examination before proceeding further and meeting their ship.

All of the men were experienced seamen. Almost all of the eight had sailed together before in various combinations, although they did not necessarily know each other. Tens of thousands of Chinese sailors worked on the Donald Line's ships, serving the various cargo and smaller passenger lines in Europe and elsewhere, so working on the same ship was no guarantee of familiarity.

Titanic's manifest listed all of the men as being from Hong Kong and many gave addresses on Des Voeux Road, likely boarding houses where they had last stayed or perhaps the offices of their employment agents. How many, if any, were born and raised in Hong Kong is not known.

Although they may not have known each other well, they were all travelling to work in North America for the first time. Changing locations back to Europe or Asia was becoming more difficult with this shift across the Atlantic.

Ah Lam was the eldest. At 38, he had built a career sailing on ships and yet he was still no more than a fireman, condemned to the engine room. At the time, Chinese sailors were not given jobs in service positions and certainly not among officers on board – a wooden ceiling. He was the group's leader, at least in the sense that he was paid £1 more per month than the others.

The writing of his name in English confounded scholars studying *Titanic* history for a century: not knowing the southern Chinese appellation 'Ah', many researchers misread the first name listed on the ticket as 'Ali'. 'Ah' is a familiar nickname, usually combined with the person's given name. 'Ah Lam', therefore, is like seeing 'Little Jimmy' on a passenger manifest, although it normally uses a different character for 'Ah' than appears with Ah Lam's name. If, instead, the character used was his actual surname, then this *Titanic* passenger had one of the rarer surnames in China.

Of the many names used throughout his life, while on ships Fong Wing Sun (方榮山) went by the name Fang Lang. Why he chose this particular name is not known, especially as he often signed the ship's register as 丙星. Sailing on *Titanic*, he listed his age as 26, although he would have been about 18 at the time.

Little is known about Len Lam beyond his age. However, he, Lee Ling and Fang Lang knew each other prior to their sailing on board *Titanic*.

Cheong Foo (張富) was born between 1879 and 1882. He was the only member of the group who signed the ship's register with an 'X', indicating he was unable, or perhaps unwilling, to sign his own name. Cheong and Lee Bing had served together before.

Chang Chip was also born between 1879 and 1882. Plagued by health problems throughout his life, there is some evidence that Chang was also from Xiachuan Island, but nothing conclusive. Chang and Fang Lang had previously been aboard a ship called *Netherpark* together.

Ling Hee was born between 1887 and 1889. He may have also been illiterate or barely literate when he boarded *Titanic*, occasionally signing ship registers with an 'X' or only writing one of his name's characters. Standing about 5ft 10in (170cm) tall, Ling had a pronounced scar on his left cheek, based on shipboard descriptions.

Lee Bing was born in Hengtang, in north-eastern Taishan, in 1879. He and Cheong Foo had served together previously on a ship called *Norwegian*, or perhaps a Norwegian-owned ship, before being assigned to *Annetta*.[4]

Despite the similarity of their names, it does not appear that Lee Ling and Lee Bing were related. Little is known about the former besides his age. However, he knew Fang Lang and Len Lam prior to boarding *Titanic* with them.

Until their arrival in New York, they had nothing particular to do on the voyage. It must have been a strange feeling for them, preparing for a ship voyage during which they were not working. It was probably the first paid vacation they had ever had. They must have realised early on that this was some special ship they were boarding, having its own train for passengers, even those travelling in Third Class. The train for Second and Third-Class passengers departed at 7.30 a.m. While they should have arrived in fewer than two hours to reach the coast, a delay caused it to take at least three.

Setting Sail

In order to reach *Titanic* on time on 10 April, the eight men woke in the small hours, finished any remaining packing and left early from their accommodation in London's Limehouse, an area on the north bank of the Thames River that had become popular with Chinese sailors in the city. They couldn't miss their train from Waterloo Station.

Arriving in Southampton, the men took their things and exited the station. While they carried their own luggage for the 200 or so metres to the ship's boarding area, porters waited to assist Second-Class passengers. A small army of assistants were already wrangling the possessions of the First-Class travellers, making sure that everything from steamer trunks to automobiles made it into *Titanic's* cargo holds.

Stepping out of the train station and turning towards the wharf, they must not have believed their eyes. For these sailors who were used to working on ships that weighed a few thousand tons, *Titanic* would have been almost incomprehensible. Here was a vessel four times longer and over twenty times more massive than the freighters and coastal passenger ships on which they served. They had stoked fires on a ship with a single funnel. How many men were needed to load and fire one with four funnels?

Boarding in Southampton as a Third-Class passenger was relatively easy, as many of the berths would be filled at later stops in France and Ireland. While there may have been some jostling during boarding, overall, it should have been a civilised affair. After a quick visual inspection by doctors upon boarding, a series of stewards directed passengers to cabins assigned by ticket numbers. As they were travelling on the same ticket, the Chinese men would have been placed together, either in the same or adjoining rooms. Some Third-Class cabins for unattached men slept as many as eight, although usually they were divided into quads, with two upper and lower bunks.

Because the coal strike had just ended, and because April was not peak travel season between Europe and the United States, *Titanic* was not full, despite this being its maiden voyage, even after taking on passengers from White Star's other departures. But even below capacity, more than 900 crew members and officers stood ready to serve over 1,300 passengers during their week-long voyage across the ocean.

On the evening of 10 April, *Titanic* arrived in Cherbourg, France, and took on mainly Third-Class passengers, although there were First- and Second-Class travellers among them. *Titanic* was far too large to enter the harbour there and so White Star tenders ferried the new arrivals out to the massive ship. On the late morning of 11 April, *Titanic* made its final stop on the eastern side of the Atlantic, picking up more passengers and mail at Queenstown (now Cobh) in southern Ireland. Once all the people and items were loaded, *Titanic* turned west towards New York.

A final photograph of *Titanic* shows her unmistakable profile – four funnels, two radio masts and swept-up stern – still accompanied by a tender, which is dwarfed by the liner. *Titanic* steamed into the flat, open sea ahead of her, with Ireland and Europe disappearing in the distance.

A Floating Microcosm of Society

On 9 April, the day before *Titanic*'s maiden voyage, some of the ship's First-Class passengers travelled to the departure city of Southampton and spent the night at South Western House. Hotel guests on the upper floors, including *Titanic*'s owner, J. Bruce Ismay, would have been able to see her from their windows.

For an off-season departure that had been rescheduled, *Titanic* was still teeming with passengers of note in First Class. Captain Edward J. Smith, despite his involvement and culpability in the *Olympic* accident, would be at the helm. Smith always took White Star's newest ship to sea. For him, this was not only a bit of redemption after

Olympic, but it was also a final bow, and after this voyage the captain would finally be retiring.

Knowing this, some of Smith's favourite passengers had made sure they were on board. They included John Jacob Astor IV, believed to be the world's richest man at the time, travelling with his new, but not first, wife Madeleine, who was also pregnant; Margaret Brown, the estranged wife of a Colorado mining tycoon; New York millionaire Benjamin Guggenheim and his personal servant, along with his mistress, Léontine Pauline Aubart; and Isador and Ida Straus, who co-owned New York's famous Macy's Department Store.

Travelling in an official capacity along with White Star's Ismay was the ship's designer, Harland & Wolff's Thomas Andrews, who would be inspecting the vessel during the journey, looking for small fixes that might be needed and where further improvements on White Star's next massive liner, *Britannic*, could be made. Ismay may have breathed a sigh of relief when he learned that his boss, J.P. Morgan, who had originally planned to be on board, had cancelled to spend more time on vacation in France. Also cancelling at the last minute was Guglielmo Marconi, inventor of the wireless telegraph and winner of the 1909 Nobel Prize for physics. Despite his company's radio equipment being installed on board and having been invited by White Star to sail on *Titanic*, urgent business required him to return earlier to New York. His family should have travelled on *Titanic* as planned, however, before the ship sailed, Marconi's son Giulio became ill and the remaining family members chose to wait in England while he recovered.

Far below the rarefied air of First Class, the Chinese men boarded via the Third-Class entrance near the bow and made their way to their accommodation. *Titanic* quartered Third-Class single or unaccompanied men in the bow; women, children and families were placed closer to the stern. For men who normally worked in engine rooms and galleys, their quiet bunks away from the ship's machinery must have been a relatively serene pleasure. Most likely, the men would have been berthed in cabins on F or G Decks, roughly at *Titanic*'s waterline. The men may not have known each other well, but they had a lot more in common than with *Titanic*'s other passengers. Except for *Titanic*'s officers and crew and a few men who had served in the navy, the Chinese men were among the most experienced seamen on board.

Life on Board

While White Star reserved most of the luxury for which its ships were known for First and Second Class; Third Class on *Titanic* also provided a higher standard of service than was available elsewhere. Even in Third Class, each cabin had electric lights and its own wash-basin with running water. Single men were given mattresses stuffed with straw and blankets, although many preferred to use their own bedclothes and linens, as most carried these with them in their possessions. As for bathing facilities, the hundreds of Third-Class passengers, male and female, had two bathtubs to share between them. However, in 1912, daily bathing beyond washing one's face was not common.

Third-Class passengers had access to a common sitting room on the poop deck – the sweeping stern of *Titanic* – and Third-Class men had a saloon they could use, complete with bar and tables for card playing and other games. There were also outdoor areas where they could get some fresh air and gaze at the passing ocean.

Perhaps the best part of Third-Class travel aboard *Titanic* was the meals. Three meals per day were served in a dining room that could seat 473 passengers, requiring the entire class to be split in two. Passengers, no matter their class, were served sit-down meals, unlike the sprawling buffets for which cruise ships are now known – buffets would have been considered impractical and undignified, even in Third Class. Diners shared common tables built for twenty. Breakfast was served in the morning, with the day's main meal, known as dinner, offered at midday. A snack, called tea, was served in the afternoon, with a lighter meal called supper in the evening. On 14 April, passengers enjoyed the following menu:

BREAKFAST
Oatmeal Porridge & Milk
Smoked Herrings
Jacket Potatoes
Ham & Eggs
Fresh Bread & Butter
Marmalade
Swedish Bread

Tea
Coffee

DINNER
Rice Soup
Fresh Bread
Cabin Biscuits
Roast Beef with Brown Gravy
Sweet Corn
Boiled Potatoes
Plum Pudding
Sweet Sauce
Fruit

TEA
Cold Meat
Cheese
Pickles
Fresh Bread & Butter
Stewed Figs & Rice
Tea

SUPPER
Gruel
Cabin Biscuits
Cheese[5]

There were no cooking facilities for Third-Class passengers, so the Chinese men would have eaten with the other passengers. Whether they enjoyed all of the dishes is unknown, but they certainly would have had plenty of choices and generous portions.

Unlike today's floating amusement parks, *Titanic's* passengers were largely left to entertain themselves. Life on board, much as with any other cruise ship of the time, followed a routine. Disciplined and energetic passengers may have risen for a constitutional walk around the deck – strolling from stem to stern three times would have been about 1 mile (1.6km). Early risers in First Class may have gone for a plunge in *Titanic*'s saltwater pool. Then breakfast, followed perhaps by getting some sun on deck or visiting other passengers. Dinner – what we now think of as lunch – would have come in the middle of the day.

The afternoon would have been filled with letter writing or perhaps a nap, and then the evening meal, for which First and Second-Class passengers would have dressed up. Afterwards, men may have gone to the smoking room for a drink or two and a cigar and chat with others, while the women moved into smaller groups in their own quarters or in other lounges set aside for them.

Third-Class options were far simpler. Single men and families were separated not only for accommodation but also for meals and recreation. These areas were found close to their quarters, again with men toward the bow and families in the stern. Aside from meals, they could organise card games, draughts or chess, play music, read books or use anything else they had brought along to pass the time. They also had their own outdoor spaces on deck. Their vistas may not have been as awe-inspiring as those for other classes, but Third-Class passengers had as much opportunity to enjoy fresh air and sunshine on the open ocean as anyone else did.

The Chinese passengers likely kept to themselves, and other Third-Class passengers did not engage with them. US Government regulations did not permit Third-Class passengers to mix with First and Second Class – this was done officially to prevent the perceived transmission of disease. Probably, the men took in as much of *Titanic* as locked gates and signs declaring areas off limits would permit them, not having ever served on a ship of this size. Their seamen's eyes would have allowed them to see details of the ship's design and its underlying operations that were missed by the layperson.

Three of the men may have talked of their future. Fang Lang, Lee Ling and Len Lam had big plans for America. Likely unbeknown to the Donald Line, the trio already had their eyes on an idea that would allow them to remain in the United States legally. For them, being transferred to the North American routes was the beginning of the fulfilment of that dream.

Fang, Lee and Len were acquainted prior to boarding *Titanic*, likely having met on other ships or possibly they were loosely related or knew each other from Taishan.[6] Together, the three had formulated a plan: pooling their own and some family resources, the three would open a store together and become merchants. At the time, due to the Chinese Exclusion Act of 1882 and related legislation, most Chinese were not permitted to enter and remain in the United States. However, along with government officials, students and tourists, merchants were a group who could stay legally. With some false identity papers, a bit of capital and some gumption, the three could fake it until they made it. Lee had even arranged to marry Sue Oi, a Chinese woman already living in Omaha, Nebraska, who would await her betrothed's arrival in their city of choice: Cleveland, Ohio.[7]

Fang was well prepared for his life after ships: in his baggage, he carried with him six shirt collars – men of the time would change their collars rather than owning more shirts or cleaning the whole shirt more frequently, both of which tended to be expensive. He also carried half a dozen neckties.[8] Fang would not have had any occasion to wear them while working in an engine room or galley, but he was certainly ready to dress for the job he wanted.

＊

For all of *Titanic*'s passengers, that week in mid-April passed pleasantly. The weather was clear, although slightly colder than normal, and the ocean remained calm, making for smooth sailing. Such favourable conditions led to talk that *Titanic* might arrive in New York early, on Tuesday night, something for which Bruce Ismay was certainly hoping so that the ship's arrival could be publicised in the morning newspapers.[9] And so on 14 April, the passengers continued in their shipboard routine of meals, games, talk and other simple amusements.

Ice warnings received in the radio room made it to the bridge, but not to most passengers. For eight Chinese men sailing across the Atlantic, their thoughts were of family back home, future business opportunities, life in a new country and how to pass the next few days, not whether they would survive the night.

6

ESCAPE

Icebergs occur at both the North and South Poles. The size of icebergs varies widely, from some bigger than Manhattan Island to smaller pieces sometimes called growlers. Approximately 90 per cent of an iceberg floats underwater; this can be seen with any ice cube placed in a glass of water. The freshwater from which icebergs form freezes at 0°C (32°F), whereas seawater normally freezes at about -2°C (28.4°F) because of the salt dissolved in it. The internal temperature of an iceberg may be -15°C (5°F), slowing the speed at which they melt into the surrounding ocean. The glaciers from which icebergs break grow over thousands of years.

Although they are made from water, striking an iceberg is like hitting solid rock. On the North Atlantic's shipping lanes, icebergs in the spring were a regular danger, a reason for concern but not cause for alarm. Smaller ships had collided with icebergs and sunk, but they were nowhere near as large as *Titanic*, nor did they have any of her innovations, such as watertight compartments with doors that sealed themselves.

The spring of 1912 was a particularly bad season for icebergs. More than usual were being swept by currents down from the Arctic into the Atlantic shipping lanes. On 14 April, due to ice warnings received by wireless telegraph from other ships, Captain Smith chose a more southerly course than normal – about 50 miles (80km) further south – to avoid icebergs that had been reported by other ships.

Many ships were now carrying wireless telegraphs, sometimes called Marconis. More than being a safety device, they were also a cash cow – wealthier passengers enjoyed receiving and sending telegrams to and from their loved ones on land, and paid extra to do so, much like airline passengers do today for inflight internet access. The telegraphs were also useful for communication between ships, sending information about conditions, weather and, in this case, the presence of icebergs.

On Sunday, 14 April, as *Titanic* continued westward, it approached an area where icebergs and field ice (shallower ice covering the water's surface) had been sighted. *Titanic* may have received as many as six ice warnings from other ships, although it's possible that not all of them reached Captain Smith or the officers on the bridge, either because the radio operator was busy or they were not marked for urgent delivery. Regardless, Smith was aware that ice lay ahead but was not sufficiently concerned to alter course further south or reduce *Titanic*'s speed from 22.5 knots.

As night fell, the air temperature turned markedly colder and was noticed by both crew and passengers.[1] This was a time before technological advances like radar or sonar. The only way that a ship knew what was in front of it was if someone saw it.

High in the crow's nest – a small place on top of the forward mast where crew could watch for ships and other dangers on the water – two lookouts stood. The cold air whistled past them. It was the night of the new moon, the darkest night of each month. There was neither cloud cover nor fog that night. The sky was filled with stars and the sea was flat calm.

Unlike contemporary automobiles, ships did not direct lights forward to illuminate anything that might appear in their path. Seeing something that lay ahead of the ship was entirely dependent on the eyesight of two men staring forward in the dark. Normally, they would have had binoculars to assist them. However, a last-minute crew change in Southampton saw a *Titanic* officer leave the ship unexpectedly, taking the key to access the crow's nest binoculars with him.

At 11.40 p.m., lookout Frederick Fleet saw 'a black mass' approaching in front of *Titanic*. He rang the lookout's bell three times, then picked up a telephone connected to the bridge. He reported, 'Iceberg! Right ahead!'

On *Titanic*'s bridge, Sixth Officer James Moody, who answered Fleet's call, told First Officer William Murdoch, who ordered the ship hard to port in an attempt to go around the iceberg. But a ship the size of *Titanic* requires a significant distance to turn or stop, especially when travelling at speed. The ship turned, turned, turned – and just when it appeared that *Titanic* might slip past, steel crunched against ice, knocking bits of ice onto the ship's deck. Fleet later said he thought it had been a 'narrow shave'.[2] Instead, it was a long, deep gash.

The Beginning of the End

When *Titanic*'s hull scraped against the massive mountain of frozen water, Captain Smith in his cabin, high above the point of impact, and the Chinese and other Third-Class male passengers quartered in the bow, all felt and heard her being fatally wounded. *Titanic*'s starboard side and keel both took damage. Fleet said he thought the iceberg rose 50–60ft (15–18m) above the water.[3] Quartermaster George Rowe heard the collision and looked starboard to see the iceberg, stating that it was at least 100ft (33m) high.[4] Like a stealthy assassin, the iceberg had appeared, inflicted the fatal wound and quickly receded into the dark and was not seen again.

Captain Smith arrived on the bridge, asking, 'What was that?'

Titanic architect Thomas Andrews went to inspect for damage and upon returning to the bridge, he informed Smith that five of *Titanic*'s watertight compartments were flooding and the ship would sink.[5] Smith gave the order to prepare lifeboats for launch. Second Officer Charles Lightoller, the highest-ranking *Titanic* officer to survive, recalled, 'I asked him: "Shall I put the women and children in the boats?" The captain replied, "Yes, and lower away".'[6]

Officers and crew were assigned to specific boats and roles in an emergency, but passengers received no advance training or guidance regarding evacuation procedures. How twenty lifeboats with insufficient capacity for everyone on board would be filled, and by whom, was left to *Titanic*'s officers to decide.

Following the sinking of RMS *Republic* three years earlier, White Star built its ships to withstand collisions with other liners, not sidelong impacts with terrain. But *Titanic's* watertight bulkheads, despite the name, extended only up to E Deck, not all the way to the top of the ship – a design choice that fostered easier movement through its passenger areas, but was ultimately a fatal flaw. Instead of crashing perpendicular into *Titanic* as another ship might have, the iceberg damaged both the ship's starboard side and the keel beneath the ship, creating a tear in the hull that led to flooding in five compartments.

The lifeboats were insufficient for all aboard, but each passenger, including Third Class, had access to a lifebelt (today, this would be called a life preserver, life vest or life jacket). Filled with buoyant cork inside a canvas shell, the vest covered the wearer's front and back. The user would slip their head through and then tie each side securely using attached cords.

Below Decks

The Chinese men had not encountered icebergs on any of their routes, having not worked so far north or on transatlantic lines at any point in their careers. But as professional seamen, they knew when something was wrong on a ship. When the engines stopped, waking many who had slept through the iceberg impact, it was a sign of something serious. A passenger liner underway in the middle of the Atlantic Ocean doesn't stop without good reason.

Third-Class passenger Daniel Buckley later testified:

I heard a terrible noise and I jumped out on the floor, and the first thing I knew my feet were getting wet, the water was coming in just slightly […] I told the other fellows to get up, that there was something wrong and that the water was coming in. They only laughed at me. One of them said, 'Get back into bed, you're not in Ireland now.'[7]

Quartered in the bow on F or G Decks with other single, male Third-Class travellers, the Chinese passengers had little time for confusion.

Having felt and heard the impact with the iceberg, they also noticed the ship starting to tilt forward.

None of the Chinese survivors of *Titanic* left behind any description of their route from their quarters to lifeboats or their fate in the water. However, based on the lifeboats in which they left *Titanic* and those boats' locations and launch times, combined with known movements and escape routes available to Third-Class passengers, we can extrapolate their most likely path up and out of the ship.

About twenty minutes after the collision, the Chinese passengers' feet were already wet. At their location, so far forward in the ship, having first felt the iceberg strike and then the bow tilt, the appearance of water was clearly no burst pipe. They dropped from their bunks and dressed, grabbed some personal items and began heading for relatively higher ground, moving towards the stern. They were among the first of a building wave of Third-Class passengers that would spend the next two hours seeking safety – most in vain.

Emerging from their cabin, the men had few choices. Watertight doors had dropped into place automatically, limiting their access to much of the rest of the deck and leading only to a nearby staircase. Going down was obviously no good; as such, the men went up.

It was immediately clear that travelling in First Class gave passengers access to the lifeboats, if not priority. That meant passengers closest to the Boat Deck – *Titanic's* top deck – would board first, followed by Second-Class passengers. *Titanic* only had enough lifeboat space for about half of the people on board. Almost every passenger – though not crew – could be saved if each boat was loaded to its rated capacity and launched successfully. Third-Class passengers had no way of knowing this, and no one from the officers or crew was about to tell them. As midnight passed, First-Class passengers, who were closest to where *Titanic's* lifeboats were stored, were alerted to the danger by ship stewards and began to gather outside, although few understood the full extent of the risk and many expressed reluctance to leave the giant ship.

Of all of *Titanic's* passengers, the eight Chinese would have been among the most obviously foreign. On board also were one Japanese passenger travelling in Second Class, Masabumi Hosono, and one black passenger, Joseph Laroche, from Haiti, also in Second Class.

During normal operation, there was a general policy barring Third-Class passengers from the upper decks of the ship, including the Boat Deck. Third-Class travellers were allowed only as high as C Deck, and even then, only to the Third-Class common room at the ship's stern. They boarded via a large door also on E Deck, then made their way to cabins or other decks. Because of this, in an emergency, Third-Class passengers trying to find their way to the boat deck were moving through completely unfamiliar territory.

On E Deck, a long corridor nicknamed Scotland Road ran almost the full length of the ship. It gave the crew a way to move back and forth, out of sight of First and Second-Class passengers. It also provided access for Third-Class passengers, especially the men in the bow, to reach the Third-Class common room in the ship's stern.

In his seminal book, *The Rescue of The Third Class on the Titanic: A Revisionist History*, former Adelphi University Statistics Professor David Gleicher outlines twenty possible routes that Third-Class passengers could have used to reach the Boat Deck.[8] Assuming that, as mariners, the Chinese men would know their way around a ship better than others, some of the less common routes perhaps become possible. However, evidence indicates that they still took paths to the Boat Deck used by many other Third-Class passengers.

As the mail room in the bow flooded and *Titanic* began to sink by the head, her stewards directed Third-Class passengers being pushed out of their cabins by water to move towards the stern via the long corridor. At about midnight, the Chinese and other male Third-Class passengers moved from their flooding quarters along Scotland Road to the Third-Class common room. Third-Class families berthed in the stern would join them later.

There in the common room, the Chinese men and other Third-Class passengers waited. Neither they nor *Titanic*'s stewards really knew what they were waiting for, since there was no plan for evacuating Third Class. But the common room was temporarily away from encroaching water and as the ship continued sinking, it became the high ground, seemingly safer than other areas. However, the common room offered no direct access to the Boat Deck, and only by reaching the Boat Deck did passengers have any hope of survival.

Launching the Lifeboats

The launch sequence and timing of *Titanic*'s lifeboats are hotly contested among historians. The British Wreck Commissioner's Inquiry, also known as the British Inquiry, held after *Titanic*'s sinking was the first to establish such a timeline. There are at least three other commonly accepted departure schedules. This book will adhere to the one developed by *Titanic* scholars Bill Wormstedt, Tad Fitch and George Behe (see Appendix).

Why does the order of *Titanic* lifeboat departures matter? *Titanic*'s history is a tapestry of eyewitness testimony stitched together with empirical evidence. Eyewitness accounts, while we as human beings want to believe them, are notoriously unreliable, especially when those memories are created in a time of crisis or emergency. They are also easily tainted as a person hears other accounts of an event in which they participated. This is a serious problem when piecing together the timeline of *Titanic*'s sinking. A person may claim that they saw a particular event, but knowing that person left in, for example, Lifeboat 6, and was already hundreds of yards from *Titanic* when the event took place – making it impossible for them to have seen it – is critical to creating an accurate and precise record of what occurred and when.

Also, which passengers occupied which lifeboats was only reconstructed years after the sinking. Many passengers thought – and testified – that they departed *Titanic* in the last available lifeboat, an observation that was most often wrong. When the rescue ship *Carpathia* arrived and began picking up survivors, its officers did not yell down, 'What lifeboat is this?' Similarly, no one stood by with a clipboard and took names as they boarded. As such, there remains some uncertainty about some passengers' exact lifeboat placement.

If the Chinese passengers spent more than a minimum of time on the Boat Deck, no one noticed them there. Unlike their presence in certain lifeboats, which is relatively well documented, there is not a single account of them being seen waiting for boats or otherwise moving around on *Titanic*'s top deck. From this, we can deduce that their time on deck was fairly short, helping to create a timeline for their movement from their bow quarters to the boat deck.

The first Third-Class male passenger to depart *Titanic* was Fahīm Rūḥānā al-Za'innī, who anglicised his name as Philip Zanni or Phillip Zenni. Despite being chased away twice, Zenni finally leaped into Lifeboat 6, which departed *Titanic* between 12.55 and 1.10 a.m. – this was the second boat lowered from the port side.[9] Two more single Third-Class men boarded Lifeboat 9 about ten minutes later. This demonstrates that Third-Class male passengers quartered in the bow could have reached the boat deck at this early stage and got off.

Titanic did not sink quickly, remaining afloat for just over two hours and forty minutes after striking the iceberg. In contrast, *Lusitania* would go down in fewer than twenty minutes in May 1915 and *Britannic*, *Titanic*'s sister ship, stayed afloat for less than an hour after hitting a mine in November 1916. The time that *Titanic* lasted saved hundreds of lives and allowed for the proper loading and safe launching of eighteen of its twenty lifeboats. So relatively leisurely was its evacuation that the first lifeboat didn't launch until an hour after hitting the iceberg.

Lifeboats were loaded primarily from the Boat Deck, giving women and children priority. On the starboard side, First Officer Henry Wilde boarded 'women and children first'. On the port side, Second Officer Charles Lightoller enforced a lifeboat loading policy of 'women and children only'. The only men permitted in boats were the *Titanic* crew members needed for rowing and steering, who were assigned and ordered by officers to enter specific boats.

The ship continued to sink, and more and more passengers realised it. The Chinese men and other Third-Class passengers could feel the angle of their position in the common room increasing and it was clear that they were in the wrong place.

At some point, the Chinese men left the common room to find their own way to the Boat Deck. Retracing their steps, the men went back towards Scotland Road. Near the stern end of Scotland Road was the aft Second-Class staircase, which was accessed via an emergency door. The men would have boarded *Titanic* near there, and although they may not have seen it then or on their way to the common room, the emergency door could have been open or at least able to be pushed open to reveal the way up. That staircase led directly to the Boat Deck and brought the men out amidst the aft lifeboats.

Lifeboats 10 and 13

These aft boats included Lifeboat 10, on the port side, and Lifeboat 13, on the starboard side. Chinese survivor Cheong Foo traditionally has been placed in Lifeboat 13, and Japanese survivor Hosono in Lifeboat 10. However, it is important to ascertain which boat Cheong Foo was in because it establishes a likely timeline of when the Chinese passengers reached the Boat Deck, and why half of them departed in the starboard side's last lifeboat.

Lifeboat 13 departed at 1.15 a.m., and Lifeboat 10 at 1.45 a.m. While it is possible that the Chinese passengers split up and tried to reach the Boat Deck in more than one group, we will assume that they stayed together until the later stages of *Titanic's* sinking. If Cheong took Lifeboat 13 at 1.15, that would place the Chinese men on deck about midway through the lifeboat loading process. But it then seems strange that four of the other seven men had to wait for the second-to-last boat, Collapsible Lifeboat C, to make their escape, and three others ended up in the water after spending so much time on deck. More importantly, the evidence points strongly to Hosono, a Second-Class passenger, leaving the Boat Deck earlier aboard 13 and Cheong arriving on deck later with the other Chinese men and getting into 10.

Hosono never suggested a number for his lifeboat. He made his way towards the Boat Deck but was sent back down for being a foreigner. Hosono was able to return to the Boat Deck on a second attempt. He would have known the aft Second-Class staircase well, as that was where he and other Second-Class passengers boarded *Titanic*. Prior to 13's launch, Second-Class passengers, both men and women, began leaving as early as 1.05 a.m. aboard Lifeboat 9.[10]

The Japanese passenger said that he was standing near a lifeboat when the officer in charge shouted, 'Room for two more!' Another man jumped aboard and, seeing his opportunity, Hosono followed. Lifeboat 13 was almost filled to rated capacity, with around sixty passengers, a number estimated by Able Seaman Frank Oliver Evans in his testimony to the US Inquiry.[11] In contrast, Lifeboat 10 was so empty that Chief Baker Charles Joughin testified in the British Inquiry that he and other crewmen descended to A Deck to find women and moved them bodily into the boat.[12]

The presence of Cheong or Hosono was not apparent to everyone involved. Lawrence Beesley, who left *Titanic* aboard Lifeboat 13 and published one of the most famous early books about the disaster, *The Loss of the SS Titanic*, did not take note of an Asian passenger in his account. Albert Caldwell, who was also in 13 and spoke often of his and his family's experience during and after the sinking, never mentioned noticing an Asian passenger being in their boat. Beesley repeats Ismay's later claim of 'four Chinamen' in his book.[13] Able Seaman Edward J. Buley said nothing about Asians in his boat, Lifeboat 10, during his inquiry testimony. Evans said he thought there was 'one foreigner' in his boat.[14]

Dining Room Steward William Burke, who was in Lifeboat 10, recalled being told there were two men in his boat:

I said, 'Are there so?' I made down in the bottom of the boat and got hold of those two men and pulled one out. I found he was, apparently, a Japanese and could not speak any English. I explained to him and put him on an oar. The other man appeared to me to be an Italian, about 18 stone. I tried to speak to him in Italian and he said, 'Armenian'. That was all he could say. I also put him on an oar.[15]

There was indeed one male Armenian passenger in Lifeboat 10 – Neshan Krekorian. If the Asian man in the boat with him could not speak any English, that would not be Hosono, who was university educated and spoke both Russian and some English. Meanwhile, Cheong was known to be illiterate, perhaps even in Chinese.

Burke's account overlaps with that of Mary Fortune, also a Lifeboat 10 survivor. 'They were put in a boat with a Chinaman, an Italian stoker and a man dressed in woman's clothing', according to one journalist.[16] 'The man dressed in woman's clothes did his best but did not seem familiar with an oar. This man wore a woman's bonnet and a veil in addition to a skirt and blouse.' Unfortunately for Mrs Fortune's imagination, there is no evidence that any male passenger donned full drag to get into a lifeboat, especially Lifeboat 10.

Shades of this account also appear in a story attributed to Elizabeth Anne Mellinger. A Vermont newspaper reported that in her boat 'were only two men, an Armenian and a Chinaman, neither of whom could speak much English'.[17] Mellinger and her daughter were ultimately rescued in Lifeboat 14, which did indeed have one Chinese man and one Italian man on board — but only after Fifth Officer Harold Lowe returned to the shipwreck area to search for any remaining survivors.

Also, there was enough room in Lifeboat 10 that when Lowe came along later in the evening, he was able to transfer '12 or 15 passengers' to it, according to Burke, and he took Evans and another crewman with him to search for survivors.

Given this preponderance of evidence, we will place Hosono in Lifeboat 13, Cheong in 10 and therefore the Chinese men on deck close to 1.45 a.m. That would have given Cheong time to reach Lifeboat 10, the last of the aft lifeboats from either side to go and the last full-sized wooden boat to leave *Titanic*. From that moment on, any chance of survival in a lifeboat lay forward, requiring a counterintuitive survival strategy: move away from the 'high ground' of *Titanic*'s rising stern and head toward the waterline, where as many as five more boats were loading.

With Lifeboat 10's departure, fifteen of *Titanic*'s lifeboats had launched. Remaining were Lifeboat 2, a cutter or emergency wooden boat on the port side, and four collapsible boats. Lifeboat 2 lowered at 1.50 a.m., clearing the way for Collapsibles C and D to be assembled and loaded.

Collapsible C and Ismay's Exit

There is some controversy surrounding the loading of both collapsible boats, especially C. *Titanic* owner J. Bruce Ismay, who escaped in C, said that there was no commotion during the loading of the boat and he heard no gunshots while that was happening. William Ernest Carter, a First-Class passenger who boarded Collapsible C at the same time as Ismay, echoed his statements, as did Quartermaster George Rowe, the crewman placed in command of C. All three indicated that there was no trouble surrounding its loading and launch, and when it was lowered, there were no women or children left in the vicinity.

Ismay and Rowe testified to this effect during the US Inquiry, and the former did so again at the British Inquiry.

However, oother eyewitnesses claimed there was a struggle to load the boat, and *Titanic* officers and crew had to keep Third-Class men out of it. Hugh Woolner claimed that he and fellow First-Class passenger Mauritz Håkan Björnström-Steffansson assisted officers and crew in removing men from the boat so that women and children could board. This and other disputes regarding the Chinese survivors and Collapsible C will be discussed in detail in a later chapter.

Peaceful or otherwise, four Chinese men – generally believed to be Ah Lam, Chang Chip, Lee Bing and Ling Hee – boarded Collapsible C, which launched at 2 a.m. *Titanic* had sunk to the point where it was only 15ft (4.5m) above the water. The ship was also listing, or tilting, so much towards the port side – the side opposite where C was launching – that the lifeboat scraped repeatedly against *Titanic*'s hull on the way down.

Where were the other three Chinese men? None escaped aboard Collapsible D, the last boat formally launched. Boats A and B were both washed off *Titanic*'s deck before they could be loaded.

Love Reveals All

A seemingly unrelated newspaper story published after the sinking seems to tell the story. The tale of a lovelorn, would-be bride from Omaha reveals a glimpse of *Titanic*'s final minutes and decisions that shattered years of dreams and careful planning. On 20 April 1912, *The Akron Beacon Journal* published 'Lover Lost; Chinese Maid Wants to Die'.[18] An alluring headline to be sure, but it risked burying the lead by only using '*Titanic*' in the subheading.

Laundrywoman Sue Oi had not only lost her lover, she had also lost him in the most famous maritime disaster of all time:

> There's a yellow maiden with a look of dead grief in her lustrous jet eyes here in Cleveland. Sue Oi, for she's a Chinese girl, is as pathetically eager to learn the final fate of the Titanic's steerage passengers as some fashionable women in New York are that of the first-class list.[19]

Residing at 1291 Ontario Street, Sue Oi's former address is now a stone's throw from the Rock and Roll Hall of Fame and the Cleveland Browns' NFL stadium on the southern shore of Lake Erie. Oi had travelled from Omaha – she was likely born in the United States, as immigration from China for a woman would have been extremely difficult – to Cleveland to marry Ah Sam Len, who was travelling there with two other friends, Sam Fang Lang and Lee Ling. According to Oi, Ah Sam Len had previously visited Cleveland, where he was going to open a store. He was importing merchandise from China and he planned to employ Sam Fang Lang and Lee Ling as clerks. By marrying Oi, he would complete his American dream, as imagined by Chinese immigrants of the time. The newspaper reported:

> Now there is nothing for Sue Oi to do but spend her trousseau money for joss sticks and incense to burn before that little picture of Ah Sam Len that she wears over her heart. There is nothing further in life for her. 'I only want now to die,' she said through an interpreter.[20]

Sad as the story is, it reveals something not previously known about *Titanic*'s Chinese passengers. At minimum, Ah Sam Len, the *Titanic* passenger registered as Len Lam, Sam Fang Lang, better known as Fang Lang; and Lee Ling all knew each other, were travelling and working together and would have been departing for Cleveland upon their arrival in New York – not aboard SS *Annetta*, as their employer, the Donald Line believed.

Faced with *Titanic*'s sinking, the three stuck together as they and the other Chinese passengers made their way to the deck. Their mutual bond sadly became a suicide pact. Fang and Lee followed their would-be employer, and when either he or they failed to find space in a lifeboat, all three ended up in the water.

In Cold Water

A popular myth ascribes numerous *Titanic* deaths to cold water, which caused spontaneous heart attacks, leading some to die in minutes.

While the water in which *Titanic* sank was near-freezing that night, cold water does not cause this kind of reaction within the human body. Instead, 'cold shock', a term first coined by Professor Mike Tipton of the University of Portsmouth,[21] can instead lead to sudden death if cold water is entered at speed and by people not accustomed to it. When humans enter icy water quickly, such as jumping in from *Titanic*'s rail, an involuntary reaction, namely inhalation that would lead to water entering the lungs, posed the greatest immediate risk. *Titanic*'s passengers and crew would not have known about this at the time, and some jumped into the water, fearing they would be pulled underwater by suction caused by the ship sinking if they waited until the last moment. Therefore, many of the ship's early victims died not from exposure but drowning, despite having sufficient floatation in the form of lifebelts.

We may never know what happened to Lee and Len beyond that they did not survive. Some of *Titanic*'s last passengers to leave the deck were struck and killed by debris or falling funnels. As described above, some may have drowned due to cold shock, but most who survived the actual sinking would eventually die from hypothermia. Depending on their dress and experience in cold water, they would have had twenty to thirty minutes of functionality, being able to swim or float, to try to locate a boat or a piece of wreckage that could save them.

Water wicks heat away from the body twenty times faster than air. A 24°C (75°F) day would be a short-sleeved, pleasant day for a healthy adult. However, that same temperature in water will start to feel cold after about an hour or less, forcing scuba divers and surfers to don wetsuits for warmth. Around *Titanic*, where the water was estimated to be just above freezing, hypothermia started to claim its first victims thirty to forty-five minutes after the sinking, with the rest to follow.

Getting out of the water was the key to survival, as the cold air was not nearly as deadly as the water. Second Officer Charles Lightoller and others survived by balancing on the overturned Collapsible B, even with wet clothing.

Fang Lang's Fight for Life

Cold and separated from his friends in the dark, Fang Lang made his way through the water, searching for the other two and looking for something to save him. He, Lee and Len had waited until the last moment to enter the water, Fang likely encouraging them to just hang on, although he knew that, unlike him, they could not swim. He honestly believed that the lifebelts would keep them afloat – they just had to find a lifeboat and get in.

Numbness gripped him. His hands were losing feeling. The cold was most uncomfortable right around his neck, where the air met the water. He thrashed, trying to keep his head above the surface, looking for a lifeboat or anything onto which he could grab. Finally, his hand hit something large. He struck it again and realised it was a piece of wood potentially large enough to hold him. Fang later said he was able to get on top of it and secured himself to it using a belt or bit of rope. For the moment, at least, he was safe but the cold continued to sap his life. The others had disappeared. Maybe he could survive.

One Came Back

Of the eighteen boats that were properly launched, only one ever went back towards the spot of *Titanic*'s sinking to try to rescue more people. Fifth Officer Harold Lowe, an experienced mariner with a short temper, who had fired his gun to scare off male passengers from boarding lifeboats, moved mostly women and children off Lifeboat 14 to make space for other survivors. Lowe took two crewmen from Lifeboat 10, Buley and Evans, and headed back to where the screams of survivors had died down.

Lowe would be disappointed. In a scene depicted accurately and poignantly in James Cameron's *Titanic* film, Lowe and his crew passed dozens of bodies as they called out for survivors. They hauled in a portly man, First-Class passenger William Hoyt, who died soon after. Floating on a piece of wood, a Chinese man moved just enough to indicate he was alive as the lifeboat rowed past.[22]

In the end, Harold Charles William Phillimore of *Titanic*'s vict-
ualling crew; Italian Second-Class passenger Emilio Ilario Giuseppe
Portaluppi, who claimed he survived resting on an ice floe after swimming for two hours; and a Chinese man listed on the passenger manifest
as Fang Lang were the only three who were successfully rescued.

The Scientific Method

To determine how long Fang would have been in the water and how
long he could have survived, your author participated in an experiment
supervised by the University of Portsmouth's Professor Tipton at the
Extreme Environments Laboratory.[23] It involved thirty-five minutes of
motionless immersion up to the neck in 12°C (54°F) water. Although
the water on the night of *Titanic*'s sinking was 0–2°C (32–35.6°F),
Professor Tipton refused to lower the temperature beyond 12°C,
believing it to be unethical and unnecessary for these purposes.

Your fully clothed writer shivered for most of the first and last ten
minutes, as my body temperature dropped consistently. That temperature was monitored using a thermometer inserted internally. By
remaining still, the body can build up a thin layer of warmer water
around itself, delaying the loss of heat.

But Fang would have had no such option, not until he found the
board and hauled himself out. The water around him was a sea of
writhing bodies, and he swam to find safety for himself – and protect
himself from others who might use him as floatation.

Most revealing from the Portsmouth experiment, was that two
manual tasks – screwing a nut onto a bolt and tying a knot around a
piece of wood – each took two to three times longer after immersion
than before. Despite understanding the task and wanting to complete
each more quickly, it simply felt physically impossible to finish more
swiftly than cold fingers and hands would allow. Afterwards, bearing
in mind that Fang was in water that was 10 or more degrees colder,
Professor Tipton estimated that Fang would have had no more than
fifteen to twenty minutes to find the piece of wood that saved his life
and clamber aboard. Longer than that, and Fang would not have had
the dexterity to pull himself out of the water or, as he later claimed,
to tie himself to it with a belt.

The Baker's Tale

One curious, similar case is that of *Titanic*'s chief baker, Charles Joughin. Joughin testified to the official British Inquiry that when he realised that the ship was going down, he ducked into his cabin for a 'drop of liqueur'.[24] This is an interesting admission under oath because it meant that Joughin was drinking on duty, during an emergency. When questioned further, he stated that he had consumed 'half a tumbler', which, while not a standard measure, was about 3oz (89ml). Joughin always denied that he was inebriated after the drink.

Although consuming alcohol makes the drinker feel warmer, it actually increases the effects of hypothermia. Joughin and members of the British Court of Inquiry believed that his drink saved his life, but if anything, the baker, who was not overweight nor had any other physical advantage, survived in spite of it. Alcohol inhibits the body's normal thermoregulatory response, and both alcohol and hypothermia diminish memory and the body's physical capacity.

Joughin claimed that he had been in the water for 'two or three hours', that he survived by keeping a hand on the upturned keel of Collapsible B and at least once he attempted to climb up, but was pushed back. He did not indicate if he had put on additional warm clothing for insulation, and even if he had, its benefit once it was wet would have been minimal.

Like many others who testified they were in the last lifeboat to leave *Titanic*, Joughin claimed he was the last person to go into the water from the ship. Having taken a big swig, the baker's perception and memory of events may have been affected. As we see throughout testimony relating to *Titanic*, survivors' recollections are often unreliable. Joughin was most likely in the water, treading water and attempting to board the upturned collapsible lifeboat, for about thirty minutes. He was assisted by another member of the cooking staff, Isaac Maynard, to hold onto the drifting lifeboat before he was finally hauled into Lifeboat 12 and saved. Despite admitting to drinking while on duty, Joughin was not reprimanded and later worked for the White Star Line again, aboard *Olympic*.

Rescue and Reunion

Just after daybreak on 15 April, RMS *Carpathia* arrived at the scene, illuminated by the first rays of the morning sun. *Carpathia*, captained by Arthur Rostron, had received *Titanic*'s distress signal, diverted from its course towards the Mediterranean and raced north-west through the night to reach the site of the sinking.

Collapsible C came alongside *Carpathia* at 5.45 a.m. Bruce Ismay exited the boat and identified himself to the crew, saying, 'I'm Ismay. I'm Ismay.' He was immediately escorted to the cabin of the ship's doctor, where he remained until the ship arrived in New York. One wonders if, among the myriad thoughts racing through Ismay's mind as he boarded the ship, he was conscious that he was being rescued by a Cunard vessel.

Over the next few hours, survivors on all of *Titanic*'s scattered lifeboats transferred to *Carpathia*. *Titanic*'s permanent lifeboats were brought on to the ship, while all four collapsibles were set adrift, including C, which was never seen again. Collapsible A was spotted and recovered a month later by White Star Line ship *Oceanic*, with three bodies still on board, as they had been when jettisoned by *Carpathia*'s crew.[25] The three men were not identified, nor did they receive a proper burial at sea from either *Carpathia* or *Oceanic*'s crew, and the boat drifted away again. Collapsible B was seen by the crew of *Mackay-Bennett*, the first of several cable ships sailing out of Halifax that were hired by White Star to recover bodies from the accident scene. They were unsuccessful in trying to retrieve it.

The six Chinese survivors finally learned of each other's fates on the deck of *Carpathia*, reunited after those harrowing hours in and on the bitterly cold water. They had beaten significant odds. Of 2,208 passengers and crew on board *Titanic*, they were among the 712 who survived. Of Third-Class men, only sixty made it to *Carpathia*. Despite the 'women and children only' policy on the port side and 'women and children first' on the starboard, some whole families died, including the Goodwins, a family of eight featured in Walter Lord's book *The Night Lives On*,[26] and the youngest of their six children, Sidney, was eventually identified as *Titanic*'s Unknown Child.

That six of the eight Chinese men lived was almost incredible. Only one of ten Danes survived. Of 327 British passengers, 223 went down with the ship. By nationality, only the Spanish (seven on board, of whom six survived) and the lone Japanese passenger Hosono had better survival rates. All fifteen Croatians on board perished and every single one of the thirty-three Bulgarians died.

Carpathia finally arrived in New York on the night of Thursday, 18 April. Under normal circumstances, any passenger ships arriving in New York would have first stopped at Ellis Island for immigration formalities, especially for Third-Class passengers. While no visas were required for entry into the United States, each new arrival was required to pass a health inspection. However, due to the unique circumstances facing *Titanic*'s survivors, *Carpathia* bypassed Ellis Island and went straight to *Titanic*'s berth at Pier 59 on the Hudson River, ghoulishly offloading its sixteen wooden lifeboats before finally proceeding to Cunard's Pier 54 for disembarkation. It was upon the remnants of Pier 54 that the New York City attraction Little Island was built. The now-rusted former Cunard archway remains in front of it, without a plaque or other indicator of its significant maritime history.

When *Carpathia* docked, thousands of relatives and onlookers gathered to witness this moment in history. Accounts from the time indicate that, at first, the crowd was silent. Only after the first passengers began to exit did the wailing begin, tears of joy for some and final confirmation that others would never arrive. Flashbulbs popped and reporters flocked to interview First-Class survivors, including Denver socialite Margaret Brown, later renamed Molly by Hollywood, who indeed declared herself 'unsinkable'. Ismay slipped away to the home of the White Star Line's vice president, Philip Franklin, on East 61st Street. Aid societies and other organisations attended to those in need, especially the children and newly widowed among the 179 Third-Class survivors, arriving without husbands or possessions in a strange land.

There was no red carpet for the Chinese passengers, not even a cup of coffee and a blanket from a local aid society. Instead, restricted from entry by the Chinese Exclusion Act of 1882, they spent another night aboard *Carpathia*. The next morning, they were escorted to the eastern side of Manhattan by US immigration officials and Donald Line representatives to their ship of employment, SS *Annetta*, and on 20 April, they sailed away with her.[27] In the following days, in their absence, the Chinese men would be blamed for the deaths of children, mothers and husbands, and accused of escaping the ship by dishonourable and shameful means.

7

COWARDS, STOWAWAYS
AND WOMEN

From the moment *Carpathia* arrived in New York, stories about *Titanic*'s Chinese passengers and their alleged behaviour on board began to filter out. Not one of them was positive. The *Brooklyn Daily Eagle* quoted 'one of the survivors of the *Titanic* tragedy', who was not named:

> One of the strangest things about the whole awful occurrence was the presence of five Chinamen in the lifeboats when they reached the *Carpathia*. No one could tell where the Chinese came from, nor how they got in the boats, but there they were.[1]

The Daily Telegraph, which was at least correct about the number of Chinese survivors, wrote:

> Among those rescued from the sinking *Titanic* were six Chinese, who had stowed themselves away in one of the vessel's boats before she left England. When the crash came the Chinese did not become excited. They knew the lifeboat would be lowered if there was any danger of the *Titanic* going down. All had shawls, and when they heard the shouts of those on board, 'Women to be saved first', they covered themselves with the shawls, leading the crew to believe they were women.[2]

In an interview with a Vermont newspaper, Mrs Elizabeth Mellinger told a whale of a tale about a Chinese man who carried a bundle and kept saying, 'Save Mellican baby' ('American', playing on the stereotypical belief that many Asian speakers of English will transpose the sounds of 'L' and 'R'), so that he would be allowed to enter Lifeboat 14. Later, she claimed, the 'baby' was revealed to be just some of the man's own clothing.[3]

Mellinger's story has more than one problem, namely that there were no Chinese passengers rescued in Lifeboat 14 – at least not until Fang Lang was pulled from the water at a time when she and her daughter had already been moved to Lifeboat 10, and so they were not present to see Fang's rescue.

These three examples are among many newspaper accounts that present the Chinese passengers negatively and claim that they acted dishonourably. It seems that few, if any, of the other *Titanic* passengers noticed the Chinese men during the cruise. It was only on *Carpathia*, when six out of the eight were among the survivors, that anyone else seemed to be aware of them. How they boarded a lifeboat was a mystery to some of the other survivors, leading them to believe that they must have done so using surreptitious means.

Three specific, although seemingly contradictory, accusations were levelled against the Chinese passengers by newspaper accounts of the time: they were stowaways, first aboard *Titanic* and then again aboard some of *Titanic*'s lifeboats; they gained access to *Titanic* lifeboats by furtive means, namely by disguising themselves as women, violating the spirit of the lifeboat boarding process and delaying or preventing the loading of other male passengers; and they forced their way into Collapsible C, then refused to leave, even when threatened at gunpoint.

The key question regarding the four men aboard Collapsible C, and Cheong Foo aboard Lifeboat 10, is did their presence in the lifeboats prevent the rescue of four other people, namely women and children? As these claims disgraced the reputation of *Titanic*'s Chinese survivors for more than a century, each will be examined in detail.

Assessment and Methodology

It is my hope that, after the Chinese passengers have lived in infamy for more than a century, you will spare some time to consider an objective analysis of *Titanic*'s Chinese passengers' actions and bear with this technical part of the book. This analysis relies primarily on testimony given at the 1912 United States Senate Inquiry and the British Wreck Commissioner's Inquiry. These are sometimes also referred to as the United States Inquiry or the American Inquiry, and the British Inquiry or the Board of Trade Inquiry, respectively.

The American Inquiry took place in New York on 19 April 1912 and was held over eighteen days between then and 28 May 1912. The hearings began in New York, ironically and ghoulishly at the Waldorf-Astoria Hotel, which had been partially owned by *Titanic* victim John Jacob Astor. They were later moved to Washington DC to allow the seven senators overseeing the inquiry to attend to other work as the inquest continued.

The British Inquiry took place after Ismay, along with *Titanic*'s officers and crew, returned to the UK. While *Titanic* was ultimately owned by the American International Mercantile Marine (IMM) Company, the White Star Line was still based in the United Kingdom, *Titanic* had flown the British flag and its place of registration was Liverpool.. As the Board of Trade oversaw all British shipping – and it could receive some blame for not requiring large passenger liners to carry more lifeboats – it was appropriate that it would hold its own inquiry.

Given the number of dead, the famous and wealthy people involved and the amount of press coverage *Titanic*'s sinking received, survivors from both sides of the Atlantic and the public demanded accountability and answers. For the time, this was the equivalent of a major air crash: a travelling public would want to know if the equipment and personnel training of the time were adequate and safe. Even if the iceberg were the sole culprit, no one was going to blame it alone for the deaths of almost 1,500 people and the loss of the world's biggest ship and leave it at that. Some person or persons had to be held responsible.

As for witnesses, *Titanic*'s three top-ranking officers – Captain Smith, Chief Officer Wilde and First Officer Murdoch – had all gone down with the ship. However, the owner, Ismay, had survived, as had Second Officer Lightoller, Third Officer Pitman, Fourth Officer Boxhall and Fifth Officer Lowe. Other important members of the crew who survived included Frederick Fleet, the lookout who spotted the iceberg, and Harold Bride, Junior Wireless Officer, who was sitting at the Marconi telegraph when *Titanic* struck the iceberg and who sent the first distress signal.

Some *Titanic* historians see the inquiries as a whitewash, official hearings that sought to place no real blame on anyone, especially the White Star Line. Those researchers instead suggest that newspaper interviews given by survivors after reaching New York and private letters exchanged between survivors, or between those who had lived and their family members, should be considered to be more honest in a time before social media, when people rarely revealed their secrets in public.

For the purposes of this examination of the evidence, the testimony given at the two inquiries receives more weight. They stand as official records of *Titanic*'s sailing, the collision with the iceberg, the sinking, and the rescue and recovery of lifeboats by *Carpathia*. Both took place within three months of *Titanic*'s sinking – Ismay's testimony at the American Inquiry began fewer than twenty-four hours after *Carpathia*'s arrival in New York and barely more than 100 hours after *Titanic*'s loss. Both led to government action and changes in the government regulation of shipping, such as additional lifeboats, emergency preparation, passenger drills and the creation of the International Ice Patrol, which operates to this day. Most importantly, both inquiries had the weight of law behind them – both were held by government bodies, and anyone found lying to either could have faced legal consequences.

Also, the vast majority of what is known and can be verified about the Chinese passengers' actions and the circumstances surrounding the launch of Collapsible C comes from official testimony. J. Bruce Ismay, Quartermaster Arthur John Bright, Quartermaster George Rowe and Pantry Steward Albert Pearcey, all of whom were in the boat or helped prepare it for launch, testified in detail regarding their experiences in and around Collapsible C.

All available materials have been considered to recreate accurately and objectively what happened at Collapsible C as *Titanic* sank.

Evidence from non-inquiry sources has provided valuable insight into that night's events. The inquiry testimony is not infallible; the embellishments, omissions and outright mistakes of the witnesses become apparent over the course of their statements. In the next chapter, each accusation against the Chinese passengers will be evaluated against the various accounts that have survived.

Sadly, we have no materials relating to that night from the Chinese passengers themselves. They were never interviewed about *Titanic*, nor did they leave behind any personal papers that recorded their version of the events in question.

One additional and exclusive source of information was used for the very first time: a full-scale reconstruction of an Engelhardt collapsible lifeboat, based on original blueprints. Other *Titanic* and White Star wooden lifeboat replicas are known to exist, but this was perhaps the first collapsible to be built in decades. This proved invaluable in solving the history of Collapsible C and what happened aboard it.

COLLAPSIBLE C

In all the treatments of *Titanic*'s history in cinema and in print, there is perhaps one group of characters towards whom there is no enmity or suspicion: *Titanic*'s band. Led by Wallace Hartley, this group of eight men all perished, and continue to be lauded for adding an air of calm and dignity as the ship's lifeboats were loaded. Despite this universal embrace, *Titanic* scholars remain sharply divided as to what the band's final song was and whether they played right up until the ship's hull cracked, or if they had stopped sometime earlier.

All of this illustrates the contention that surrounds deeper discussion of the *Titanic* narrative. Even in matters relating to *Titanic*'s beloved band, there is disagreement. Therefore, it is unlikely that all *Titanic* historians will agree on an issue as controversial as the actions of the Chinese passengers in Collapsible Lifeboat C. However, careful examination of inquiry testimony, eyewitness accounts and the application of science and rational thought narrow the number of possible realities on the night.

One Hundred Years of Shame

In 1955, Walter Lord's book *A Night to Remember* reminded Europeans and North Americans of the cultural and societal impact that *Titanic*'s sinking had in the early part of the twentieth century. Then, almost exactly as many years from *A Night to Remember* as that book was from *Titanic*'s sinking, in 1997 James Cameron's global blockbuster *Titanic* made the story of the ship perhaps even more popular than the real vessel had been in its day.

The discovery of the wreck of *Titanic* in September 1985 had revived the story. The ship had clearly cracked, with the bow and stern sections landing hundreds of metres away from each other. The bow had remained remarkably intact but parts of the stern were almost unrecognisable. Some of *Titanic*'s survivors were still alive, and renewed interest in its history led to a *Titanic* renaissance, including a slew of new books and documentaries, and culminated in Cameron's film. The film presented much more of the Third-Class passengers' story than previous cinematic adaptations, such as glimpses of the diversity of that group, including a Chinese passenger.

As part of that revived interest, almost every aspect of *Titanic*'s history has been re-examined. Who was the Unknown Child – the only child's body recovered after the sinking? Could the *Californian*, which was stopped nearby at the time of the sinking, have saved *Titanic*'s passengers? Walter Lord himself kicked off the new wave of re-evaluation with his 1986 book, *The Night Lives On*.[1]

However, despite this surge of new scrutiny, the survival of six of *Titanic*'s Chinese passengers never landed in the spotlight, at least not in any languages besides Chinese. Whole books have been written in English about *Titanic*'s Irish, Jewish, Arabic-speaking and even its sole Black passenger.

In 2013, University of Chinese Academy of Social Sciences Professor Cheng Wei wrote a book entitled *Titanic's 'Chinamen'*,[2] examining the socioeconomic conditions and treatment of the Chinese passengers. Journalists in China did some research into the men and were able to identify Chinese names for them using documents available at the United States National Archives in New York, but even these works did not investigate whether the accusations against the Chinese passengers had any basis in fact.

The Testimony

What follows are the only official statements given to the American and British inquiries regarding Chinese passengers. Most of this testimony relates to the passengers in Collapsible C and a bit more addresses the presence of Asian passengers in Lifeboats 10 and 13.

The senators conducting the American Inquiry, led by Senator William Alden Smith of Michigan, were trying to make political hay by placing themselves at the forefront of investigating a disaster that was still front-page news. They were trying to paint J. Bruce Ismay as a coward who stole the place of a woman or child in one of *Titanic*'s last lifeboats. Ismay was attempting to maintain that he acted as a gentleman and found himself in Collapsible C almost by chance.

Ismay and Quartermaster George Rowe, who was ordered to take charge of Collapsible C by Captain Smith, testified at both inquiries about the presence of four 'Chinamen' or 'Filipinos' at daybreak. No Filipinos or other Asians, besides Japanese Masabumi Hosono, were on board *Titanic*, either as passengers or crew, so only the Chinese men could have been in the lifeboat. Rowe, testifying on Day 7 of the United States Inquiry, mentioned them first:

8080. The passengers, aside from you sailors, were all women and children?

Except Mr. Ismay and another gentleman. When daylight broke, we found four men, Chinamen, I think they were, or Filipinos.

8081. Were those additional to the 39?

Yes, sir.

8082. All the rest of the 39 were women and children, except two, Mr. Ismay and another gentleman?

Yes, sir.

8083. When day broke, you found four Chinamen or Filipinos under the seats?

Not under the seats then, sir. They came up between the seats. Ours was about the ninth boat which was unloaded upon the Carpathia. The night was very cold; but those who were in the boat were very well wrapped up and did not suffer.[3]

Ismay mentioned the Chinese men briefly on Day 11:

14410. How many men were in the boat?

Three - four. We found four Chinamen stowed away under the thwarts after we got away. I think they were Filipinos, perhaps. There were four of them.[4]

The same two witnesses echoed their American testimony when they appeared again at the British Wreck Commissioner's Inquiry, with Rowe first on Day 15:

17648. Why? Tell me about that?

I found four Chinamen aboard.

17649. Where were they?

I could not see at the time.

17650. They were in the boat somewhere?

They were in there at daybreak.

17651. How they got in you do not know, I suppose?

No.

17652. (The Commissioner.) Were they all women and children, with the exception of three Chinamen?

Four Chinamen and Mr. Ismay and Mr. Carter.

17653. I have the two male passengers. Were the rest all women and children with the exception of the crew and the four Chinamen?

And the two gentlemen.[5]

Ismay followed the next day, Day 16:

18563. Am I right, then, in this, that there were women and children and some members of the crew to man the boat and two passengers, yourself and Mr. Carter?

Yes, and four Chinamen were in the boat.

18564. Four Chinamen who, we have heard, were discovered after the boat was lowered?

Yes.[6]

These are the only mentions of the Chinese passengers in Collapsible C in the American Inquiry. Pantry Steward Albert Pearcey, who also left Titanic on C, did not refer to them in his testimony.[7]

The Rescue of Fang Lang

Fifth Officer Harold Lowe returned to the area of *Titanic*'s sinking aboard Lifeboat 14 to search for survivors. During his cantankerous testimony in New York, Lowe never pointed out that one of the four men he rescued was Chinese (Fang Lang), nor did he mention the order in which he and his crew retrieved them from the ocean. Lowe said only that one of the men, First-Class passenger William Hoyt, died soon after being pulled into the lifeboat. He added that he did not see the bodies of any women in the water, which seems strange although not impossible.

At the American Inquiry, Harold Lowe testified, 'So I transferred all my passengers – somewhere about 53 passengers – from my boat, and I equally distributed them between my other four boats', meaning boats 10, 12 and D, which had tied up with 14. Lowe wanted passengers out of 14 so that he could go back closer to the wreck site and search for survivors.[8]

Steward George Crowe survived in Lifeboat 14 and returned with Lowe to search for anyone still alive. He mentioned Fang Lang briefly in his testimony to the American inquiry:

Senator BOURNE. Did [Steward Harold Phillimore] survive?

Mr. CROWE. Yes, sir; also a Japanese or Chinese young fellow that we picked up on top of some of the wreckage – it might have been a sideboard or table – that was floating around.[9]

The most detailed account of Fang's rescue comes not from Lowe or Crowe, but from a magazine interview given by Second-Class passenger Charlotte Collyer, who had been travelling with her husband Harvey and their daughter, Marjorie. Charlotte and Marjorie left *Titanic* in Lifeboat 14. Collyer insisted that she remained in 14 after the transfer of passengers back to other boats, and that she returned with Lowe to the wreck site:

[Lowe] then, with great difficulty, distributed most of the women in our boat among the other craft. This took perhaps half an hour. It gave him an almost empty boat, and as soon as possible he cut loose, and we went in search of survivors.

It is not known why Lowe would have kept a few women in his boat instead of transferring all of them:

A little further on, we saw a floating door that must have been torn loose when the ship went down. Lying upon it, face downwards, was a small Japanese. He had lashed himself with a rope to his frail raft, using the broken hinges to make knots secure. As far as we could see, he was dead. The sea washed over him every time the door bobbed up and down, and he was frozen stiff. He did not answer when he was hailed, and the officer hesitated about trying to save him.

'What's the use?' said Mr. Lowe. 'He's dead, likely, and if he isn't there's others [*sic*] better worth saving than a Jap!'

He had actually turned our boat around, but he changed his mind and went back. The Japanese was hauled on board, and one of the women rubbed his chest, while others chafed his hands and feet. In less time than it takes to tell, he opened his eyes. He spoke to us in his own tongue; then seeing that we did not understand, he struggled to his feet, and in five minutes or so had recovered his strength. One of the sailors near to him was so tired that he could hardly pull his oar. The Japanese bustled over, pushed him from his seat, took the oar, and worked like a hero until we were finally picked up. I saw Mr. Lowe watching him in open-mouthed surprise.

'By Jove!' muttered the officer. 'I am ashamed of what I said about the little blighter. I'd save the likes o' him six times over, if I got the chance'.[10]

Collyer's account is both accurate and outlandish at the same time. Her description, 'Lying upon it, face downwards, was a small Japanese. He had lashed himself with a rope to his frail raft, using the broken hinges to make knots secure',[11] matches Fang Lang's own description of his predicament almost exactly, except of course that he was not Japanese. After swimming away from the wreck and through survivors and victims, he had climbed up on a large piece of floating wood and used a belt or bit of rope to tie himself to it.

The rest of Collyer's description is quite strange. If Fang appeared dead and did not respond when hailed, what made Lowe think he was alive, enough to turn around and haul him into the boat? Especially when he seems to have so little regard for Fang that he refers to him in a derogatory way.

In Lowe's testimony in New York, he speaks bluntly, including using 'Italian' as a catch-all term for passengers that Steward Crowe described as 'some foreign nationality other than English or American'. Lowe used 'Italian' so callously that the Consul General of Italy in New York demanded an apology and the fifth officer publicly apologised for using the word in such a way. Yet, in that same testimony, Lowe never mentions his rescue of an Asian passenger among the people he pulled from the water. According to Collyer, Lowe spent significant time and energy in first identifying the 'Japanese', and then saying aloud that he would not rescue a man that appears to be dead, then for some reason turns the boat around and brings him in. When that man springs back to life and starts pulling an oar, Lowe praises him, again out loud, but Crowe makes no mention of Lowe saying any of these things.

It was not the first time that Lowe had rescued an Asian passenger from the water. In 1904 or 1905, while working for the Blue Funnel Line, a passenger shipping company that sailed between the UK and Asia, Lowe jumped into the water to save a Chinese passenger who had fallen overboard.[12]

Also peculiar is Collyer's claim that 'The Japanese was hauled on board, and one of the women rubbed his chest, while others chafed his hands and feet'. The veracity of this is difficult to assess. Lowe mentions his men attempting to revive William Hoyt, but the others rescued do not seem to receive any attention. Crowe did not include it in his account. It is certainly possible that the women on board Lifeboat 14 came to his aid, but this kind of physical contact between unrelated women and a man, especially of different races, seems out of the ordinary for the time, even in an emergency.

Collyer's account has received significant scrutiny since it was first published in April 1912. At that time, she was destitute. She and her husband, Harvey, had sold all of their possessions to move to the United States, and Harvey went down with the ship with $500 in his pocket, the money they needed to start their new life. Collyer accepted payment from the *San Francisco Call* newspaper, which, along with *Semi-Monthly Magazine*, published her story. That Collyer took money to tell her story makes some believe that she felt the need to exaggerate or make the tale more detailed and exciting. She later received $1,965 in donations from readers of *Semi-Monthly Magazine* who were moved by her story and touched by her and Marjorie's desperate situation. Regardless, Collyer's uncanny use of some bits of the description of Fang's rescue leads us to believe that she was actually in Lifeboat 14 at the time.

Cheong Foo: Barely Noticed

In Chapter 6, we stated that historians have traditionally placed a Chinese survivor identified as Cheong Foo in Lifeboat 13 and Japanese survivor Masabumi Hosono in Lifeboat 10. However, based on a preponderance of evidence presented in that chapter, from here on, we place Cheong in Lifeboat 10 and Hosono in 13.

We cannot say with any confidence that this Chinese passenger was Cheong; it may have been Cheong or it may have been one of the four men traditionally placed in Collapsible C. We do know definitively that this passenger was not Fang Lang. For simplicity's sake, we will continue to refer to this single Chinese man in Lifeboat 10 as Cheong Foo. His presence there was noticed, barely, but it aroused far less negative sentiment than the Chinese men in Collapsible C.

On Day 7 of the American Inquiry, Able Seaman Edward John Buley mentioned the presence of an Asian passenger or passengers in his boat, Lifeboat 10:

Senator Fletcher. Do you think there were no male passengers in No. 12 [*sic*]?

Mr. Buley. I was told afterwards that there were a couple of Japanese in our boat. They never got in our boat unless they came in there dressed as women.

Senator Fletcher. Do you know if they actually were there?

Mr. Buley. I can say I never saw them there.[13]

Buley never saw an Asian man in his boat, but here introduces into the official record the idea that an Asian passenger may have dressed as a woman to enter a lifeboat.

Saloon Steward Frederick Ray, who escaped in Lifeboat 13, remembered an Asian passenger in his boat clearly:

> Senator SMITH. I would like to know how many first-class male passengers there were.

> Mr. RAY. I could not say, sir. There was one Japanese. I remember a Japanese, very well, being there. I have no idea, because I could not discriminate second from third class passengers.[14]

Other survivors who gave official testimony failed to notice, or at least mention, an Asian passenger in Lifeboat 13.

Despite being absolutely grilled about various other subjects during the British Inquiry, Leading Stoker Frederick Barrett never mentioned any Asian passengers in Lifeboat 13, of which he was briefly in charge.[15] Third-Class passenger Daniel Buckley never mentioned seeing any Asian passengers during his testimony, although he too left *Titanic* in Lifeboat 13.[16] Lawrence Beesley, who published *The Loss of S.S. Titanic* within months of the sinking, repeated Ismay's claim of four 'Chinamen' under the thwarts but did not seem to notice any in his own boat.[17] Albert J. Caldwell, also saved in Lifeboat 13, did not note the presence of a Chinese or Japanese passenger either, despite having just spent two years in Bangkok. Caldwell also never mentioned seeing an Asian passenger to his niece, who wrote a biography of the Caldwells' time prior to and on *Titanic*.[18] Neither Beesley nor Caldwell testified at either inquiry, but even in later spoken or written accounts, they did not mention an Asian passenger in their respective boats.

The Collapsible Lifeboats

Before evaluating the above evidence and testimony further, it will be helpful to understand more about *Titanic*'s collapsible lifeboats, and how they were different from the wooden lifeboats in which most survivors escaped. During the half an hour before *Titanic* sank, only four lifeboats remained – collapsibles designed by the Engelhardt Boat Co. of Denmark and built for the White Star Line by R. McAlister & Sons of Glasgow, Scotland.

Each boat was 28ft (8.53m) long, 8.5ft (2.6 m) wide and 3ft 1in (0.94m) deep. The latter measurement is from the bottom of the keel to the top of the gunwale (side) of the assembled boat. In their folded and stowed position, the collapsible lifeboats' cork and kapok bottoms and canvas sides compacted down to about 1ft (30–35cm). The boats were rated to hold forty-seven passengers safely.

If needed, the boats could be assembled in about twenty to thirty minutes. Their canvas sides, or gunwales, would be lifted and fixed in place with pegs. Passengers sat on thin wooden benches, or thwarts, which were as wide as the boat.

However, while relatively compact, the boats still weighed more than 1,000lb (450kg) each, requiring several people to assist with their assembly and moving them into position for the lifeboat davits to handle it.

Collapsibles C and D were stored flat on the deck underneath the lifeboat positions for the two cutters, Lifeboats 1 and 2. Lifeboat 1 and C were placed on the starboard side; 2 and D on the port. The placement of Collapsibles A and B was far less advantageous, both being stored on top of the wheelhouse. To deploy them, crew would have to climb on top of the wheelhouse, free each boat, bring them down to the boat deck and then assemble and prepare them for loading and launch.

No Way Stowaways

It is a common misunderstanding and accusation that the Chinese on board *Titanic* were not passengers. Some reports list them as members of the crew, or worse, as stowaways who had sneaked onto the ship. As stated earlier, all eight were travelling as Third-Class passengers on ticket No. 1601, for which a fare of £59 9s 11d was paid. At no time were they illegal or undocumented on *Titanic*.

The Daily Telegraph reported, 'Among those rescued from the sinking *Titanic* were six Chinese, who had stowed themselves away in one of the vessel's boats before she left England.' For this report to be valid beyond the number of Chinese passengers, who were the most obviously foreign of all foreigners on board, they would first have had to board *Titanic* without being noticed by crew. Then the men would have had to find their way up to the Boat Deck, which was off-limits to Third-Class passengers; choose a hiding place that happened to be within almost direct sight of *Titanic*'s bridge and top officers; and ensconce themselves there, all in daylight, with *Titanic*'s richest passengers and highest-ranking officers among the few passengers having access to that deck. They would also have needed to bring a week's worth of provisions, unless they planned to starve themselves to reduce the bodily functions that they also would have had to address during that time. And the men would have allegedly undertaken this adventure despite having a valid ticket for warm, clean berths below, complete with three square meals per day. These kinds of reports were not misunderstandings or exaggerations. They were complete fabrications.

The cutters – Lifeboats 1 and 2 – were always ready to be launched in the event of someone being lost overboard, with the collapsible on the deck below them. Early photographs of the collapsibles from 1904 taken by the manufacturer show men standing in a floating boat, sides not erected, each with the folded gunwales rising to no more than ankle height. There was simply not enough room for any human being to hide in the available space, and certainly not four to eight adult men.

Even stowing away in Collapsible C after *Titanic* began sinking would have been an impossible feat of deception and endurance. To do so would have required them to reach the Boat Deck, optimally within the first hour of *Titanic* striking the iceberg. Amidst the chaos of an evacuation order, that deck would have been swarming with senior officers, crewmen and First-Class passengers, none of whom would have welcomed the presence of the Chinese passengers.

Four men would then have had to conceal themselves in an unassembled collapsible lifeboat while the cutter at the same davit was being prepared, loaded and launched. They would have had to continue hiding while the boat itself was prepared, loaded and launched, without anyone noticing their presence for four hours. Again, one would have to have a very sharp axe to grind against the Chinese men to believe such an utterly implausible story. Those who remain sceptical about such theories may wish to purchase a large piece of flat-pack furniture, attempt to insert themselves into the packaging and then remain there during delivery and assembly without being discovered.

Frankly, this kind of tall tale might at least be conceivable if it related to men found in one of the wooden, fixed-side lifeboats. Covered in canvas, hanging from the davits and with more room at the bottom of the hull, such a story of four men concealed there might cross the line into possibility, instead of languishing in absurdity.

There is one documented incident of a passenger hiding in a lifeboat. Phillip Zanni, mentioned earlier as the first Third-Class passenger to enter a lifeboat successfully, said in an interview granted to the *Dayton Herald* newspaper of Dayton, Ohio, that he had hidden underneath a thwart after foiling a *Titanic* officer's attempts to prevent him from boarding what is believed to be Lifeboat 6.[19] The newspaper wrote:

> The greatest confusion was evident on all sides, and men were lowering the lifeboats. Zenni made an effort to leap into one of the boats, but an officer of the boat stood with a drawn revolver in his hand and all of the men were compelled to stand back at the command 'Women first'. Zenni made a second unsuccessful attempt to leap into the boat and was again ordered back by the officer, but a moment later the officer turned, and he made a leap, landing in the middle of the boat. He took refuge under one of the seats and the boat was pulled away.[20]

Even though he repeatedly disobeyed the *Titanic* officer's orders not to enter the boat, neither the quartermaster in charge of Lifeboat 6 nor Zenni's fellow passengers seem to have admonished him, nor did they report him to the officer who tried to prevent his boarding.

Not only did Zenni feel comfortable telling his story to a local reporter, but he also even took the opportunity to criticise a female passenger in his boat. Elizabeth Jane Ann Rothschild had rescued her dog, a Pomeranian:

When the survivors were being raised into the *Carpathia* a woman who was in his lifeboat pleaded with him to save her dog, which she had clasped tightly in her arms since leaving the *Titanic*. Zenni informed her politely that human beings came first, and she clung desperately to the little animal until someone lifted her [the dog] to the deck of the boat.

Mrs. Rothschild's husband, Martin Rothschild, was not rescued. Zenni later gave lectures featuring his account of escaping the ship, earning him the nickname 'Mr. Titanic'.

Interestingly, Margaret 'Molly' Brown, a First-Class woman who claimed she was thrown into Lifeboat 6 by an unseen male, made no mention of a man jumping in nor any other non-crewmen in her boat when she wrote an account of her escape for *The Denver Post* on 5 May 1912. 'The only man in our boat was the quartermaster. He was at the rudder and standing much higher than we were,' Brown wrote. She didn't mention Mrs Rothschild's dog, either.

The Map Is Not the Territory

The most important and illuminating statement regarding the Chinese men during the US Inquiry came in this exchange involving Quartermaster George Rowe:

Senator BURTON. When day broke, you found four Chinamen or Filipinos under the seats?

Mr. ROWE. Not under the seats then, sir. They came up between the seats.[21]

There was only way to prove once and for all whether it was even physically possible for four men to conceal themselves under or between a collapsible lifeboat's seats: by building a full-sized model and putting people into it.

A 9-Year-Old Solves a Century-Old Mystery

In one short statement, a 9-year-old survivor solved two key mysteries that have haunted the Chinese passengers for more than 100 years. Frankie Goldsmith's father, also named Frank, escorted his wife Emily and son to Collapsible C, along with a family friend, Alfred Rush. Frankie and his mother boarded the boat, but Alfred, who was 17, declared that he was a man and would not go with the children. Rush and the elder Goldsmith were both denied entry to the Boat Deck.

The lifeboat was cut loose after reaching the surface, and to young Frankie it was a great adventure. He remembers particularly looking toward the rear of the boat and seeing four Chinese crouching there. 'Their long black coats and round caps probably passed them as women in the confusion,' he believes. 'They sat very quiet with the arms folded in flowing sleeves and faces expressionless,' Goldsmith said in a 1943 interview.[22] What Ismay, Rowe and others did not see, a young boy observed and recalled clearly.

Recall that there was no moon on the night of 14 April, so the iceberg was much harder to spot than it would have been if some moonlight were present. The lifeboats, at least the primary, wooden lifeboats, may have had lanterns for light, but chose to extinguish them. Except for a few flashlights and matches carried by men and women who smoked, there were few light sources and the night would have been pitch dark. A quartermaster like Rowe would barely be able to see the bow of his own boat, never mind be able to make out individual faces or ethnicities.

None of the observers who saw the Chinese mentioned that they spoke to each other, unlike Chief Steward Second Class John Hardy in Collapsible D, 'There were a number of third-class passengers, that were Syrians, in the bottom of the boat, chattering the whole night in their strange language.' If the Chinese passengers spoke to each other in Collapsible C, no one seems to have noticed.

Frankie Goldsmith may be mistaken about where the men were in the boat, as he stated that Collapsible C launched from the port side when it was the final boat launched from starboard. Collapsible C departed *Titanic* around 2.00 a.m. That time matches the approximate point to which *Titanic* had sunk, based on the description of

Quartermaster George Rowe, who was in charge of C, describing the difficulty with which the boat was lowered:

Senator BURTON. What side was your boat on?

Mr. ROWE. The starboard side, sir. All the time my boat was being lowered the rubbing strake kept on catching on the rivets down the ship's side, and it was as much as we could do to keep her off.[23]

Senator BURTON. She must have sunk soon after you left?

Mr. ROWE. Twenty minutes, I believe.[24]

Titanic's 2.20 a.m. sinking time is not disputed.

Clothes Maketh Woman

This book does not accept the suggestion that *Titanic*'s Chinese passengers ever attempted to disguise themselves as women, either to gain access to a lifeboat or for any other reason. Young Frankie Goldsmith's statement – 'Their long black coats and round caps probably passed them as women in the confusion' – tells us what they were wearing.

The same accusations of being dressed as women do not survive daylight. When Ismay and Rowe finally became aware of the four men, they never stated that they came up from between the seats 'dressed as women'.

In order to believe that the Chinese men disguised themselves in this way to gain access to the lifeboat, there are a number of questions that must be answered in order for that to be credible. Where did these men – travelling in a part of the ship where only men were quartered and having no other known acquaintances or friends on *Titanic* – get enough women's clothing for the four of them to fool *Titanic*'s officers and crew?

It also fails to explain why only five of the eight managed to find women's clothing and make it into lifeboats, while the disguise doesn't seem to have worked for the other two who perished. Don't forget, when Fang emerged from the water, he was not wearing a shawl or a skirt.

That the men, who had worked on ships in and out of the UK for a number of years, would own dark coats makes perfect sense. These are men who would have spent time on deck, on watch and otherwise outside in less than perfect weather, both at sea and on land in the UK or Continental Europe. In an age before synthetic fabrics, a big wool coat would have been an effective and affordable bulwark against the elements, although it's surprising that other Third-Class men were not similarly dressed and, therefore, similarly accused.

At least three passengers did dress as women to gain or keep their places in lifeboats, and none of them were Chinese. Daniel Buckley, who testified at the US Inquiry, openly admitted it:

> I was crying. There was a woman in the boat, and she had thrown her shawl over me, and she told me to stay in there. I believe she was Mrs. Astor. Then they did not see me, and the boat was lowered down into the water, and we rowed away out from the steamer.[25]

Irishman Edward Ryan told his parents of his deception in a letter dated 6 May 1912:

> I stood on the *Titanic* and kept cool, although she was sinking fast. She had gone down about forty feet by now. The last boat was about being rowed away when I thought in a second if I could only pass out [i.e. get into the boat] I'd be all right. I had a towel round my neck. I just threw this over my head and left it hang in the back. I wore my waterproof overcoat. I then walked very stiff past the officers, who had declared they'd shoot the first man that dare pass out. They didn't notice me. They thought I was a woman. I grasped a girl who was standing by in despair, and jumped with her 30 feet into the boat.[26]

If a towel around one's neck were enough to convince *Titanic*'s deck officers that one was a woman, they were very easily fooled indeed.

Fifth Officer Lowe said during his testimony that he found an 'Italian' dressed as a woman in Lifeboat 14:

Mr. LOWE. I then asked for volunteers to go with me to the wreck, and it was at this time that I found this Italian. He came aft, and he had a shawl over his head, and I suppose he had skirts. Anyhow, I pulled this shawl off his face and saw he was a man. He was in a great hurry to get into the other boat, and I caught hold of him and pitched him in.[27]

These are the only documented cases of men using women's clothing to gain access to lifeboats or to try to do so.

What's intriguing about the accusations of stowing away and the men changing their appearance is that they negate each other. If the men were able to hide, they would not need to disguise themselves. If they could effectively appear as women enough to enter a lifeboat, then they would not need to conceal themselves once on board.

Would the eight Chinese men, who had worked aboard foreign ships out of European ports for at least a couple of years, still have had their traditional long braids or queues, possibly leading to them being identified as women? Likely not. Evidence indicates that most Chinese men who worked outside of China would have been eager to move towards shorter, more contemporary and practical hairstyles. Especially for these mariners, for whom exposure to open flame and spinning machinery was a regular occupational hazard, having any kind of long hair would have been a significant liability.

As such, the two claims of stowing away and dressing as women respectively are disproven. There is simply no evidence to support either accusation, but ample proof to show that they were aboard Collapsible C as normal passengers who had entered via conventional means.

Entering Collapsible C

Frankie Goldsmith's recollection about the Chinese men was a boy's objective observation of an event. His mother Emily was far less charitable in her statements about them:

Except when some of the foreign steerage passengers attempted to rush the boats there was little excitement. Several of these men forced their way to the upper deck and jumped into our lifeboat, but the officers were firm and drove them back. One of the men on our boat pointed a revolver at them and then fired three shots in the air. That brought them to their senses, and as they evidently preferred a chance with the *Titanic* to certain death by shooting if they remained in the lifeboat, they scrambled back on deck. Four Chinamen refused to get out, but crept down among the women and remained there. The officer did not dare to fire at them for fear of hitting the women, and the boat was lowered with these four in it.[28]

Collapsible C is one potential site of pistols fired by *Titanic*'s officers or crew, either to warn men – always labelled 'foreigners' in accounts – from entering lifeboats, or in one or more cases, to kill such men when they were clambering aboard.[29]

There is no dispute that firearms were both distributed to *Titanic*'s senior officers after the collision with the iceberg and later discharged. Second Officer Charles Lightoller said in his testimony that he had one and Fifth Officer Harold Lowe indicated to the US Inquiry that he both received a pistol and fired warning shots from it during the loading of his boat, Lifeboat 14.

Emily Goldsmith's statement shows that there was no chance for anyone to enter the boat and hide before its launch. Therefore, the four Chinese passengers could only have entered Collapsible C legitimately – that is, stepping into the boat like every other passenger. Accounts such as Mrs Goldsmith's claim that attempts succeeded in removing other men but not the four Chinese men.

Some passengers state that it was during the loading of C that guns were brandished at and/or fired at 'foreigners' who attempted to enter the boat. However, neither Ismay nor Rowe makes any mention of guns at C. Rowe knew enough about guns and what they sound like – he had just assisted Fourth Officer Joseph Boxhall prepare and fire *Titanic*'s emergency flares. Rowe himself was not one of the crew members to whom firearms were issued.

None of the four of the White Star men with a connection to Collapsible C who testified – Ismay, Rowe, Pearcey and Bright – indicate any kind of trouble with the loading and launch of C. Other officers testified about male passengers attempting to board lifeboats, including Lightoller while loading Collapsible D, and Lowe went on at length about issues on Lifeboat 14. So there was certainly no gag order on White Star officers testifying about doing their duty and preventing male passengers from boarding lifeboats. If Ismay, Rowe, Pearcey and Bright had seen any commotion in or around C, there was no reason for them to remain silent about it. Fending off male passengers, especially Third-Class male passengers, from boarding lifeboats would simply have demonstrated that they carried out their orders as officers and crewmen to ensure priority was given to women and children.

The Troublesome Testimony of Hugh Woolner

In contrast to those men's statements, Hugh Woolner testified on Day 10 of the US Inquiry that he and fellow First-Class passenger Mauritz Håkan Björnström-Steffansson took it upon themselves to assist officers and crew in removing other men from Collapsible C so that women and children could board.

Born in the UK, Woolner was the son of a successful sculptor who worked in finance. His testimony paints a picture of Steffansson and him patrolling the decks, looking to be of service throughout the sinking, and then finally, miraculously, ending up in Collapsible D as it was being lowered. He testified that he and Steffansson, who Woolner had met on board *Titanic*, helped load all of the lifeboats on the port side except one. Why they were needed to help load the boats is unclear:

Senator Smith: You mean that the men stood back and passed the women and children forward?

Woolner: Yes.

Smith: There was no crowding?

Woolner: None.

Smith: No jostling?

Woolner: None.[30]

If there was no crowding and no jostling, what 'loading' were Woolner and Steffansson doing and why? That is, unless they were waiting for an invitation into one of the lifeboats. If that was their intent, they should have done their 'loading' on the starboard side, where at least the rule was women and children first, not women and children only.

Woolner claimed, however, that the loading of Collapsible C was not so orderly. On switching sides of the ship, apparently disorder suddenly reigned on the starboard side. Woolner claimed:

Steffansson and I went up to help to clear that boat of the men who were climbing in, because there was a bunch of women – I think Italians and foreigners – who were standing on the outside of the crowd, unable to make their way toward the side of the boat. So we helped the officer to pull these men out, by their legs and anything we could get hold of.[31]

Apparently, those did not include Chinese legs, if there were any Chinese legs to get hold of. Woolner claimed that he and his friend pulled out 'five or six' men each from the boat.[32]

Although *Titanic* historians are quick to note that Steffansson, who did not testify at either inquiry, corroborated Woolner, this is meaningless, like two bank robbers who provide each other's alibis. Just as Ernest Carter backed Ismay's story about entering Collapsible C, it would be surprising if Woolner and Steffansson's stories didn't match.

Why would *Titanic*'s crew deployed to Collapsible C to prevent male passengers from entering think that two large men approaching the last lifeboat on the starboard side had any intention except to board it? If either man indicated to the crew that they were there to assist in removing other male passengers from C, that statement was not recorded.

Most unfavourable for Woolner and his friend is that none of *Titanic*'s personnel, neither on the port side nor around or in Collapsible C, including Ismay, made any mention of the pair's presence in assisting them in fending off crazed male passengers attempting to enter a lifeboat. They reported no disturbance; why would there be any need for other men to assist?

Lastly, not once in his self-aggrandising testimony does Woolner indicate that he ever thought of anything other than escape. Not once does he mention contemplating staying aboard *Titanic*, with or without Steffansson. Even when he and Steffansson decided to try to get into Collapsible D, he hedged, 'I said to Steffansson, "There is nobody in the bows. Let us make a jump for it. You go first."'[33] You go first, Steffansson, and make sure the boat doesn't give way, Woolner seems to say.

This has not gone unnoticed by historians. Author Richard Davenport-Hines, in *Voyagers of the Titanic*, wrote:

> The veneer that [Woolner] put on his actions was devised to stop any surmise that his survival had been unmanly. He was a public school and Cambridge man, trying to revive his credit and reputation after his bankruptcy, and needed to show that although he had saved himself, he was as fine a gentleman as Jack Astor or Archie Butt.[34]

After illuminating the details of Woolner's claims, Davenport-Hines wrote:

> With this tale Woolner established his superiority over the panicky foreign men who tried to save themselves before the women. Although he had survived, unlike few if any of the ejected foreigners, he surpassed their level because he had shown Anglo-Saxon self-mastery.[35]

David Gleicher echoes these ideas in his own analysis of Woolner and Steffansson's actions, coming to a similarly unfavourable conclusion:

> When stripped of veneer, the two were seeking a way to gain entrance into one of the last boats being launched from the forward

end. Having given up on Lifeboat 2 and Collapsible C, they went down to A Deck and encountered the loading of Lifeboat 4 under Second Officer Lightoller.[36]

Gleicher adds later, 'For Woolner to have been honest about his motivation would have been tantamount to aligning himself with the Third-Class men; the very people he claimed to have removed from Collapsible C.'[37] Finally, he writes of Woolner's account, 'Woolner thereby converted a confession of guilt into an adventure story with him and Steffansson as the conventional heroes.'[38]

Cancelling Each Other Out

The claims appear to cancel each other. If Woolner and Steffansson heroically jumped into the boat to assist the officers, tossing out 'five or six' men each, why was there any need to use guns to scare men off? Why would Woolner, Steffansson and *Titanic*'s crew leave the job unfinished with four Chinese men still in the boat?

Once again, a rational explanation must apply. Why would only the four Chinese men in Collapsible C – the most foreign of *Titanic*'s foreigners – be willing to risk getting shot rather than get out of the boat? And if they were sufficiently small that others believed they could pass as women just by covering themselves in shawls or hide under the seats for hours without being noticed, how is it that they could not just be physically hauled from the boat by crewmen on deck or assigned to the boat? It is illogical that the Chinese passengers went, in a period of only minutes, from being threatened at gunpoint to being invisible in the lifeboat, only to be 'discovered' by Ismay and Rowe hours later at daybreak.

The survival of Ismay, Carter and the Chinese men in Collapsible C seems to indicate that getting access to that boat was dependent on people already being on the Boat Deck at the time of loading. The Chinese men's arrival on the Boat Deck no later than 1.45 a.m., and probably earlier, put them in a position to see which boats were left and which could still be boarded.

The Middle-Eastern Passengers

Titanic's passenger list included dozens from the Middle East, namely Lebanon and Syria, all of whom were travelling in Third Class. Among the relatives of Middle-Eastern passengers, many have maintained since *Titanic's* sinking that officers and crew shot and killed a number of Syrian male passengers attempting to board lifeboats.

Scholar Leila Saloum Elias, author of the book *The Dream and Then the Nightmare: The Syrians who Boarded the Titanic, the Story of the Arabic-Speaking Passengers*, wrote:

> There is also a Syrian survivor, steerage passenger Mubārak Ḥannā Sulaymān Abī'sī, who claimed to have been shot at six times by two of the *Titanic's* officers while attempting to board a lifeboat. Yet another Syrian saw a passenger shot dead by one of the sailors. Two of Fāṭimah Muslamāni's cousins, she claimed, did not drown but rather were killed by the crew, one as he attempted to board a lifeboat, the other while in it. Syrian survivor Sa'īd Nakid also saw a man shot dead as he attempted to board a lifeboat. When several men in steerage tried to rush the officers in charge of the lifeboats, they were initially kept at bay 'by fist blows.' But as the passengers grew more terrified, the officers made use of their revolvers, first firing in the air, then directly at the men, hitting one passenger in the arm. Before the stern of the *Titanic* submerged, the occupants of the tenth boat saw scores of men struggling in the water.[39]

These accounts speak to a hail of carnage and gunfire that is simply not corroborated by the majority of other passenger or crew accounts and recollections. Throughout the books, interviews and letters written by *Titanic* survivors, stories are repeated by passengers who were not in a position to hear or see the events they describe. Even under these circumstances, most do not mention any gunfire beyond that indicated in official testimony. If *Titanic* crew resorted to shooting male passengers, then they were highly accurate, killing almost every man they shot – only Mubārak Ḥannā Sulaymān Abī'sī reported himself to be injured by gunfire, and only in one of his accounts. All of the shooting victims are alleged to be 'Italian' – a catch-all phrase for southern European and Middle-Eastern passengers – there is no mention of any Asians among the supposed victims.

While the presence of passengers from this group is confirmed in both Collapsible C and D, it is unclear if there were adult male travellers among them. In the end, no *Titanic* officer was ever directly accused or formally charged with injuring or causing the death of any passenger or crew member. No wrongful death claim – a type of legal action permitted under British law in 1912, although not American law – was ever filed. Of the 332 bodies recovered from the water around the *Titanic* wreck site, none were noted as having bullet wounds. None of *Titanic's* officers ever admitted to this kind of action in later writing about their time aboard her, and no deathbed confessions by *Titanic* officers have ever surfaced.

As we have seen regarding the Chinese passengers, due to anger, emotion and ignorance, *Titanic* passengers and crew believed many things about their experience that had no factual basis. This did not stop many of them from repeating those beliefs to newspapers, family members, other *Titanic* survivors and official bodies. Only careful evaluation of each and every claim, along with the speaker's location and motivations at the time the event took place, can bring us as close as possible to the truth.

Conclusions

The launch of Collapsible C was problematic, given *Titanic's* list to port. Even if there was a commotion, the lifeboat still departed slightly below capacity, with enough space for Ismay and Carter to step in just as it was leaving.

It may seem strange that the last lifeboat on the starboard side was not overloaded or rushed, only twenty minutes before the ship's final plunge. But by 2 a.m., *Titanic's* stern had become the relative high ground and many remaining passengers had moved up and away from the waterline. Also, by that point in the sinking, all of the ship's fixed lifeboats had been launched and passengers may not have been aware that four collapsible boats remained. The ship's list to port may have also obscured any view of the assembly of Collapsible C, blocked by structures on the top decks.

In the end, Collapsible Lifeboat C left *Titanic* with an estimated forty-three passengers and crew, four fewer than its rated capacity. For all the purported struggle, pistol shots and skirmishing over who should or should not be allowed into this boat, the last lifeboat that left the starboard side did so with room for more. To emphasise the point, Collapsible D launched five minutes later from the port side, only half full.

While the Chinese passengers certainly received a lot of criticism from their fellow travellers for the supposed ingenuity and tenacity displayed in saving their own lives – hiding on board a lifeboat, disguising themselves as women and resisting being shot at by *Titanic* officers – the evidence indicates their departure aboard Collapsible C was as uneventful as possible under the circumstances.

There is nothing wrong with any *Titanic* passenger, crew member or officer wanting to survive, male or female; adult or child; American, British, Chinese, Swedish or Syrian. If there had been enough available lifeboat seats, no one, likely not even Captain Smith, would have chosen to go down with *Titanic*. The will to live is our most basic desire and drive.

Some men and women adhered to an Edwardian ideal and lost their lives; their courage and determination will always be remembered. However, hundreds of men had the opportunity to survive *Titanic* – and did. They do not deserve infamy simply because they survived. Do we remember the average crew member or Third-Class passenger any more because they are dead? No, we do not. Through the lens of *Titanic* history, most Third-Class passengers are no one more than names on a list. Better, then, that they ended up on the list of survivors than the list of victims.

Almost 1,500 people died that night, but not because six Chinese men survived. Ultimately, too few lifeboats; a lack of emergency planning; poor lifeboat management and the unwillingness of *Titanic* boats to return and take on additional passengers cost the lives of at least 400 people who could have been rescued. Even if every lifeboat was filled to capacity and launched successfully, more than 1,000 people still would have died.

The vicious rumours listed here have tarnished the memories of *Titanic*'s Chinese passengers for a century, but despite their persistence, they are not supported by careful analysis and rational evaluation. They are also primarily levied at the four men in Collapsible C, although stories like Elizabeth Mellinger's nonsensical 'Mellican baby' tale were told in relation to phantom Chinese passengers in other boats.

The Chinese bore the misplaced enmity of some of their fellow passengers and the press because they survived when so many others died. After the initial wave of newspaper reports, though, the six Chinese survivors faded quickly from the *Titanic* story. Despite being held overnight on *Carpathia* upon arriving in New York, it appears no one attempted to interview them.

Besides Ismay, one of the only other passengers who was harried for the rest of his life for surviving was Japan's Hosono. He was fired from his job with Japan's railways (then later rehired) and was haunted by the zero-sum perception that his survival directly caused the death of a child or woman. In contrast, the Chinese passengers were accused, blamed and then simply forgotten.

Under this cloud of derision and suspicion, the Chinese survivors arrived in New York, in a country that offered them no welcome, only exclusion.

9

EXCLUDED

After *Titanic* sank, survivors who had floated on Collapsibles A and B during the night were rescued by wooden lifeboats, mostly by boats commanded by Fifth Officer Harold Lowe in Lifeboat 14. When *Carpathia* arrived at the accident site around 4 a.m., it met first Lifeboat 2, which confirmed *Titanic*'s sinking. Over the next four or so hours, lifeboats pulled alongside *Carpathia*.

Most passengers and crew were able to climb onto the rescue ship using rope ladders. Others had to be hauled up by *Carpathia*'s crew. All accounts of these procedures state that the process was entirely orderly. As *Titanic*'s survivors came aboard, the first rays of the sun illuminated icebergs and field ice in the distance, appearing pink in the early morning light.

Only after all the *Titanic* survivors came on board, received either medical attention or hot drinks, food and blankets, did *Carpathia* begin taking their names and creating a list. *Carpathia* then sent an official survivor list to the White Star office in New York by telegraph.

Since passengers were not assigned to particular lifeboats, they would not have known their boat's number. The lists of passengers and on which boat they left *Titanic* was assembled later from passenger recollections and scholars' research; as such, they are incomplete and imperfect.

On *Carpathia*

On board *Carpathia*, the more than 700 *Titanic* survivors had to find space for themselves among the ship's 740 passengers. J. Bruce Ismay immediately found the ship's doctor, Lengyel Árpád, and said, 'I'm Ismay. I'm Ismay.' The doctor gave *Titanic*'s owner his quarters, where Ismay went and remained for the entire trip to New York.

Some First and Second-Class passengers were lucky to find friends aboard *Carpathia*. Henry Sleeper Harper recognised Louis Ogden, who was watching survivors coming on board *Carpathia*. Wallace Bradford saw Washington Dodge and his family come aboard and accommodated them in his cabin.

Carpathia's crew and passengers did everything they could to make *Titanic*'s survivors feel more comfortable. But for the majority of those who had escaped, there was no comfort during the three-day sail to New York. The arrival of the last lifeboat, Lifeboat 12, with Second Officer Charles Lightoller aboard, was the final hope for many that their loved ones had made it to a boat and were saved. But it also dashed that hope when all lifeboats were accounted for and there were no further survivors to take on. Aboard *Carpathia*, they were tired, cold, and in some cases, injured. Some Third-Class passengers, including the Chinese men, had lost everything: spouses, parents, possessions, their life savings. Until the ship arrived in New York, they had nothing to do but contemplate everything they had lost and what the future might bring.

If they had been invisible on *Titanic* until they boarded lifeboats, the Chinese men were noticed a bit more on *Carpathia*. 'Six Chinamen dressed themselves in ladies' clothing and managed to get into the lifeboats,' said Third-Class passenger Edward Dorkings, speaking about his *Titanic* experience to an Illinois audience in May 1912.[1]

The Daily Telegraph, which had so viciously portrayed the Chinese passengers' behaviour on *Titanic* and in the lifeboat, wrote, 'It was not known that they were Chinese until they were taken on board the *Carpathia*. Then some of the *Carpathia*'s crew wanted to toss them into the sea, it was said, but the officers of the Cunard vessel put them in irons instead.'[2] There is no evidence to support any of these statements. There are no corroborating statements that suggest that

Carpathia's crew said anything to or about the Chinese passengers, and nothing to show that they were in any way confined on board the ship before arriving in New York.

The *Brooklyn Daily Eagle* newspaper published the most distasteful of all the press reports. In an article with the title, 'Heroism of Anglo-Saxon Sailors Stands Out in Disaster', the newspaper wrote:

> The one thing upon which Anglo-Saxon sailors pride themselves today, the single leaven in the bitter loaf, is the fact that heroism was paramount at the climax of this greatest of marine disasters. The one dark spot is the fact that in the bottom of one lifeboat which left the Titanic were found, wedged beneath the seats, the bodies of two dead Chinese coolies and eight living ones. These were creatures on their way to New York to join a sailing ship for the Orient, and who, at the first sign of danger, had sprung into the lifeboats before they had left their davits and concealed themselves beneath the seats. They were trampled upon by the women who were lowered into the boats later, and two of them crushed to death. Not until this boatload had been taken aboard the *Carpathia* were the bodies of these dead and living Chinese discovered.[3]

Again, there is no factual basis for this. There were not ten Chinese passengers on *Titanic*; at most, four survived in the same boat; and there were no dead bodies discovered in the bottom of Collapsible C. Ismay and Rowe testified clearly that the four Chinese men were found in the boat prior to their arrival alongside *Carpathia*. The *Brooklyn Daily Eagle*'s report cites no sources and quotes no one.

The hostility shown toward the Chinese survivors really knew no bounds. Elizabeth Dowdell, a governess travelling in charge of a 6-year-old child, was rescued along with the child in Lifeboat 13 or 15. In a long, whining interview with the New Jersey newspaper *Hudson Dispatch*, Dowdell, not grateful simply to be alive, finds time to complain about both the food on *Carpathia* and other survivors:

> On the *Carpathia* we were looked over by the officers, and those who apparently had nothing were all ordered down into the steerage. With my charge I was put in with the rest. We were fed on

hard-tack. Many of us refused to eat, and when the *Carpathia*'s officers saw this, they let us come into the second cabin. Before this we had been down in the steerage for a full day, rubbing arms with Chinese emmigrants [*sic*].

Dowdell's account of *Titanic*'s sinking and her escape in the lifeboat are so wild and distant from the facts that one wonders about her state of mind. She claimed to see the iceberg clearly from her lifeboat, when it was in fact miles away by the time lifeboats were lowered. Her boat had twelve sailors aboard, at least double the number assigned to any *Titanic* lifeboat and she clearly saw the time of *Titanic*'s sinking at 1.30 a.m., almost a full hour before the ship's actual final plunge.[4]

Carpathia's Dr Árpád wrote in a long letter in May 1912, 'The story of the two Chinamen who hid under the seat of the lifeboat and were thus saved is true; one of them had a small parcel.'[5] Strangely, Árpád never mentions in this account that Ismay was in his care for the duration of *Carpathia*'s trip back to New York.

Instead, very much like their time on *Titanic*, on *Carpathia* the men most likely kept to themselves. They were suddenly destitute, with their few sets of clothes and personal items gone down with the ship. Fang Lang's dreams of a life and a business in the United States died with his two partners, Lee Ling and Len Lam, at least temporarily. However, they were better off than some of their female, Third-Class counterparts: they were arriving in New York with employment aboard *SS Annetta*.

Arrival in New York

Carpathia arrived in New York on the evening of 18 April, a day after *Titanic*'s scheduled arrival. Bad weather had slowed *Carpathia*'s journey, and her top speed was about half that of *Titanic*.

The rescue ship's late arrival is somewhat ironic. Although Ismay and *Titanic* officers denied during their inquiry testimony that their ship was travelling too swiftly through ice, the British Wreck Commissioner's Inquiry found that the collision with the iceberg was due in part to the ship's 'excessive speed'. The bad weather near New

York that slowed *Carpathia*'s arrival may have prevented the early *Titanic* arrival for which Ismay had hoped. A few knots slower on 14 April and *Titanic* might have reached its destination close to schedule, instead of not at all.

As *Carpathia* entered New York Harbour, a boat full of journalists and photographers sailed out to meet her to get the first pictures and quotes from *Titanic* survivors. It was early evening, so any such news could be published in the following morning's newspapers. During the voyage, *Carpathia*'s captain, Arthur Rostron, did not allow journalists to send messages to passengers requesting interviews. However, travelling on board *Carpathia* was St Louis-based reporter Carlos Hurd and his wife, Katherine. Hurd interviewed numerous survivors and filed the first article to include actual survivor accounts of *Titanic*'s sinking.[6]

Normally, any inbound passenger ship arriving in New York would have stopped at Ellis Island Immigration Station so that foreign passengers could be processed. Third-Class passengers especially would have been subject to medical inspections, and in the case of Chinese passengers, temporary detention and questioning. Because White Star Line performed medical inspections on its Third-Class passengers prior to departure from the UK, and due to the special circumstances surrounding its arrival, *Carpathia* was not required to stop at Ellis Island.

As a Cunard ship, *Carpathia* would normally have alighted at Pier 54 on the west side of New York, where all Cunard ships loaded and unloaded. But on 18 April, *Carpathia* sailed to Pier 59 first. In one of the *Titanic* saga's most ghoulish moments, with passengers and survivors and the New York news media watching, *Carpathia*'s crew unloaded the thirteen wooden lifeboats that had been recovered. Why it was so important that these boats were not only recovered but then returned before passengers in need of medical treatment disembarked is still unclear. In retrospect, it was an exceptionally callous and macabre procedure that the otherwise noble Captain Rostron should have avoided.

With this gruesome duty completed, *Carpathia* moved to its own berth at Pier 54. A crowd of hundreds to thousands had gathered to witness the arrival, some hoping that their family members would soon come down the gangplank. Wisely, Rostron allowed *Carpathia*'s original passengers to depart first. This process was orderly and did not stir the crowd. Only when the first *Titanic* survivors came into view did cries begin to go up from people in the crowd: in some cases tears of joy; in others, anguish.

Wealthy families sent cars and representatives to fetch their loved ones. Aid societies like the Salvation Army arrived with doctors and others ready to provide assistance and a place to stay for Third-Class passengers who were arriving in New York with no relatives or means of support. Reporters cornered passengers they recognised – and anyone else who would talk to them – to get more information about *Titanic*'s sinking and its circumstances.

Awaiting J. Bruce Ismay were representatives of US Senator William Alden Smith, who held subpoenas for him, *Titanic*'s surviving senior officers and a number of crew members and passengers. By this point, Smith had prepared to hold a US Inquiry into *Titanic*'s sinking and had arrived in New York from Washington earlier that day.

Ismay had little time to collect his thoughts, and even less time to discuss matters with White Star representatives or *Titanic*'s surviving officers. He took the witness stand on the morning of 19 April at the Waldorf-Astoria Hotel. The choice of that venue likely was not lost on anyone, with one of its owners, John Jacob Astor IV, having gone down on Ismay's ship less than a week before.

Last to Leave

As Ismay began his testimony, the six Chinese survivors, four of whom he had shared a lifeboat with, were on their way across Manhattan. On that morning, they received a different kind of welcome than the other *Titanic* survivors. No family sent anyone to meet them. No aid society offered them any comfort. No reporters tried to interview them. Instead, they were met by agents from the Chinese Bureau of the Department of the Treasury, who were assigned to handle matters relating to the Chinese Exclusion Act of 1882. These agents were there to make sure that the men went to their assigned ship, which was waiting for them along the East River. That ship,

SS *Annetta*, was the same one that years before mistakenly believed it had spotted *Titanic* victim John Jacob Astor IV's missing yacht in the Caribbean.

Simultaneously, newspapers containing some of the baseless and most vile accusations against the Chinese men were appearing in New York City and elsewhere. There they were, the accused, in the custody of US immigration agents, and yet no action was seemingly being taken against them. Vilified in the court of US public opinion, US Government officials conveyed them across Manhattan on their way to points along the Atlantic coast.

Thirty years after the Chinese Exclusion Act went into effect, Chinese labourers were still actively prevented from entering the United States. While *Titanic*'s passengers and crew largely seemed to be ignorant of the presence of the Chinese men, the Chinese Bureau was clearly aware of them being on board and was present to meet them upon arrival.

The *New York Times* got most of this story right:

> The Chinamen were taken in hand by the immigration authorities and were placed in charge of one of the Inspectors of the Chinese Bureau of the service. They are all said to be in transit, and will be constantly under the eye of immigration officials during their journey across the country.[7]

The *New York Times* must have thought that the men were being deported back to China, which was not correct. As a historical foot-note, Fang Lang may have been the last person rescued from *Titanic* and was amount the last *Titanic* survivors to leave *Carpathia*.

One wonders what the men, particularly Fang, thought as they watched the buildings and people of New York pass by. This is where Fang had planned to slip away, with Lee Ling and Len Lam, to start his new career and new life. Now he was not only in the custody of American immigration officials, but also a prisoner of circumstance.

For the Chinese men, this passage through New York was a cruel stopover. Had they arrived aboard *Titanic*, they would have had a day to get a meal or two in Chinatown and perhaps buy some needed items before they went to sea again. Now, they had nothing – no steamer trunks with even basic clothes, no personal items and very little cash. There was no time to mourn their lost travelling companions or send a quick letter to family letting them know what had happened.

At least on *Annetta* they had somewhere to go that would offer them a place to sleep, three meals per day and a chance to earn some much-needed money. Of all the thousands of American dollars and British pounds that were raised for *Titanic*'s survivors, especially Third-Class passengers, there is no record of any of that money ever being distributed to the Chinese men.

Insurance No Guarantee

Only one bit of the *Titanic* story remained for them. In 1913, five of the six men filed claims for lost property to the White Star Line. In relative size, the Chinese men's claims were small compared to those made by some of *Titanic*'s First-Class passengers (such as Collapsible C survivor William Carter, who claimed the loss of his Renault automobile in *Titanic*'s cargo hold). The difference was that the Chinese men lost everything on the night that the ship sank.

They were represented by the law firm of Hunt, Hill & Betts of 165 Broadway.[8] Once again, some of the Romanised names of the men varied – Fang Lang became Yong Lang, Lee Bing became Lee Ping.[9] Why the variation occurred is uncertain.

Their claims are similar: bed linen, underwear, a pocket watch or clock. However, Fang's claim is most interesting. Among his personal items were six shirt collars and six neckties. At the time, while owning separate shirts was expensive, changing to a more visible, clean collar gave the well-dressed man a more affordable opportunity to look presentable. But what was a man who worked in a ship's engine room going to do with so many shirt collars and ties? Clearly, these were items for Fang's life away from the sea in his planned work as a merchant with Lee and Len.

At the end of 1915, a US court authorised repayment of US$664,000, over $20 million in 2024 dollars, to be divided among all claimants, a fraction of the US$16 million that survivors and victims' families sought. However, in a final decree signed July 1916 by United States District Judge Julius M. Mayer, White Star Line was found to be not liable for the sinking and any loss of life or property.[10] The survivors and the victims' families received nothing.

On 21 April, CS *Mackay-Bennett*, hired by the White Star Line, arrived at the site of *Titanic*'s sinking. Her task was to recover the bodies of as many of the almost 1,500 dead as her crew could find. Still wearing their white lifebelts, so many of *Titanic*'s bodies were found that *Mackay-Bennett* quickly realised more ships were needed. Ultimately, four cable layers participated in the search and recovery, bringing in 337 bodies.

As they had been in life, the dead were governed by the class system of the time. First-Class passengers' bodies (determined by their dress if identification was not available) were packed in ice and retained for return to Halifax, Nova Scotia, in Canada. The same was true for Second-Class passengers. Third-Class bodies were kept if they were in good condition (i.e., had not been damaged or rapidly decomposed), otherwise they were photographed and buried at sea.

John Jacob Astor IV's body was found, identified and returned to New York, where it was buried at Trinity Church Cemetery in Manhattan. His and Madeleine's son was born four months later.

Also among the bodies was a blond-haired child, who would be known for a century as the Unknown Child. DNA would eventually solve that mystery, ultimately identifying the boy as Sidney Goodwin.

Bodies that were unclaimed and unidentified were buried in three cemeteries around Halifax, based on the apparent religion of the dead, Catholic, Christian or Jewish.

On 20 April, Harold Thomas Cottam, *Carpathia*'s Marconi radio operator, began the second day of US Inquiry testimony. By that time, *Annetta* had already sailed out of New York Harbour, heading south. It was not a grand passenger liner like *Titanic* or even *Carpathia*, just a one-funnel, single-propeller cargo ship. Whether they liked it or not, six Chinese men were back on a ship on the ocean, on the schedule they had intended to keep all along. At the moment of their greatest association with *Titanic*'s story, the men sailed off, seemingly into oblivion, their historical trail dissipating like the wake of their ship.

SCATTERED TO THE FOUR WINDS

The Donald Steam Ship Company, which employed the Chinese men and had sent them to the United States for work, wasn't going to take any chances that the six men would run off after their brush with death:

> Immigration policies placed Chinese seamen under the control of employers who, after 1902, were required to take out security bonds indemnifying them against unauthorized immigration. Alternatively, ship captains could deny Chinese sailors shore leave altogether. When Chinese seamen arrived in American ports on contracts that had ended, they were still not free to come ashore – unless they could finance their participation in the American labor markets by arranging for security bonds on their own accord.[1]

SS *Annetta* was so much smaller than *Titanic* that the men could walk from stem to stern faster than the time it took to walk to meals on the great liner. Their quarters were as basic as they had remembered: cramped and dark, nothing like the relative luxury they had enjoyed before the sinking. Now they were back in the engine room and back to regular watches as before, as if the whole event had never happened:

> While Chinese seamen could be found working in any number of jobs on vessels, they were disproportionately employed as stewards, cooks, and firemen – positions that white sailors shunned for

more skilled positions that earned higher pay. Freight and passenger lines prized Chinese sailors as workers who could be enlisted to do grunt work for low wages, a willingness that [the shipping lines] attributed to race rather than to economic need and discrimination.[2]

The men carried papers that would have identified them as sailors and limited their travel options while on shore.

More than 100 years later, little has changed for merchant seamen who otherwise would not qualify for visas to many of the countries their ships visit. The two main differences are that after the terrorist attacks of 11 September 2001, most major port areas are now enclosed and secured with services such as restaurants and shops available within that area, eliminating the need for sailors to leave the port. The other difference is that, where China was once a major source of mariners for international shipping companies, Chinese sailors now work almost exclusively for Chinese shipping lines, with men from the Philippines providing 20–25 per cent of the global seafaring workforce.

Ports of Call

Even if they wanted to, the Chinese men had no chance to renege on their commitment to work on *Annetta* in New York, ending up under the watchful eye of US immigration officials. However, they may have considered their options elsewhere along their route.

After stopping at some coastal American cities, *Annetta* would arrive in Cuba. In 1912, Havana, Cuba, had the largest Chinese population in Latin America, with about 200,000 Chinese, almost entirely men, living in the country.[3] Since the mid-1800s, Chinese labourers were recruited to work on the island's sugar plantations, in part to replace African slavery, which was by this point banned in both Spain and the UK's Caribbean colonies. Cuba received another immigration boost in the 1880s, when the passage and implementation of the Chinese Exclusion Act in the United States temporarily stopped Chinese immigrants going there, and some chose the island nation instead.

Fewer of the migrants to Cuba were from Taishan, with the majority being either Hakka, from north-east Guangdong, or from the area around Guangzhou. Most Chinese arrived in Cuba as indentured servants – workers who either agreed to a period of employment of eight years in exchange for pay, or eight years of largely unpaid labour, with the promise of a piece of land at the end. As almost all the workers came from southern China, the climate and conditions of Cuba were reminiscent of their homeland.

However, the terms of employment were not always fair, transparent or voluntary:

> In 1859, 15-year-old Tung Kun Sen, a native of Dongguan County in Guangdong Province, was kidnapped and taken to the Spanish Caribbean colony of Cuba as part of the infamous coolie trade. He signed a contract of indenture that obligated him to work for eight years on a sugar estate. There he was baptized and given a Spanish name. After completing his term of service, he was forced to recontract for another eight years.[4]

If the Chinese *Titanic* survivors were looking for a life on land, Cuba presented one option, but it would have been a difficult one. One scholar observed:

> The Chinese in Cuba did not experience institutionalized discrimination to the same extent as their counterparts in the United States, which maintained a policy of exclusion from 1882 to 1943, or Mexico, where anti-Chinese campaigns led to their violent expulsion from the northern state of Sonora in 1931. Nor were they victims of sustained anti-Chinese riots, as in Peru and Jamaica. Rather, Chinese participation in the Cuban wars for independence spanning 1868 to 1898, their successful formation of cross-racial alliances, and the professed dedication of the Cuban republic to an ideal of a racial democracy, created the conditions of their incorporation into the national citizenry. At the same time, however, a negative view of Chinese developed in the Cuban press, in government and police reports, and in popular attitudes.[5]

A 1920 Ellis Island immigration record shows a 'Chang Chip Kok' arriving there from Havana, Cuba.[6] However, the age of this man does not match the *Titanic* survivor of the same name closely enough to indicate that person ended up living in Cuba.

Another *Annetta* destination was Port Antonio, Jamaica. Jamaica followed a similar pattern to Cuba in regard to Chinese immigration. With similar conditions and similar products, such as sugar, the British Government required would-be Chinese immigrants to pay a fee of £30 (almost £4,300 in 2024) and pass a literacy test. Indentured servitude was still an option in 1912, although it would be banned in 1917.

Paper Sons and Daughters

When Fang Lang, Lee Ling and Len Lam made their plan to become merchants in Cleveland, they had to solve a basic problem: how could they transform themselves from being merchant seamen, who were not eligible for entry or residence in the United States, into merchants, who were?

When the Chinese Exclusion Act became law in 1882, a virtual border wall went up to keep out Chinese labourers. However, would-be workers did not suddenly give up their aim to reach the United States. There was no amenable land border, such as Canada or Mexico, where Chinese migrants could go first and then cross over – entering those two countries was as difficult as arriving in the United States, and sometimes more so. Also, after 1888, an addition to the Chinese Exclusion Act, the Scott Act, mandated that even Chinese who had established themselves in the United States were legally barred from re-entering the country without authorisation if they went back to China or another country.

It was not until 1898 that a Chinese man born in San Francisco established birthright citizenship not only for himself and other Chinese, but for all future children born on US soil. The 14th Amendment to the Constitution of the United States was enacted primarily to ensure that Black Americans, especially former slaves, were granted full American citizenship after the end of the US Civil War (1861–65). Although Chinese people who were already in the United States at the time that the Chinese Exclusion Act went into effect were allowed to remain, they were not eligible to become citizens via naturalisation.

The first sentence of Section 1 of the 14th Amendment states, 'All persons born or naturalized in the United States, and subject to the jurisdiction thereof, are citizens of the United States and of the State wherein they reside.'[7] Wong Kim Ark was born in the United States in 1873 to parents who were in the United States but were citizens of China. He travelled to China in 1890 and returned to the United States later in the same year.

In 1894, he went to China again, but upon returning the following year, was denied re-entry to the United States, with customs officials in San Francisco stating that because Wong's parents were citizens of China (technically subjects), he too was a Chinese citizen, not an American one. Wong decided to challenge that assertion in court.

While he waited on various ships offshore for five months, friends and the local Chinese community in San Francisco pushed the case forward, until it eventually reached the US Supreme Court. The Supreme Court affirmed Wong's US citizenship in a 6–2 decision. Birthright citizenship still did not apply to Native Americans until 1924. The issue of granting to US citizenship to children born in the United States of non-citizen parents remains contentious to this day, more than 100 years after Wong's case.[8]

Chinese immigration to the United States therefore became a battle of wits. Taking a weeks-long journey by ship from Hong Kong or Shanghai to San Francisco, only to be turned away, was dangerous and expensive. Anyone going that far would want a reasonable guarantee of success. Pretending to be a diplomat, scholar, teacher, traveller or even a merchant was simply not going to be possible for most Chinese labourers seeking work in the United States. Over time, the easiest way, relatively, to evade these restrictive laws was to prove that someone was the child of an existing citizen or resident.

A disaster opened the 'golden door' for many Chinese immigrants. On 18 April 1906, a huge earthquake near San Francisco damaged large parts of the city. The earthquake ignited a fire that vaporised much of what the shaking had not. Because San Francisco at that time was the epicentre of Chinese immigration to the United States, almost all relevant Chinese arrival and birth records were stored there and therefore burned along with much of the city.

Hundreds of Chinese people were killed. But from the literal ashes of that event rose new hope for the Chinese community in the United States. The destruction of the birth and immigration records, coupled with the Wong Kim Ark ruling, now made it far more difficult for US immigration officials to prove whether a particular Chinese person was born in the United States.

It then became much easier for Chinese wishing to go to or remain in the United States to claim that they were born there and the relevant paperwork had been destroyed. Although at first, this was simpler for male children than female, given the small number of Chinese women born in the United States, eventually it also became easier for women.

From these circumstances, the concept of the 'paper son' was born. When a young Chinese man wanted to go to the United States, his claim usually took one of two common forms. Either he was portrayed as having been born in the United States, who had been sent back to China at a young age for education and now wanted to return to the United States, or he was a son born in China to a father in the United States, who had citizenship or legal right to residence and to which the son was now entitled. Also, when Chinese men with a legal presence in the United States returned from a trip to China, they would often file paperwork indicating that a son had been born recently, creating a future opportunity for their own son or another person to travel to the United States at a later date. While many 'paper sons' were blood relatives of the person sponsoring them, possibly a nephew or cousin, in some cases, the 'sons' were also neighbours of families with members in the United States or even total strangers who had purchased their identity papers.[9]

Much like the 'witness protection program' in the United States, which gives new identities to participants in the prosecution of high-profile criminals, or even identity theft, where one person completely assumes the digital identity of another, the 'paper son' had to know the details of his new identity perhaps even better than they knew their own.

Even before the 1906 earthquake, these tactics had been employed – a bit too often, according to the statement of one US Government attorney. 'If all these fellows were really born in the United States every Chinese woman in American twenty-five years ago must have had at least 500 children,' said Duncan E. McKinlay, Assistant US District Attorney, in 1901.[10]

The difficult ocean voyage from China to California (or in some cases, Seattle) was a boon for would-be 'paper sons': it gave them weeks of unbroken time to learn their new names and backgrounds backward and forward, before finally tossing any information sheets relating to these assumed identities overboard, lest they be discovered.

Angel Island

Beginning in 1892, many immigrants to the United States from Europe passed through the Ellis Island Immigration Station in New York Harbour. To handle a new surge of arrivals from Asia, and to sift them through a finer filter than before, the US Government opened a similar facility on Angel Island in San Francisco Bay. Angel Island had previously been used to quarantine incoming passengers from Asia as early as 1891, but now became an official immigration checkpoint beginning in 1910.

Unlike Ellis Island, which is basically an overbuilt rock in a harbour, Angel Island itself is a hilly oasis covered with trees, with beautiful views of San Francisco, Oakland and the Pacific Ocean.[11] Despite the beauty, however, the experience was more like Alcatraz.

On Angel Island, Chinese arrivals would be identified and separated from other passengers. Immigration officials first administered a health examination. One later immigrant recalled the process:

> When we first came, we went to the hospital building for the physical examination. The doctor told us to take off everything. Really, though, it was humiliating. The Chinese never expose themselves like that. They checked you and checked you. We never got used to that kind of thing – and in front of whites.[12]

Provided the applicant was in good health, he (or she) later waited in dormitory accommodation to face questioning. One scholar wrote about the interrogation of her grandfather, who was from the Taishan region:

> He answered questions about his name, age, the Yee family, and the Yee family village. He had studied these details, including how many rows of houses there were in Lok Oh Lee village, the name of the nearest market, how often his father came to visit, the occupations and family makeup of various neighbors, and the size and location of the family's clock.[13]

Despite the draconian detention and the need in many cases to adopt a false identity, 75 per cent or more of all immigrants who passed through Angel Island were ultimately admitted.[14] Angel Island officials processed about 1 million immigrants in the thirty years the station was used; approximately 175,000 of them were Chinese.[15] Just as millions of European Americans now trace their families' arrival in the United States to Ellis Island in New York, the same is true of hundreds of thousands or more Chinese Americans whose ancestor or relative first landed on Angel Island. Ellis Island, by contrast, saw only about 5,000 Chinese pass through it.

In the spring of 1912, the best option for six sailors on a British-owned banana boat in North America was probably to stay aboard their ship and ride the wind and tide until something better came along.

The Scattering of the Six

Of the six men, the first to leave *Annetta* was the eldest, Ah Lam. Ah Lam departed the ship when it arrived back in New York on 29 July, three months into *Annetta*'s voyage. The ship's log indicates that he declined to report for an ability and conduct inspection or review and received a negative report as a result. Possibly due to this disciplinary problem, Ah Lam left *Annetta* by mutual agreement when it returned to New York.[16]

Annetta's Chinese crew list upon arriving in Philadelphia on 11 August 1912 provides some insight into the men and their situation. By this point, they had already gone to the Caribbean and returned to New York since their departure in April. Ah Lam had just left after the completion of the first full voyage.

Ten Chinese men were on board, including five of the six *Titanic* survivors. Interestingly, Fang Lang was now using the name Bing Sun (彭星), yet another variation on his known aliases. Yum Hee/Ling Hee is listed as Nim Hee. Although he signed his name in Chinese in the same way on most shipping records, in this case, he made a '++' mark instead. Why he did that is not known. He is described as having a 'scar on left cheek'.[17] Identifying marks were often included on Chinese crew lists: American or European officers on ships may have found these helpful to recognise individuals, especially when new crews came on board.

At this stop in Philadelphia, Chang Chip, plagued by poor health throughout his career at sea, was left in hospital. *Annetta*'s log indicates that Chang was treated for pleurisy, a type of lung infection.[18] Later, he rejoined *Annetta*, but in March 1913 the ship's log lists him as being discharged in Port Antonio, Jamaica – again being sent to hospital.[19] Despite his time on and off the ship due to medical problems, Chang is believed to be the last of the six *Titanic* survivors to leave *Annetta*.

A ship's cook named Chang Chip, of similar age to the *Titanic* survivor and *Annetta* crewman, appears in records as dying in London on 3 July 1914 from pneumonia, at the approximate age of 24.[20] That he would have returned to the UK from North America via Jamaica is entirely plausible. Aside from being close in age, dying from pneumonia, although common both then and now, matches with Chang, as he suffered from pleurisy earlier in his time on *Annetta*. If this man was Chang Chip, then he was the first of the Chinese *Titanic* survivors to die, barely two years after the sinking.

Chang is buried at East London Cemetery in London's West Ham. The space above Chang's grave was reused in the 1980s and the grave marker removed as a result. It is believed to be at or near the site of a memorial erected in 1927, which reads, 'In memory of the Chinese that have died in England'.

When research into *Titanic*'s Chinese passengers began, a promising lead made it appear that Chang Chip's story would be known more fully. An American-born Chinese businessman with the surname Lee in Taishan indicated that his wife's family, all of whom were from the area, was related to Chang and his story of surviving the sinking had been passed down. However, this gentleman never provided any more than these few basic facts and eventually stopped responding to all contact. Perhaps someday, he or another member of his family will tell Chang's story in greater detail.

On 27 December 1912, *Annetta* discharged Fang Lang and Ling Hee in New York, leaving only Lee Bing and Cheong Foo from the original six. It appears the men never served together again, as a group nor even in pairs and there is also no indication that they remained in contact later in life. Therefore, it is likely that if any of the initial eight Chinese men aboard *Titanic* were related, they were not close relatives.

The First World War Interrupts

A coal strike sent Chinese sailors across the Atlantic Ocean, but two parallel events brought them back. During the summer of 1914, five of the six Chinese men were still working on ships, with the remaining one probably already deceased. However, their time in North America was about to end as the demand for Chinese sailors shifted from the American coast to Europe.

In June 1914, the start of the First World War in Europe, with the UK, France and Russia – the Allies – on one side, and Germany, the Austro-Hungarian Empire and the Ottoman Empire – the Central Powers – on the other, suddenly meant that Britain and France required every able-bodied sailor to serve in their countries' navies. With the United States remaining neutral during the first three years of the war, and Canada still a British Dominion, merchant vessels needed any available sailor to help keep goods and supplies moving from North America to Great Britain and its allies on the European continent.

Once again, Chinese sailors had a critical role to play in maintaining regional and global shipping. Although military participation by Chinese soldiers and naval personnel was limited during the war, along with their countrymen on the high seas, another 140,000 Chinese served in non-combat roles on European battlefields as part of the Chinese Labour Corps.

From the start of the war, Germany attempted to blockade the UK. For an island in the age before widespread air transport, this was a real threat. The Royal Navy was the largest naval force in the world at that point, but the Imperial German Navy had become a formidable foe. And while Germany had not invented the submarine, it believed very much in its power not only to be an effective weapon, but also to inspire fear in a country reliant on seaborne cargo and passengers who travelled internationally by sea.

Previously, Chinese sailors only faced standard sailing and workplace hazards, such as being injured by machinery or collision with an unexpected iceberg. Now they would be sailing on ships that were actively being hunted by German submarines.

For Britain, having a large and effective navy was the only way to ensure the safety and security of the home islands and its sprawling empire. With British sailors shifting into military roles aboard naval ships, British merchant ships needed all the experienced mariners they could get, and for a few years, they weren't too picky about where they came from. Suddenly, the jobs for firemen and cooks were back in Europe and shipping records show the *Titanic* survivors migrating back to ships serving British if not European waters, or at least ships that were based on that side of the Atlantic.

The Seamen's Act of 1915

As if demand in Europe were not sufficient to push Chinese sailors back across the Atlantic, the message from the United States to them was clear: go away. Alongside the Chinese Exclusion Act, which remained in force, new legislation designed to 'protect' the jobs of American mariners and increase shipboard safety became law. This legislation was actually a reaction to *Titanic*'s sinking. It contains numerous provisions regarding the number of lifeboats that ships must carry, that each lifeboat must have certified men to man them, and that regular lifeboat drills be undertaken to ensure successful loading and launch.

Officially and exhaustively known as the Act to Promote the Welfare of American Seamen in the Merchant Marine of the United States,[21] the Seamen's Act of 1915 did not single out any ethnic group or nationality. However, the act strongly reduced the opportunities for many foreign sailors by enforcing certain requirements for the qualifications and language abilities of crew members.

Ships were required to have 75 per cent of their crew who 'are able to understand any order given by the officers of such vessel', and within five years of enacting the law, 65 per cent of crew members must have at least achieved a rating of able seaman. Both of those demands were outside the reach of most non-native, English-speaking sailors. A formal rating such as able seaman requires the performance of 'deck service', or must 'involve the mechanics of conducting the ship on its voyage, such as helmsman [wheelsman], lookout, etc., and which are necessary to the maintenance of a continuous watch'.[22] In other words, not working in the boiler room, engine room or the galley (kitchen).

In 1915, Chinese crew could be hired for work below decks, but they were not being assigned tasks such as navigation or functions required to run a ship. Suddenly, most Chinese sailors were unqualified to serve aboard not only US-registered ships, but also foreign ships sailing into US ports to which the law also applied.

The Chinese *Titanic* survivors' employment shows how they rode the tide back to Europe. From their transfer to North America in the spring of 1912, by 1914 all the living survivors were back where they started, with most based once again in London's Limehouse area, still a hub for Chinese sailors in the capital.

As war approached, British shipping operations began shifting to Liverpool. Moving the centre of British shipping away from the English Channel to the Irish Sea offered relative, although not complete, safety from German submarines and put shipping closer to a centre of British shipbuilding. Liverpool already had Europe's oldest Chinatown, offering an easy base of operations for incoming Chinese sailors.[23]

Tracing the history of these six men – who expended significant effort first trying to hide their identities and origins, and then later trying to prove them – requires carefully pulling at strands of information: a name on a crew list here, a similar name in an immigration file there. Sometimes, those threads break and cannot be reattached. However, without known relatives or published personal stories, pulling at threads is all that can be done to try to reveal a history they never intended to share.

LING HEE, AH LAM AND CHEONG FOO

Ling Hee/Yum Hee

During the 1910s, all merchant seamen travelling in and out of the United Kingdom had an identification record called a CR10, a crew registry document. These cards included basic personal information, such as the seaman's name, date of birth, place of birth, nationality, the person's rating or occupation on board ships, height, weight and distinguishing marks. The back of the card included a photograph of the sailor.

One CR10 record that relates to *Titanic's* Chinese survivors is for Ling Hee/Yum Hee. His birthdate is listed as 22 January 1889, and it identifies him as being from Hong Kong. His position is listed as fireman.[1] In the photograph on the card's back, a younger man wears a suit and tie. On his left cheek, he clearly sports a large scar – exactly as he was described in his crew listing on *Annetta*.[2] The photo is a rare opportunity to look into the eyes of one of *Titanic's* Chinese survivors.

Despite his frequent name changes in English, Ling's unique Chinese name identifies him clearly. Ling was sufficiently literate to sign his name, although in some instances he made only a mark. While men's names frequently changed or were spelled differently on crew lists in English, the Chinese name is almost always the same.

Ling appears to have continued in shipping and appears on a crew manifest as 'Yum Hui' in 1920 aboard the *Keelung*, sailing from London in May and returning in December.[3] However, it did not return with the sailor identified as Ling Hee or Yum Hui, who was listed as deserting the ship in Calcutta (today's Kolkata), India, in October.

Why Ling Hee deserted is not known. Desertion is a serious offence for any mariner, and he would have known that, so he likely made that decision carefully. Calcutta might seem like an odd choice, but it was *Keelung*'s furthest east port of call, so if he were trying to return to Hong Kong or elsewhere, this is as close as that ship would take him. Also, Calcutta, which had been the capital of British-governed India until 1911, had a small although mostly Hakka Chinese community, which still exists today. Ling cannot be confirmed in any British shipping records after his desertion from *Keelung* in October 1920.

That may not be the end of Ling's story. A Ling Hee of the correct age arrived on board SS *Talthybius* from Hong Kong at an unspecified US port, likely San Francisco, in July 1927. This Ling Hee was employed as a fireman. However, his distinguishing marks do not mention a scar on his left cheek.

A man named Ling Hee resided at 30 Beckett St, in the northeastern corner of San Francisco's Chinatown, in the early 1940s. His age of 54 is close to that indicated on the CR10. The census information also indicates that Ling Hee was a widower. His residence's other occupant, a man named Ah Fong, provided the information, which might possibly account for any discrepancies.

Shortly afterward, in 1942 and 1943, Ling spent time in Monterey, California, south of San Francisco, on the coast, based on an alien registration card from that time, which lists his birthdate as 27 October 1886. Jobs were plentiful there, canning fish caught from Monterey Bay and other local waters. These were the kind of jobs that often attracted Chinese immigrants – dirty, smelly work with reasonable pay that other Americans weren't willing to do. A Chinese grocer features as a main character in the famous novel *Cannery Row*, which John Steinbeck wrote about the place and time in 1945.

In 1946 this same Ling Hee – by this point, he had settled on Ling Hee as his permanent name – began applying for US citizenship. The Chinese Exclusion Act was finally repealed in 1943 and many Chinese immigrants in the United States became eligible for citizenship. However, because Ling and other Chinese immigrants had spent decades attempting to conceal the circumstances of their arrival and their identity, proving how and when they had arrived and what they had been doing since then was difficult.

Ling Hee's Alien File – or 'A File' – from the US Citizenship and Immigration Services (USCIS) lists him with a birthdate of 1 October 1886, being born in or near Hong Kong and a subject of Great Britain. The undated file states that he entered the United States on 10 October 1918 as a crew member aboard a ship owned by the Adick Holland Steamship Co., a company name that does not appear in existing records. The file also shows he was a member of the Alaska Cannery Workers Union and the On Ping Association. Although unemployed at the time of the application, he had most recently worked as a cook.

If he entered the United States via San Francisco, then Ling Hee is likely the only Chinese *Titanic* survivor to come through Angel Island, although those records did not survive or provide any assistance in his efforts to legitimise his residence. While the file does not include a photo of the applicant, it does include his signature. This signature appears different from the one associated with the *Titanic* survivor.

This Ling Hee died on 17 July 1975. Even on his official death certificate, his information varies, with the certificate listing his date of birth as 1 October 1887. He is buried in the Chinese Six Companies Cemetery in Colma, California, south of San Francisco. He had no known children and either had never married or lost his wife at some point.

Ah Lam: A Fresh Start?

About the time that Chang Chip departed *Annetta* in March 1913, a man named Lam Choy or Lam Choi joined the crew of a ship named *Norhilda*, also owned by the Donald Line. Boarding on 3 March 1913, this Lam indicates *Annetta* as his previous ship. Is this Ah Lam, using a different name?

No other Lams had served aboard *Annetta* in the interim, and Lam Choi is the same age as Ah Lam. Perhaps whatever disciplinary problem had caused his departure was forgotten by both Lam and the Donald Line, and a familiar face was better than one who had to be retrained or at least reintegrated onto the ship. Given his senior age, Lam might have been a welcome, if not slightly cantankerous, addition to the crew.

One of the surviving CR 10 cards linked to a *Titanic* survivor is for a Chinese sailor named Lam Choi. His card does not include his name in Chinese or his signature, nor does it include a list of ships upon which he has served, so there is no way to confirm if this is the same person who was on *Norhilda*. But the Lam Choi depicted otherwise matches the age of Ah Lam, with a birthdate of 1 April 1874. He is listed as being from Hong Kong, as he had been since being on *Titanic*.

Most powerful is the photograph. The man looks healthy, but clearly older than his approximately 40 years. The lines on his face could be waves upon the ocean. He is not smiling. He has done his work as it came, seemingly always on the sea. We don't know enough about Ah Lam/Lam Choi to know if all his years on ships went to support a family back in China, Hong Kong or elsewhere, or whether he just started on ships early and never stopped.

Lam Choi later served mostly on ships owned by Elder Dempster and Company, a shipping line that primarily handled international mail. Those ships included *Kaduna*, *Bendu* and finally, in the summer of 1920, *Achilles*, owned by the Ocean Steam Ship Company.

Achilles departed from Birkenhead, very close to the English city of Liverpool, on the western bank of the River Mersey. From Birkenhead, it made its way gradually east, passing through the Mediterranean Sea and the Suez Canal, and then across the Indian Ocean before reaching major destinations including Singapore, Hong Kong and Shanghai, where the entire Chinese crew was discharged and not rehired for the return journey. At this point, Ah Lam/Lam Choi does not appear again in similar British shipping records, with British lines being the primary employer of Chinese crew in global shipping.

However, it is possible that Lam's career continued on ships elsewhere. An Ah Lam, aged 50, appears as a cook on board the ship *Strath* or *Br. Strath*, which was calling in at Seattle, Washington, on 29 July 1926. Although slightly younger than his age given on *Titanic* would have indicated (he should have been 52), the name, age and occupation are sufficiently similar that it merits consideration. He does not appear in shipping records again after this date.

Too Many Cheong Foos

Chasing historical shadows sometimes leads to dead ends. Cheong Foo's anglicised name made him one of the most difficult to track. Its variations – Cheong Foo, Chang Foo, Cheung Foo, Chung Foo – could point to any number of Chinese names in several dialects. Which Cheong? Which Foo?

One other obstacle made tracing this man even more onerous: being illiterate, Cheong left behind no signature against which other records could be compared. Would finding another Cheong Foo who signed shipping records with '++' mean that this was the same person? In places, he does sign a Chinese name. Did he eventually learn to write his name? How could that person be matched to earlier records?

Cheong Foo remained on *Annetta* the longest of the *Titanic* survivors. In March 1914, he appears on the *Crown of Toledo* as a fireman. After that, his trail grows somewhat cold. However, one interesting lead connects to a Cheong Foo in the United Kingdom.

Unlike other British possessions and former colonies, the United Kingdom never adopted anti-miscegenation laws, which forbid people from different races to marry. That said, marriages between white women and non-white men were still rare and usually frowned upon.

A case that appeared in a June 1936 newspaper article put such relationships, and the name 'Chung Foo', front and centre in the public's attention. The case involved a woman born with the name Georgina Bellman, who had married a man named Chung Foo:

An inquest was held at the Howbeck Institution, West Hartlepool, this afternoon, on Ah Chung-Foo (46), a Chinese laundryman, of 22 Musgrave Street, who was found in an unconscious condition, early on Sunday morning, apparently suffering from gas poisoning.

Mrs. Georgina Chung-foo said at 2:30 on Sunday morning her husband came into her room and got into bed. Chung-foo, she said, then got hold of her and tried to strangle her. He struck witness [Georgina], and she ran out of the house into the street.

A man who was passing on a bicycle went for police assistance.

The Coroner (Mr. Norman Graham) showed Mrs. Chung-foo a letter and asked if it was in her husband's handwriting.

'IT IS ALL LIES'

Mrs. Chung-foo, pointing to the top half of the letter, said that portion was in her husband's writing, but she was certain the remainder of it was not in his writing.

Asked about the meaning of the contents of the letter, the wife said, 'It is all lies.'

[Police Constable] Meek said when he was called to the house, Mrs. Chung-foo was standing outside in her nightdress. The man was lying in a corner of the back bedroom, which smelt strongly of gas. He was in an unconscious condition. Beside him there was a gas pipe.

A verdict of 'Suicide' was returned.[4]

It was not the first time that the Chungs had attracted the attention of the police. The two had previously been sentenced to one month's imprisonment for possession and smuggling of opium.

As sensational a story as this is, the Chung Foo that married Georgina Bellman was most likely not the man who was on *Titanic*. Even with the discrepancy in ages seen through the records of the Chinese that survived *Titanic*, this Chung Foo would have been too young by about ten years.

Removal

It is possible that both Ah Lam and Cheong Foo were swept up in a little known and dark chapter of British immigration history, one that only became known in recent years. Chinese sailors served on British merchant ships throughout the First World War, along with British officers and other crew members from the Caribbean, Africa, the Middle East and India. They also died on them, their cargo vessels attacked by German surface ships or torpedoed by German submarines. The best-known sinking involving Chinese sailors was the SS *Vinovia*, a Cunard-owned cargo ship that was torpedoed near Cornwall in south-west England in December 1917. Nine men died, including six Chinese.[5]

Other victims included *Achilles*, on which Ah Lam/Lam Choi served, which was sunk by a German submarine in 1916, although it is believed he had already moved on by then. *Norhilda*, another Lam Choi ship, was also sunk by a submarine in 1917.

At the end of the First World War, sailors – including Chinese sailors – who had served on at least one mission through a combat zone were eligible to receive the Mercantile Medal, awarded in 1919. An exact death toll of Chinese sailors on board British ships during the war is not known. In 2006, a memorial to the Chinese merchant seamen who died during the First and Second World Wars was erected in Liverpool. According to records that have survived to the present day – many records were destroyed as a result of bombing during the Second World War – at least 493 Chinese sailors received these medals. However, if any of the Chinese *Titanic* survivors were decorated in this way, those records no longer exist.

This spirit of gratitude for the service of Chinese sailors did not last long. As early as 1916, with the war still being fought, 'the Sailors' and Firemen's Union organised protest meetings around Limehouse and Poplar in London, against the increasing use of Chinese labour on British ships'.[6]

In response to the need to employ thousands of British sailors demobilising from the war, in the summer of 1919, the UK's Ministry of Labour and other government departments proposed to begin removing unemployed Chinese seamen back to China. This was part of a larger effort to remove people from Britain's colonies and possessions, including Black labourers from the Caribbean and Arabs from the Middle East, in response to a series of violent race riots in various UK port cities at the same time.

However, this was problematic. If the Chinese men were from Hong Kong (or Malaya/Singapore), then they were British subjects and could not be sent back there without having been convicted of a criminal offence. Even if they were natives of other parts of China, there were no specific grounds for removing them from British soil. This was not deportation in the sense of being ejected from a foreign country due to improper status or a criminal offence. It was instead a plan by government departments to get large groups of unemployed, non-British men out of Britain and make it extremely difficult for them to return.

Police conducted a large-scale survey of British Chinatowns, namely in Liverpool and London, to assess how many Chinese were there and how willing they would be to leave voluntarily. One of the people interviewed during this survey was Lam Choi, age 42, living at 20 Pitt Street in Liverpool – 'Seaman; claims to be a native of Hong Kong; arrived here on February 2, 1919, on S.S. 'Kaduna', since unemployed; owes £9 for board and lodgings.'

After preparing to conduct secret repatriations by rounding up the Chinese men and herding them on to ships at night, then giving them £7 upon arrival in China, the British Government cancelled the plan when China's Ambassador to the UK objected to the move. Relations between the Republic of China Government and the UK were already frosty after the Allies had ignored China's demand to resolve territorial disputes with Japan, relating to post-First World War settlement of these claims.

Even with the repatriation plan cancelled, the friction between British seamen and foreign sailors was not going away. The British Government took action in two ways.

First, it extended the 1919 Alien Restriction Act. This law was enacted in 1914, at the beginning of the war, to allow the British Government to keep tabs on non-Britons, especially those from enemy countries such as Germany and Austria–Hungary. It also made it more difficult for British shipping lines to employ foreign seaman, including Chinese sailors.

The second is not entirely proven but appears to have occurred. British shipping companies operating between the UK and China, perhaps encouraged or even ordered by the government, started to remove Chinese seamen, slowly but surely, in late 1919 and throughout 1920. There would be no night raids, no bundling of men onto ships, kicking and screaming. Instead, shipping companies employed Chinese crews as normal, including accommodation and pay. Upon arrival in Shanghai, the chosen destination for these operations, the Chinese sailors, whether they were from Shanghai or not, were paid and discharged from the ship. No Chinese sailors were rehired for the return journey to the UK.

Whether this course of action was endorsed officially or not, the effect was the same. During 1920, the UK's Chinatowns emptied out, with populations in Liverpool dropping from the thousands into the hundreds.[7] Couples in which Chinese men had married British women were permanently divided; the children from these unions never saw their fathers again and never knew what happened to them.[8] Dad went to sea and never came back.

Both Ah Lam/Lam Choi and Cheong Fu may have been removed from the UK in this manner. Lam seems the most likely, having appeared in the 1919 police report, followed by his one-way journey to Shanghai on *Achilles*. Cheong Foo, having been based in the UK, may also have fallen into this trap, although his common name has made him too difficult to trace over long periods of time.

The year 1920 marked the end of a significant Chinese presence in global shipping. American shipping companies began rivalling British ones for supremacy on the waves, and the restrictions imposed by both made it difficult for Chinese sailors to continue to work outside Asia.

This period of 1850–1920 cannot be called a golden age. Although it provided employment for thousands of Chinese men, it was dangerous and difficult work, with no insurance and no pension. A man earned only his wage, and if he did not save it or use it to assist his family in China, there was nothing more. Illness, injury, shipwreck or simple discharge could leave a man stranded in a foreign port with little or nothing. Men like Ah Lam stayed at sea because there was nowhere for them to go on land.

It is entirely possible that Ah Lam, Cheong Fu and Ling Hee all eventually returned to China voluntarily. The vast majority of Chinese labourers who sought work overseas between the mid-1850s and 1920 did so only as a short- to medium-term plan, with the intention of returning to China once they had made enough money to ensure their families' or their own personal financial future. Many, however, never went back, either because they could not afford it or because circumstances took their lives in other directions.

It was the pair of Chinese *Titanic* survivors who went to the two most difficult countries to enter – Canada and the United States – whose stories were discovered most completely. From one of the world's great maritime disasters to rejection in New York, the two continued their lives on the sea just long enough until they could seize their chance on land.

LEE BING:
THE CANADIAN

To understand Lee Bing and his story of survival, we must begin at the end:

> Lee Coon, one of the city's best-known Chinese, died [2 June 1943] at Freeport Sanatorium. Long known by many restaurant patrons as the 'Big Chief,' he had been ill for about a year and was a patient in the sanatorium for about 10 weeks prior to his death. Lee Coon came to Galt from Canton [now Guangzhou], China, about 25 years ago. After being in the laundry business for a short time, he became associated with the City Café which was located for many years at 4 South Water Street and in recent years at 14 South Water Street. The deceased was about 64 years old.[1]

A later notice specified, 'Funeral service at the T. Little and Son Ltd. Funeral Home, 39 Grand Ave. N. on Friday, June 4, at 3 p.m. Interment Mount View Cemetery'.

Based on its condition, no one appears to have visited the grave in Mount View Cemetery in Cambridge, Ontario, Canada, for decades. The headstone itself is a Rosetta Stone of sorts for his life. He was born in 1879 and, although he was known in English as Lee Coon or Coon Lee, his birth name was Lee Yun An (李雲安). Above even his Chinese name appears his place of birth, Hengtang, an inland village in central southern Taishan, Guangdong Province. So, using the grave marker as a reference, as Eliot stated, we start from the end.

From Hengtang, Lee made his way to Hong Kong like many young men from his area, seeking work and ending up on ships. Early shipping records indicate that at one point he, using the name Lee Bing, listed 25 Des Voeux Road West, now in Hong Kong's Sheung Wan area, as a residential address. Many Taishan sailors found lodging there while waiting for assignments aboard ships. These stops in Hong Kong are what led some of the Chinese passengers aboard *Titanic* to be listed as being from there, even though they were from elsewhere in China.

Described as being 5ft 5in–5ft 8in (165–73cm), Lee sported a tattoo on his left forearm, likely a butterfly. Lee is listed in some sources as being married to a woman named Too Bing, although the source of this is disputed. If they were married, it is assumed she remained in Hengtang while Lee went elsewhere to work.

Prior to *Titanic*, Lee appears on crew lists for the freighter *Norwegian*, not to be confused with the later luxury cruise ship. Lee served on board *Norwegian* with Cheong Foo. During this time, he listed 51 or 57 Pennyfields Road in London as his address, in the Limehouse area. As previously noted, this part of London had a small Chinese community, including boarding houses where sailors working on the European freighters would stay while in port.

He was in the employ of the Donald Steam Ship Line, which maintained offices in both Bristol, England, and New York City in the United States. Not to be confused with the Donaldson Passenger Ship Line, the Donald Line operated freighters for clients including United Fruit Co. and Atlantic Fruit Co., around Europe and more specifically, along the North American coast. These freighters were known as 'fruit boats' because of their most common cargo but could carry other foodstuffs or material based on a client's charter.

In the spring of 1912, Lee Bing joined the seven other Chinese sailors on *Titanic*, sailing on White Star ticket No. 1601. As *Titanic* sank, Lee Bing boarded Collapsible C with Ah Lam, Chang Chip and Ling Hee, and made it first to *Carpathia* and then to their assigned ship, SS *Annetta*.

About six months after *Titanic*'s sinking, Lee filed a claim for

US$99.43 in lost possessions, almost entirely clothing. That would now be more than US$2,600. The figure would be understandable in the context of losing all of one's possessions, but hard to fathom in an age without personal electronics, for men who carried neither cosmetics nor jewellery, except for the odd watch or clock. In a time before personal insurance, getting back anything would be better than losing everything. However, there is no indication that he or four of the other five Chinese survivors who filed claims were ever recompensed for their lost property.

Lee appears in *Annetta*'s crew log until at least January 1913.[2] The following year, a Lee Bing begins to appear on Canadian census records in a small Canadian town called Galt, Ontario.

Canada and Chinese Immigration

Canadian anti-Chinese immigration policy followed the United States but was no less comprehensive or insidious; in fact, in some ways it was more restrictive and intrusive. Canada's economic expansion mirrored that of the United States, with the west coast at first trailing behind the eastern half of the country. The discovery of gold in British Columbia in 1858 led to a surge in Chinese and other immigration. That event, as it had in the United States, pushed the government in the east to want to unite the landmass with a transcontinental railroad. The desire and opportunity to expand the exploitation of various natural resources, especially in the west, required more labour, particularly workers willing to do dirtier, harder work in remote areas.

The opposition to Chinese immigration was ironic in that while overlapping gold claims could create tension in mining areas, for the most part, Chinese workers were at least not directly taking the jobs of any other group. Although wage levels were an issue, there was simply too much work to go around and more hands were needed to do it, be they Chinese or any others.

Once the Canadian Pacific Railway was completed in 1885, the usual anti-immigrant litany of disease and moral inferiority was weaponised against Chinese workers, and Canada's Parliament passed the Chinese Immigration Act of 1885. Opposition to Chinese immigration stemmed almost entirely from British Columbia on Canada's west coast, since that was the destination for almost all Chinese immigration to Canada.

Instead of restricting entry to Canada merely by statute, the 1885 act put a price tag on it. The price of entry into Canada, called a head tax, was therefore set at C$50, about C$2,200 today, which would have been about two and a half months' salary for a Chinese worker at the time. Also included in the act were ethnic Chinese with British nationality, despite Canada not having full independence from the United Kingdom at that point.

While the head tax was not the only limitation placed upon would-be Chinese immigrants, it created a somewhat easier process than in the United States. As long as one could pony up the $50 – often paid by someone in Canada, who would hire the applicant and then get them to work it off – the process was fairly straightforward. Realising this, Canada's legislature first raised the tax to $100, and to $500 by 1906.

Paying the fee gave one entry into Canada and the opportunity to work, but there was no path to citizenship. Chinese immigration dropped to a trickle, at least in the near term after the tax went up by five times, but it eventually returned to such a level that Canada banned Chinese immigration almost entirely.

In 1923, Canada implemented the Chinese Immigration Act, which was essentially similar to the US Chinese Exclusion Act. The opportunity to pay the head tax was revoked, and like the American legislation, Canada's legislation made exceptions for diplomats, scholars, merchants and tourists.

One onerous but historically valuable aspect of Canada's immigration policies is the Canadian Immigration Form No. 9, also known as a CI9 or a certificate of leave. Canadian officials required this paperwork for any ethnic Chinese wishing to return to China or otherwise depart Canada, to prove that he (or very rarely, she) had legal status to return. The result is an almost complete catalogue of over 40,000 records that provide not only personal information, but also photographs of each person.[3]

Unfortunately, no single CI9 matches a Lee with sufficiently similar characteristics, such as name or age. Several records for 'Lee Bings' were located, but neither the age nor description were close to the *Titanic* survivor and eventual restaurant owner. It's possible that Lee never went back to China and therefore didn't need the document.

Life in a Northern Town

Cambridge, in the Canadian province of Ontario, could pass for a quaint English town. Actually, it does so professionally – Cambridge is regularly used as a stand-in for English or European settings in North American film and television productions, including *Designated Survivor*, *American Gods* and *The Handmaid's Tale*. About 62 miles (100km) south-west of Toronto, before it was ready for its close-up, the area was previously part of the town of Galt. Originally settled by Six Nations Native Canadians, Scottish settlers acquired land from them and established Galt in 1816. It was incorporated in 1973 with the nearby towns of Hespeler and Preston to form present-day Cambridge.

Not surprisingly for a road with its name, Main Street, in the former Galt itself, looks like a movie set, a spot where one imagines cars from the first half of the twentieth century driven by men wearing hats filling the streets. At the intersection of Main Street and Water Street, which runs along the east bank of the Grand River, stand four banks. That quartet of financial institutions became a meeting spot for the town's young people, who met at Four Corners or Four Banks before moving to other locations in search of merriment. Local writer and artist Bob Green recalled in his memoir *Eavesdroppings*, about life in Galt during the twentieth century:

> On any Saturday night in downtown Galt back in the 1930s, automobiles bumper to bumper on Main Street between the unsynchronized traffic lights at Water and Ainslie chugged up such a din that jaywalkers had to shout to one another. And the sidewalks were so crowded that the fit and able walked on the pavement. Most people weren't out to shop but just to walk and talk, a luxury of the Great Depression. Patrons of Gone With The Wind lined two abreast from the Capitol Theatre on Water Street to the Imperial Bank at Main and around the corner to jostle with people pushing in and out of Walker Stores.[4]

Green wrote:

> Directly across from Walker Stores, Lee Bing's second-floor res-
> taurant enclosed its patrons in mutual green upholstered enclaves
> affording such privacy and quiet that diners in each cubicle peered
> out a lot to see who might be in the next. Bing McCauley, whose
> Bing is not to be confused with Lee's Bing, said that Lee once told
> him he had survived the sinking of the *Titanic*. He had been a
> steward but wouldn't discuss how he got off with the women and
> children. Years after he departed and the book about the disaster,
> *A Night to Remember*, was published, Lee Bing appeared in the sur-
> vivors' list.[5]

The Grand River has an unpleasant habit of overflowing and disrupt-
ing daily life. In footage from an April 1929 flood, cars still manage
to navigate the inundation, but it is clearly causing pedestrians some
trouble. Some of those passersby could have taken refuge for lunch
at a place upstairs. Next to the Bank of Montreal, an I-shaped sign
hanging from the second floor of 16 Main Street denoted the White
Rose Café, standing above all of it.[6]

By the time that the White Rose Café was operating, Lee Bing was
one of several male Lee family members who had put down roots in
Galt. Lee Coon's brother, Sam Lee, was established in the area's small
but growing Chinese community. Lee Coon is listed as arriving in
1911. Coon and Sam had another brother, See Lee.

Sam Lee originally operated a laundry in the area, the family's first
business there, before getting into the restaurant industry. Sam had
two sons, Yes Lee and Chong Fong Lee. These sons were probably
born in China and then joined their father in Canada, as there is no
record of any wife or mother being with the other Lee men there in
Galt. Lee Bing is believed to be Lee Coon's son.

Bing McCauley knew Lee Bing and dined at the White Rose Café.
Marjorie Bartholomew, a Galt resident, recalled that he was a kind
man. During quiet times, he would pour glasses of milk and bring
them downstairs to children that he saw playing in the streets below
the café.[7] As described by McCauley, the White Rose leaned towards
fine dining, with its privacy and upholstery, and its menu shows

it was anything but a Chinese restaurant, although it offered both Western and Chinese dishes.

Lee Bing pops up more than once in peculiar tales of Galt. A 1938 item distributed by the *Canadian Press* news service appeared on the front page of *The Winnipeg Tribune* with an accompanying cartoon, 'Cops Rue the Day Lee Bing Ran Away':

Kitchener, Ont., June 18 – City policemen are operating a Chinese laundry here, much to their sorrow. Lee Bing, a laundryman here, fled after he was summoned to court to answer a criminal charge. Police took all the laundry to the police station and since have been trying to match laundry slips.[8]

Nearby Kitchener certainly could have been served by a Galt-based laundryman. However, while the *Canadian Press* recorded the humorous side of the supposed events, no corresponding crime that required Lee Bing's answer could be found.

Despite the Lees' seeming success in Galt, with a laundry and two restaurants, Lee Coon's death in June 1943 ended the family's tenure there. Later that year, the White Rose Café closed and Lee Bing moved to Toronto, where he worked at the Lychee Gardens Restaurant, although Sam Lee and his sons remained in the area. After Lychee Gardens, Lee Bing's trail goes cold.[9]

The Lees appear to have owned another Galt restaurant, the City Café. It is mentioned as 'the Chinese place' in one account. One of the most famous Canadians of his day, 'Mr Hockey', Gordon 'Gordie' Howe, played for the Galt Red Wings farm team before going on to goals and glory with the Detroit Red Wings. Howe recalled going for hayrides that year, and 'going down to the little malt shop where we would have Boston cream pie'. Fellow Red Wings player and Howe teammate Marty Pavelich had not forgotten the Boston cream pie either. '"Oh sure, the Chinese place (City Cafe, which formerly sat beside the CIBC bar the corner of Main and Water Streets at the Four Corners). Hell, we used to go there all the time. We'd go there especially on Sunday and have Boston cream pie",' Cambridge author David Menary wrote in a self-published book about Howe's time in Galt during the 1944–45 hockey season.[10]

Why Lee Bing would leave Galt while his other family members remained, and where he had at least one successful business, is not known.

Similar to Chang Chip, while I was researching this story, the American son-in-law of a Chinese family from Shanghai came forward to state that his mother-in-law had long told a story about a relative of hers being on *Titanic* but the woman's husband regularly ridiculed both the story and the idea that any relative had been on *Titanic*. The Chinese members of the family ultimately declined to tell their version of the story.

Who was Lee Bing?

The relationship between Lee Coon and Lee Bing is problematic. Coon is the correct age of the Lee on board *Titanic*, but of course, it is his apparent son who uses the name Lee Bing in public. Is one of them a *Titanic* survivor, and if so, which one?

It is hard to believe that a Chinese immigrant in Canada would make up a story about having survived *Titanic*. There is little upside to White Rose Café's Lee telling a tall tale about being on board *Titanic* if it were not true. Certainly, in the 1920s and 1930s, Ontarians knew about *Titanic*; Toronto had a number of both survivors and victims.

The wealthy Allison family, travelling in First Class – Hudson, Loraine and Bess – of Chesterfield in eastern Ontario, along with their butler, George Swane, all drowned in the sinking. They died because the parents Hudson and Loraine refused to leave without their youngest son, Trevor, who unbeknownst to them had already boarded a lifeboat with their family's servant, Alice Cleaver. Although they were members of Montreal society, the Allisons were buried in Hudson's native Chesterfield underneath a huge obelisk, where Trevor joined them in 1929, when he died from food poisoning.

Despite the notoriety of *Titanic*'s sinking and Ontarians' involvement with it, it was not widely known that Chinese passengers travelled on the ship, and certainly any awareness of that would have related to the negative accusations of them stowing away. It's unclear how Chinese people in North America who were not among the six survivors or their families would have even known that their compatriots had been on the ship. Therefore, it can be concluded safely that the Lee story is truthful.

So is Lee Coon *Titanic*'s Lee Bing? Or is Lee Bing the *Titanic* Lee Bing? Lee is the only one of the Chinese survivors who spoke about his *Titanic* experience publicly, insofar that he told people outside of his family.

Birthdates alone point toward Lee Coon as the *Titanic* survivor. Lee Bing appears on the passenger list as aged 32, aligning correctly with an 1879 birthdate. The person known as Lee Coon, rather than Lee Bing, is clearly the *Titanic* survivor. In 1920, that same person would have been in his 40s. A glass photographic plate of 'Lee Bing' found in the Cambridge Archives shows a young man, perhaps in high school – someone who was too young to have been on the famous ship.

It's not known why the younger Lee would have taken the moniker Lee Bing, or why the elder would have used it in the first place. *Titanic* records, both for boarding and rescue, clearly indicate the name Lee Bing, along with the Chinese characters 李丙 or 李炳, both pronounced the same way and sounding like the English iteration. This Lee Bing also filed a claim for personal property lost aboard *Titanic*. And the same person served aboard *Annetta* and other vessels, appearing in shipping records that also include a Chinese name that corresponds to the Lee Bing that was on *Titanic*.

Curiously, Lee Bing's story disproves one of the early assumptions of research conducted into *Titanic*'s Chinese passengers, namely that Lee Bing and Lee Ling, who did not survive, were related – likely brothers. Lee, or Li, is one of the most common surnames in China. This is despite the fact that most Chinese names in the late nineteenth and early twentieth centuries were three characters, and all of those on the *Titanic* list were only two, that the Lees' names are so similar, that one follows the other on their *Titanic* ticket, and the difference in ages is only four years, which all still suggest kinship on first glance.

However, the Sue Oi article – which suggested that Fang Lang, Lee Ling and Len Lam were travelling together and intended to start a business in Cleveland – never mentions Lee Bing as part of that plan. Of course, it's entirely possible that the two were brothers or cousins, but that one had made future arrangements with two non-family members for the future. If Lee Bing were indeed related to Lee Ling, he does not seem to have mentioned it as part of any *Titanic* account remembered or recorded by McCauley or Green.

One possibility for Lee Bing's seeming disappearance from Canada is that he returned to China. Despite having run successful businesses in Canada, without their elder family member, at least one of the remaining Lee men may have felt his place was not there. It's also possible that relatives in China may have asked him to return. As none were known to be married and were only related to each other, the death of Lee Coon may have led to him deciding to leave Canada altogether.

If, in 1943 or shortly afterward, Lee chose to return to China, it would have been either an exceptionally brave or exceptionally strange decision. Aside from being in the middle of the most anti-Chinese period of Canadian immigration policy, both Canada and China were deep in the Second World War. Canadian troops, under British command, were fighting both in Asia and Europe; and Japan already occupied swaths of China, with the Americans and British supporting Chinese armies in the south-west, and the Soviet Union backing Chinese armies in the north-east. For a family that had arrived prior to Canada's ban on Chinese immigration and established itself, 1943 would have been the worst possible moment to leave.

Except, of course, if patriotic sentiment compelled Lee Bing to return and help a China under attack. Japanese forces occupied most of eastern and southern Guangdong. There would have been no reason to think the Taishan region wouldn't be next. The family they left behind to help may have needed them present and presently.

There would have been no way to foresee a post-war future. But had Lee Bing hung in until 1947 – and perhaps he and other Lees did, despite a lack of records – they and other Chinese there suddenly would have been eligible for citizenship in the new, fully independent Canada.

Lee Bing arguably prospered more than the other five *Titanic* survivors. By all accounts, he and his family members opened at least three successful businesses and managed to create a foothold in a community that did not have a significant Chinese population. Most likely, that survivor's journey ended in a small Ontario town in 1943. It's unclear whether his extended family in China benefited more from his absence or his presence.

13

FONG WING SUN: THE AMERICAN

Ancestral temples all over Xiachuan Island display banners that indicate that while the residents were born and raised there in the south, they trace their roots to today's Henan Province, the birthplace of Chinese culture, where the first Song Dynasty capital stood in Kaifeng before, under increasing pressure from the Mongols of the north, later shifting to Hangzhou in Zhejiang Province. For a boy growing up on the island in the dusk of the nineteenth century, all of that would have seemed very far away in space and time.

Fong Wing Sun was born on 21 June 1894. An avid reader and a good student, by the time he was 15 the young man was already heading elsewhere, toward a life that for most of the next fifty years kept him moving almost constantly, across oceans and continents, according to a plan that he clearly had in his head but rarely, if ever, uttered from his lips.

Like others from the Taishan region, he travelled by boat to Hong Kong to look for work. No matter what the assignment was, the hours would be long, the labour strenuous and the salary not great. He wasn't going to be inheriting any land on Xiachuan Island, so there was no point working his brother's or someone else's land. Fong's fortune was his own to make, but he was never miserly and always remembered to send some of his earnings back home to support his family.

Despite growing up on an island, the Fong family had no history working on ships or in other maritime trades. They were farmers for the most part. At least Wing Sun knew how to swim, something he had learned earlier in his life in one of Xiachuan Island's quiet bays.

By 1912, Fong had served on ships for three or four years, mostly as a fireman in the engine room, and occasionally as a cook. But he was clearly biding his time, waiting for a bigger opportunity in a better place. When and why he began using the name Fang Lang is not known. Fong does appear in at least one photo later in life with the name Fong Sen (方森) written beneath. While I was researching this book, more than one speaker of Toisan saw this name and pronounced it first as 'Fang Lang' before correcting themselves.

Prior to going to North America, he worked with future *Annetta* sailor and *Titanic* passenger Chang Chip aboard *Netherpark*, a cargo ship.[1]

As described in the Sue Oi article, when finally together with his would-be business partners Lee Ling and Len Lam, the trio must have spent hours on board *Titanic* discussing the details of their plans. How would they get away from immigration officials and their employer's representatives from the Donald Steam Ship Co.?

First, they and the other Chinese men would pass through immigration inspection at Ellis Island. This was likely an advantage: if they had arrived on the American west coast, they would have been stopped and interrogated at the Angel Island Immigration Station, which thousands of arriving Chinese experienced from 1910 to 1940. Only about 5,000 Chinese ever came through Ellis Island, unlike the millions of European immigrants who passed through it.

Once cleared through Ellis Island, Fong, Lee and Len would have to get away from their employers, who had paid their passage across the Atlantic. And all of that had to happen before they made it to a train station and bought tickets to Cleveland. Best-laid plans, indeed.

When *Titanic* struck the iceberg, Fong and the others made their way first toward *Titanic*'s stern, then up to the Boat Deck. There is no indication that they too tried to reach Collapsible Lifeboats C or D. Perhaps they separated from the others and, at some point, chose to move toward *Titanic*'s stern as it rose higher out of the water. That the three were the only Chinese passengers who didn't make it into lifeboats is likely no coincidence, as they were sticking together. Soon, they were out of options and out of time. They ended up in the water, and only Fong lived, in one of *Titanic*'s most dramatic, and perhaps its last, tales of rescue.

Somewhere in his travels, Fong acquired a taste for fine clothing. The son of local farmers who found work in the engine rooms and galleys of ships, to him, a man was not properly dressed unless he wore a Western suit and tie. Although he would have worn a work uniform more appropriate to getting covered with the grease of machine parts or the slop of a ship's kitchen, when Fong had his choice, he dressed up. No photo of him exists that does not show him in at least a shirt and tie. Perhaps he was dressing for the job he wanted.

Fong's claim for property lost on *Titanic* gives us insight into the man and his plans. Along with work clothes and boots, which he listed separately, he claimed three suits; six shirts; two pairs of boots; six neckties and shirt collars; a clock; a watch and watch charm; and a bracelet.[2] The Chinese men would have been carrying all their possessions with them. With no reason to wear such formal clothing on board ship, and with little time for shore leave, Fong was clearly carrying these items for the future.

Following *Titanic*'s sinking, Fong and the others went straight back to work, boarding *Annetta* and sailing away with the other Chinese survivors. If he knew Lee and Len's families, he had no chance to notify them or Sue Oi of their loss. A mountain of ice in the middle of the Atlantic Ocean had sunk his dreams – and a piece of wood had saved his life. Maybe he pondered that as he found his bunk on *Annetta*. Maybe he just looked into the future and wondered how much longer it would take to realise his dream.

Fong continued working on ships using the name Bing Xin or Fang Lang or some variation, both as a fireman and occasionally as a cook. He left *Annetta* in late 1912 but went on to work on other ships. Prior to arriving in the United States, Fong may have served as Ah Fang on a ship based in Le Havre, France, called SS *Strathorne*. In later US immigration documents, Fong indicated he had lived in Le Havre immediately prior to going to the United States. Fong's youngest son, Tom, recalled seeing a photo of his father taken in front of famous Paris landmark the Arc de Triomphe.[3] Fong's last assignment at sea was aboard SS *Rondo*, which sailed from Batavia, today's Jakarta in Indonesia, to New York City.

Farewell, Fang Lang

On 18 August 1920, SS *Rondo* docked in New York, its final destination. It was an end and a beginning. As he carefully and quietly packed his trunk, Fang Lang knew that his time at sea was at last over, years later than he had initially planned.

New York was not new to him. He had arrived there on board *Carpathia* in 1912, his two friends and future business partners drowned in the cold ocean hundreds of miles away. He left *Annetta* there in late 1912.

That day in New York City, the Chinese Exclusion Act remained in effect. A Chinese sailor was no more welcome than he had been as a survivor of the world's most famous shipwreck eight years earlier. But this was 1920 not 2020, and the anti-immigration infrastructure, namely border checkpoints, enforcement agents and identification documents that the United States now has, especially post-2001, didn't exist to the same degree. A Chinese mariner could make his way to Chinatown for a meal in a restaurant or a bed in a boarding house. Sure, he'd better have his papers ready to show in the event of a raid, but raids didn't happen that often.

The fireman and cook known as Fang Lang, aka Sam Fang Lang, picked up his things and walked down the gangplank of SS *Rondo*. As the man stepped from the ship's walkway onto the dock, Fang Lang ceased to exist. With that first step on to dry land, Fong Wing Sun was reborn. Fang Lang may as well have gone down with *Titanic* because he no longer existed. Fong was taking back his name and taking back his dream of a new life in this new land. No more greasy overalls. Now this man would wear a suit and tie.

In the late summer of 1920, Fong would have been 26 years old. Although not necessarily a 'paper son', he would likely have carried false identity papers. He was not deserting a ship, but he was attempting to disappear into the United States. Getting caught with no papers meant deportation. At least with a credible identity, he had a chance.

Fong may have made a brief stop in New York, but it wasn't long before he was on his way to the American Midwest, although not quite where he originally intended. It wasn't to Cleveland that he headed, as he would have in 1912, but to Chicago. After spending his formative years on board ships, his next three decades would be lived on the run on dry land, an undocumented immigrant from America's least popular immigrant group.

Life on dry land was not so different for Fong. He was still an illegal immigrant with limited formal education, and while by this point he spoke some English, it was far from fluent. Moving forward as he always had, Fong quickly found his way into Chicago's Chinese community, joining the local Fong Family Association. Luckily for him, Toisan was still the Chinatown lingua franca, so he could find work and live – and blend in.

During his time aboard ships, along with his sartorial interests, Fong became interested in politics, namely developments in post-imperial China. He quickly converted that into activism on behalf of China's Nationalist Party (Kuomintang) and began to build his own personal and political network around it. To live illegally thousands of miles from home, a man with no nearby family and no degree needed to build a solid network of people he could trust, and do so quickly.

Fong had already left Xiachuan Island when the Xinhai Revolution took place, learning about it from other Chinese sailors on board ships and from the newspapers and books he could pick up while sailing from port to port. But clearly, he was fascinated by and supportive of this new political direction for China. At the same time, Fong had almost no way in which to participate. Stuck on ships far from where the action was, like so many other emotions, he could only hold them in his heart and hope that one day he would have the chance to express them. There is no indication that he ever intended to return to China to participate more fully in a post-imperial government and society. Throughout his life in the United States, he remained active in local Chinese community politics, never running for office but raising money for charitable and community causes.

A Life in Pictures

One of the earliest-known photographs of Fong Wing Sun was taken some time in the early to mid-1920s. Fong is by himself in the photo, clearly in his early 20s, wearing a white or light-coloured shirt and a black or dark pinstriped suit and a dark tie. His hair is neatly parted on the left. He also appears to be wearing a Republic of China flag pin on his left lapel, or similar insignia. The photo, which has a sepia tone to it, was taken at Jaenel Studio, 4108 Milwaukee Avenue in Chicago. Between December 1922 and December 1930, Fong lived near this photo studio, with a residence at 4032 Milwaukee Avenue.[4]

A second, black and white photograph is dated 7 April 1931. Fong appears with two other men, named Hu Yifu 胡艺圃 and Huang Biying 黄比瀛. Fong's name is written here as 方容山. He looks like he's in his mid-20s, wearing a light-coloured suit, perhaps grey, with a matching vest, striped tie and a white or very light-coloured pocket square. The photography studio is not identified.

The third photo, also black and white, is a portrait taken with three other men at a photo studio in Chicago in the late 1920s. Here, a slightly older Fong, maybe now in his early 30s, stands on the right side of the photo in a grey three-piece, single-breasted suit and tie. He has gained a bit of weight since the previous photo.

On two separate copies of this photo owned by the Fong family, handwritten identifications of the men in it use the name Fong Wing Sun on one and Fong Sen on the other. More than once during the research for this book, Toisan speakers saw this name and pronounced it as 'Fang Lang', perhaps mistaking it for Fong Sen, and offering a possible explanation for his use of the name on ships.

The names of the other men are the same on both, most notable among them being Chang Fa-kuei. Although the occupations and origins of the other two men are not known, Chang served as a Kuomintang general before eventually retiring to Hong Kong. Chang would have been allowed to enter the United States as a tourist or perhaps as a diplomat if he were travelling on official business, unimpeded by the Chinese Exclusion Act. The photo was taken at Peter Schneider's photo studio, 2222 State Street in Chicago, which opened in 1892.

Life in Chicago

In his first years in the United States, Fong Wing Sun gave the addresses 2020 West Madison Street and 4032 Milwaukee Avenue in Chicago as both his residence and employment addresses for September 1920 until December 1930. His occupation is not known, but he may have worked as a waiter.[5]

From December 1930 until June 1935, Fong finally got his chance to run a business, not as a merchant but as a partner in Sam Lee Laundry, operating at 2833 West Van Buren Street. However, Fong left that business from June 1935 until December 1938 for unknown reasons and returned to restaurant work as a waiter at the Happy Inn at 4739 Broadway. He returned to the Sam Lee Laundry from December 1938 until June 1942 before departing for the final time. This location no longer exists, as the building at that address was demolished in the early 1950s to make way for the construction of the Interstate 290 highway into Chicago.[6]

He repeated this pattern, working again as a waiter from October 1942 to March 1945 at a restaurant called the Paris Inn at 2744 North Clark Street. From March 1945 to August 1945, there is an unexplained gap in his employment record. It is not known what Fong did or where he was during this time.

Fong then moved to a different restaurant, the Paradise Inn at 4007 West Madison Avenue, also in Chicago, from August 1945 to August 1951. After a two-month gap, he returned to the Paris Inn in October 1951 until February 1952.

Moving to Milwaukee

By early 1952, Fong Wing Sun had been working almost continuously since he was a teenager and was now well into middle age. Almost forty years had passed since the ship on which he had been travelling scraped an iceberg and sank in the middle of the Atlantic Ocean. For more than thirty years, he had been on the run, staying and working in the United States illegally. During that time, he had faithfully supported his family on Xiachuan Island, along with the Chinese community in Chicago.

But he still had no wife, children or business of his own. In 1943, the United States finally rescinded the Chinese Exclusion Act, but even then, there was still no opportunity for Chinese immigrants who had entered the country illegally to become citizens.

With his plans still unfulfilled, Fong moved from Chicago to Milwaukee, Wisconsin, in February 1952. The reason for the move is not known. Some 90 miles (145km) north of Chicago, Milwaukee was known as America's 'Beer City', and was home to four of the world's largest breweries in the 1950s. Milwaukee had a small but distinctive Chinatown, with an array of laundries, restaurants, medicine shops and a theatre.

Fong went to work at Lotus Restaurant, 731 North Third Street – again as a waiter. He then moved to Gay Garden, nearby at 2242 North Third Street in November 1955. It was there that the missing pieces of Fong's life began to fit together.[7]

Becoming a Citizen

In the early 1950s, following the founding of the People's Republic of China, the US Government began to fear that Chinese immigrants in the United States who had not become citizens might become spies for the new communist government. As such, the United States Immigration and Naturalization Service (INS) initiated what was called the Chinese Confession Program. If Chinese non-citizens in the United States came forward and gave a complete account of their time in the United States – specifically, where they had lived and worked, and the names they used, family members' names and the names of employers – they could become eligible for citizenship. However, if the INS believed the person to be untruthful, they could be deported.

Fong considered that possibility and, believing it was his best opportunity to become an American citizen, he submitted his application. This is how we know the complete list of his employers and residential addresses from September 1920 until when he applied in 1956.

Fong's application does not include a complete financial accounting from 1920 until 1956. However, it does show that in October 1922 he opened a bank account with $500, and closed it in December 1925, having saved a bit more than $2,000. Today, that amount would be valued at more than $30,000 – not bad for a former seaman working as a waiter.

The documentation supporting Fong's application also included names he had used throughout his working life in the United States. Along with Fong Wing Sun, he used the name Frank W. Jee or Frank Jee Wee-Won Hon for almost his entire working life, including his waiter jobs and even in his partnership in the Sam Lee Laundry. The document makes no mention of the name 'Fang Lang'. Even letters from employers verifying Fong's identity for his citizenship application state that he used the name Frank W. Jee into the 1950s. Throughout the document, the applicant referred to himself as 'Fong Wing Sun' and signed that in English.

On 29 June 1956, Fong Wing Sun became an American citizen, eight days after his sixty-second birthday. With this dream now realised, Fong turned his attention to other areas of his life that were unfulfilled – namely, finding a wife and getting married.

A May–December Relationship

Fong's American citizenship finally gave him the stability he wanted to start a family. But finding a wife as a 62-year-old Chinese man in the United States was difficult. He turned to friends in Hong Kong, who introduced him to 23-year-old Tom Ah Fong. Also born in the Taishan region of Guangdong, she later moved with family to Hong Kong.

As she would later say, at the time she had a boyfriend, but her brother encouraged her to marry Fong Wing Sun and go to the United States. Tom was uncomfortable with the age difference, but he had a stable job and a good income. So she broke up with the boyfriend, and on 6 February 1957, the two were married in Hong Kong. The couple remained in Hong Kong for the next two years, during which he may have purchased a piece of property there. While in Hong Kong, their first son, John, was born.

The couple returned to the United States in February 1959, via Honolulu, Hawaii, and took up residence in Milwaukee. Their second son, Tom, was born in December that year. Finally, at age 65, all the pieces in Fong Wing Sun's life had fallen into place, or so it seemed.

However, the marriage was not a particularly happy one. Fong continued to be devoted to his family overseas, and unbeknownst to his wife, he assisted another Chinese family to come to the United States. When the new family arrived in Milwaukee and Tom Ah Fong discovered Fong Wing Sun had promised them they could share their small apartment, she threw the new arrivals – and her husband – out.

The couple never reconciled. A possibly apocryphal story from their divorce was picked up by United Press International (UPI) and published in newspapers throughout the United States on 4 July 1966:

It's This Way in America

Milwaukee, Wisconsin – UPI – Mrs. Marie Fong, 32, wanted a divorce. She said her husband, Wing Sun Fong, 72, made her sleep on the floor, gave her almost no social life and relegated her to the 'status of a house keeper.' Fong said it was the Chinese way. The judge said this is America and granted the divorce.[8]

Broken Dreams

One of Tom Fong's first memories of his father was going with him to visit a nearby rental property. The elder Fong, who was about 70 at the time, rang the bell, which was answered by the landlord. Fong asked if the house was still for rent. The owner looked at Fong and said, 'I would never rent to a yellow dog like you.' Without hesitation, Fong punched the man in the face, and the landlord fell to his knees. 'My father was a man who never backed down from anything,' his son recalled.[9]

Fong continued to live and work as a waiter in Milwaukee and shuttled between the Chinese communities in Milwaukee and Chicago. In 1973, he moved back to Chicago permanently, to be closer to other family and friends as his age advanced and health declined.

Even late in his life, he maintained contact with his family in China, writing letters and when possible, sending money or photos. The following letter, written in Chinese and sent to his sister, is typical of his correspondence:

Dear Sister,

I know my niece, and the grandson and daughter-in-law of Hongpin are sending a package of photos from the post office today. Please look out for it. If you receive it, please reply and let me know. There are photos in it, for Zhou Xia's niece, please pass them on. It has been two months since I sent a letter back to you on October 2 this year, but I don't know if you received it or not. I do not know if you wrote back. Please read the letter carefully. On September 12 I was admitted to the hospital due to nasal inflammation, all without incident. I went home on my own, but so far the surgery on the left nostril is a little unsuccessful. The doctor said it would take time for things to heal. In the New Year this year, Qu Gaoqing and Zhou Meiyue said they will send a letter soon, and they will convey it to Zhou Youfu. But I don't worry about my personal safety, and just hope for happiness and world peace. As the old saying goes, it's good to spend a thousand days at home, but it's always difficult to get out. There is nothing wrong with this sentence. I asked about sending letters at the post office. It takes 15 days for any letter or photo package to be sent from the United States, and it may be sent to Guangdong, China and then transferred to people in Xiachuan, Taishan. A package of photos will be sent to you from the post office and should take 15 days to reach you. Today is November 26, and if it goes well it will arrive on December 15. Fortunately, everything is fine here with me. Kuoguang [John] and Kuomin [Tom] worked elsewhere, about a hundred miles away. I don't see them often, we only talk long distance sometimes. I will write again soon, and wish the whole family peace and happiness.

Your Brother,

Fong Wing Sun

November 26, 1979[10]

In another letter, written in English, Fong told a 25-year-old relative that he could not sponsor the young man to come to the United States. The younger man's English was too poor and Fong felt that he would not be successful applying to university at that age without at least better language skills.

Before moving to hospice care in his final years, Fong lived in an apartment upstairs from a Chinese restaurant, close to 2100 South Wentworth Avenue in Chicago's Chinatown. That building was demolished in 2014 to make room for the new Chinatown branch of the Chicago Public Library.

Tom Fong stated that his father always carried a notebook in his jacket pocket and would write in it frequently. Fong Wing Sun told Tom that after he was gone, if his son wanted to understand his life, he should read the book. Sadly, the notebook and its contents were lost after Fong's death, perhaps thrown away when his belongings were sorted.

In 1974, Tom Ah Fong and her son, Tom Fong, bought the Cozy Inn, Wisconsin's oldest and longest-operating Chinese restaurant, in the town of Janesville, which the family still owns. Tom Ah Fong is the youngest-known former spouse of a *Titanic* survivor; Tom Fong is the youngest-known child of a *Titanic* survivor; Tom's son and daughter are the youngest-known grandchildren of a *Titanic* survivor. In 2024, the youngest-known great-grandchild of a *Titanic* survivor joined the family.

Fong Wing Sun died on 21 January 1986, and is buried in Mount Auburn Cemetery in Stickney, Illinois, near Chicago, a popular burial site for Chinese residents. A flat marker indicates the site of the grave. Aside from his name in Chinese and English and the dates of his life, it says, only in Chinese, that he was from Shuiyang Village, Xiachuan (Island), Taishan. Even at the end, Old Fong did not give away any of his secrets.

Establishing the histories of Fang Lang and Fong Wing Sun, and demonstrating that they were the same person, meant placing them in the same place at the same time. Researchers Cynthia Lee in New York and Clothilde Yap in London used shipping records to trace the Fang Lang of *Titanic* to *Annetta* and beyond, and then placing him arriving in New York at the same time that Fong Wing Sun stated that he arrived there on board an unknown ship. That ship, SS *Rondo*, arrived in New York with Fang Lang aboard, just at the time that Fong Wing Sun said he was there, at last uniting the two parts of the man's history.

14

THE SEVENTH

Fairview Lawn Cemetery doesn't resemble its depictions in *Titanic* documentaries. It is not a memorial to a distant disaster on a wind-swept bluff overlooking an angry sea; the 'fair view' to which its name alludes is not the Atlantic Ocean. Nor is it in the best area of Halifax; it abuts a large railyard. There are no guards or security aside from a chest-high, chain-link fence. The *Titanic* graves, well-marked by signage, are close to its centre.

No one will ever accuse the White Star Line of overspending when it came to burying these *Titanic* victims: the markers are small, utili-tarian, dark grey granite, with a name or number and disturbingly close to each other. Some families chose to erect their own headstones for identified loved ones, and they stand in stark contrast to the White Star Line's basic offerings. At least passenger line Cunard, which pur-chased what remained of the White Star Line in 1947, has the decency to pay for the upkeep of these graves. Regardless of its circumstances, this cemetery marks the unintended destination of over 100 *Titanic* passengers whose lives ended more than 700 miles (1,000km) away, but whose journey terminated here.

Before the six Chinese and other *Titanic* survivors even arrived in New York aboard *Carpathia*, CS *Mackay-Bennett* was already heading back to the wreck site for a grim but noble task. Following the sink-ing, the White Star Line procured the services of four ships, whose usual work was laying transatlantic telegraph cables. The North

Atlantic was well known to these ships and their crews, but this time, instead of the painstaking labour of submerging cables in miles-deep water, the crew would be engaged entirely on the surface, searching for and recovering any bodies they found, then returning them to the ship for embalming, preservation and transport to Halifax, where they could hopefully be identified and claimed.

Mackay-Bennett was loaded up with canvas, embalming fluid and ice, among other things, to receive their macabre cargo, enough to handle the retrieval of 70–100 bodies. Three other ships – CS *Minia*, *Montmerency* and *Algerine* – received the same orders and later followed *Mackay-Bennett* to the site of the sinking.

Aside from the obvious act of mercy – recovering bodies for proper burial and offering closure to the families – there was a tad more at stake. Some of *Titanic*'s most famous passengers, including some of the world's richest men such as John Jacob Astor and Benjamin Guggenheim, had declined to board lifeboats and were subsequently lost. That meant some of the most famous names of the time, or at least their remains, were left floating out in the middle of the Atlantic. Trying to bring them back was the least the White Star Line could do under the circumstances.

Although the cable ships had *Titanic*'s last-known position as a target, they were really looking for floating needles in an expansive, liquid haystack, one with wind and currents that would most certainly move anything on the surface away from where it had been a few days earlier. Considering that *Titanic*'s wreck was ultimately found about 13 nautical miles (14.9 miles/24km) away from its last reported location, it is amazing that any bodies were retrieved at all.

Working in the recovery ships' favour was the near-freezing water. Aside from helping to preserve the bodies, the North Atlantic in mid-April is also nearly devoid of creatures such as sharks or even active microbes that might consume human corpses.

Passengers who entered the water wearing the lifebelts provided by *Titanic* had no reason to fear drowning, unless they were pushed under by a struggling survivor or the belt happened to be defective. The front and back design of the lifebelt would keep the wearer's head and shoulders above the surface, making recovery easier. This unsettled members of the retrieval team as they came upon groups of dead passengers who looked like they were standing or sleeping upright in the water. 'Hauling the soaked remains in saturated clothing over the side of the cutter is no light task. Fifty-one we have taken on board today, two children, three women, and forty-six men, and still the sea seems strewn,' *Mackay-Bennett* Cable Engineer Frederick Hamilton wrote in his diary.[1]

Instead of finding few or no bodies, *Mackay-Bennett* came upon more than it was equipped to handle. Eventually, it still picked up 306 of the 337 bodies recovered. In death, as in life, there just wasn't enough space for everyone. And just like *Titanic's* evacuation, a class system decided which bodies returned to land and which remained at sea.

Triage began immediately. Instead of waiting to see how many would ultimately be retrieved, twenty-four of that first group were buried at sea.[2] The decision on which remains to retain and which to commit to the deep was based on two things: a body's condition and its apparent class. It wasn't women and children first this time, as there were few women and almost no children. Instead, it was First Class first, in this case meaning access not to a lifeboat but to a coffin and proper embalming.

The poor condition of many bodies surprised *Mackay-Bennett's* crew – many had been damaged or disfigured rather than decomposed, likely due to being hit by wreckage such as collapsing funnels. Although the cold water and lack of predatory marine life reduced decomposition or consumption, extended immersion in saltwater would have taken its toll, gradually disfiguring the dead. Band leader Wallace Hartley was identified from his violin case; John Jacob Astor's collar monogram apparently identified him, not his moustache.[3]

The treatment of the dead also followed a pecking order. Accustomed to finery in life, passengers identified as First Class received coffins and embalming, as did Second-Class bodies. Third-Class passengers were wrapped in canvas and crew members were stored on deck.

Burials at sea continued. Hamilton wrote:

The funeral service is conducted by the Reverent Canon Hind, for nearly an hour the words 'For as must [*sic*] as it hath pleased' – 'we therefore commit his body to the deep' are repeated and at each interval comes, splash! as the weighted body plunges into the sea, there to sink to a depth of about two miles. Splash, splash, splash.[4]

On 30 April, *Mackay-Bennett* arrived in Halifax. In late April and May, the three other ships also searched and returned from the area, aided in part by sightings of bodies and debris reported by passing liners. Each of the subsequent search boats retrieved far fewer bodies than *Mackay-Bennett*, with *Algerine* finding only one, who was positively identified as one of *Titanic*'s stewards.

Given that only about 20 per cent of *Titanic*'s dead were recovered, and about 40 per cent of those were buried at sea, what is the likelihood that the body of either Lee Ling or Len Lam, or possibly both, was located, retained and ultimately buried at Halifax's Fairview Lawn Cemetery? The simple answer is unlikely – but it was similarly unlikely that six of the eight Chinese male Third-Class passengers travelling without families would survive the sinking of *Titanic*.

The early flooding of the Chinese passengers' quarters in the bow put them on the move in the first half an hour following *Titanic* striking the iceberg. Their experience working on board ships and the quick realisation that *Titanic* was in peril pushed them to move quickly towards the Boat Deck. That five of the six survivors got off in lifeboats and Fang Lang was rescued from the water points to all eight having been on deck in the late stages of the sinking. The link between Fang, Lee Ling and Len Lam, and Fang ultimately being plucked off floating wreckage, suggests that the three stuck together until the end, perhaps entering the water together when lifeboat places were not available. If all three went into the water from the Boat Deck wearing lifebelts, their bodies would have remained on the surface after they had succumbed.

Fang safely entered the water and was not injured or struck by funnels or other parts of the ship. He also was not pulled down by any suction from the wreck. Assuming Lee and Len died from exposure and not injury, and that they did not sink, their bodies would float like hundreds of others following the sinking. That means they were just as likely to be found as any other *Titanic* body – about a one in five chance of discovery and recovery.

Records from *Mackay-Bennett*'s crew and others make no mention of the ethnicity of any bodies recovered, only passengers of note, such as John Jacob Astor; women; or children like the Unknown Child. Therefore, there is no reason specifically to exclude the possibility that the body of one or both Chinese victims made it aboard the cable ships. From all the four recovery ships, a total of 209 bodies were landed in Halifax.[5]

While Third-Class bodies were more likely to be buried at sea, some were also retained, returned to Halifax and buried, with many later identified from descriptions, photographs or, eventually, DNA testing.

Families of First-Class passengers used their means to claim their loved ones' remains and send them to their final resting place for burial, usually a family cemetery plot. That left Second Class, Third Class and crew to be buried in Halifax. In the end, 121 graves were dug in Fairview Lawn Cemetery, a non-denominational burial ground, with Roman Catholic and Jewish bodies laid to rest in their respective dedicated cemeteries elsewhere in Halifax. One of those bodies belongs to the so-called Unknown Child, who was first misidentified as Eino Panula[6] and later positively identified as Sidney Goodwin.

That leaves 120 bodies that could potentially be Lee or Len. Of particular interest is body No. 233.

Two lists were created of the returned dead: one in alphabetical order for those positively identified,[7] and another based on the number given to each body as it was brought aboard its recovery ship. Upon return to Halifax, crewmen took the bodies to an ice-skating rink that had been temporarily designated as a morgue. There, each body was photographed and catalogued, including personal effects, identifying marks and the contents of pockets, in the hopes that the description would resonate with someone reading it at a White Star office in New York or the UK or in a newspaper and restore to that person their rightful name.

The first list describes body 233:

NO. 233. – MALE. – ESTIMATED AGE, 25. – HAIR, VERY DARK. – CLOTHING – Grey pants; print shirt. – NO MARKS. – PROBABLY GREEK.

However, the other list states that body No. 233 was:

233 Male – Estimated age, 24 to 26.
Height, 5 ft. 8 1/2in. [174cm] Weight, 140 lbs. [63.5kg]
Hair, black; eyebrows, black (look [*sic*] like Japanese).
Marks, low forehead; prominent eyebrows; very large head.
Buried at Fairview Cemetery, Halifax, N. S.
No aids to identification.

That the observer ascribed Asian features to the body is noteworthy. While lumping together southern European and perhaps even Middle-Eastern passengers as similar in appearance might be ignorant but understandable for the time, those traits would have been more familiar to someone in 1912 Halifax. To state that someone looked 'Japanese' is a different ball of wax, especially at a time where class and ethnicity were so closely linked to social status.

If body 233 is truly of Asian descent, then it would not be Japanese. Second-class passenger Masabumi Hosono left *Titanic* in Lifeboat 10. Therefore, an Asian body in grave 233 could only be Lee Ling or Len Lam.

DNA could provide the answer. Although a positive identification would be difficult because neither Lee nor Len's descendants are known currently, a DNA typing that demonstrated Asian descent would be sufficient to show that the body is either Lee or Len.

With fewer than fifty of the Fairview Lawn bodies still unidentified, grave 233 among them, new DNA methods, while more comprehensive and able to test smaller traces of organic material, face a difficult path. Fairview Lawn is a large cemetery, the final resting place of not just *Titanic* victims, but hundreds of other former residents of Halifax, including some of the city's first Chinese immigrants – almost all of whom hailed from Taishan, just like Fong Wing Sun and Lee Bing. Relatives of local families buried at the site are increasingly opposed to new work in the cemetery that might include soil samples or any degree of exhumation.

During initial attempts to identify the Unknown Child and two other Fairview Lawn *Titanic* passengers, scientists made a frustrating and unpleasant discovery. Sometime over the last century, the *Titanic* graves had been flooded, leaving no usable genetic material behind to be tested. Because the Unknown Child had been buried with a large metal plaque that read 'Our Babe', the presence of that item prevented some organic material from degrading, leaving enough for a DNA sample to test.

However, current methods would require only core sampling – a small hole made into a grave to try to retrieve samples of bone or hair. Also, despite the flooding of the graves, new techniques could identify genetic material in soil surrounding each plot. Those methods and the testing have yet to be approved by Halifax cemetery officials, despite broad support from *Titanic* family groups wanting to know for sure the fate of their relatives. Until then, the final mystery relating to *Titanic*'s Chinese passengers remains to be solved.

SECTION II

15

THE SEARCH FOR
THE SIX

Every search begins with a question. Some of them are resolved quickly, by Googling or a phone call. It isn't often that one defies a simple answer, bypassing the daytime mind and burrowing into the subconscious, supplanting more important thoughts, pushing aside other subjects and re-emerging in the small hours for further, deeper consideration.

The search for *Titanic*'s Chinese passengers initially had nothing to do with the world's most famous shipwreck. It *did* have to do with Chinese passengers involved in a major maritime disaster and huge loss of life. But that ship sank near Shanghai, and was sunk by a mysterious explosion, not an iceberg.

The *Poseidon* Adventure

In 2005, I found a lost British submarine using Google.

HMS *Poseidon* sank in 1931 off the coast of China following a collision with a freighter. The sub went down in about five minutes, yet more than half of its officers and crew were able to escape. Three hours after the sinking, six men broke the surface: five Royal Navy submariners and a teenage Chinese cabin boy. One died at the surface, but the other five lived.

The four navy men were decorated. A feature film was made. And then the men, the Chinese teenager and the submarine they left on the ocean floor were forgotten. Until an American journalist living in Beijing, who had a side hustle as a scuba instructor, stumbled on the story and wanted to investigate it.

Pursuing the story in my free time, it became clear that it might make a good documentary, along with the book I was planning to write. As a Yank who was researching a British sub in China, I felt out of place as the storyteller, but my friend and *Variety* colleague Arthur Jones, who lived in Shanghai, was from the UK. He had shifted away from pure journalism and was making documentary films.

Arthur and I had been introduced by another Englishman, Mark Kitto, publisher of the seminal China expatriate magazine *That's Shanghai*. Arthur was the inaugural managing editor for the publication. At Kitto's weekend-long fortieth birthday party at a mountain resort near Shanghai, I introduced Arthur to *Poseidon*'s history and even passed him a couple of related books in the hope that he would share my interest. Four years later, *The Poseidon Project* documentary premiered at the Hoboken Film Festival (which was held in Middletown, New York), and *Poseidon: China's Secret Salvage of Britain's Lost Submarine* was published.

More than discovering the unknown history of a sunken vessel and putting out a couple of satisfactory end products, we travelled to, filmed and researched on two different continents, and laughed our heads off. We didn't make any money, but it hadn't cost too much, and it was so much fun. Immediately, we talked about what our next project would be.

Beijing Dreams

When I was 3 years old, I saw Jacques Cousteau on television. 'I want to do that,' I announced – *that* being swimming with sharks, diving with dolphins and finding shipwrecks. The name 'China' was not in my lexicon and wouldn't be for several more years.

A product of the New Jersey Shore, the ocean was always nearby. I loved the beach, the sand, the waves. In the backyard, we had a pool.

There was only one problem: I didn't like to get my hair wet. Even though I learned to swim early, wet hair? Yuck. Instead, I held onto the side of the pool and pulled myself around in a circle.

That was until my grandparents bought me a diving mask. A US Divers diving mask, complete with a sticker of Jacques Cousteau in the middle of the faceplate. It remained in place until too much exposure to water finally caused it to float off. But when that mask went on my face and I could see what was underwater, suddenly I didn't care what happened to my hair.

'A marine biologist' was my standard answer to what I wanted to be when I grew up. I even met Cousteau when I was 13. But heading into my early teens, and having participated in a few 'young biologist' programmes, I started to realise that marine biology was a lot more lab work than I wanted to do. While still keen on all things ocean, my professional interest shifted toward journalism. Journalism seemed like a way to keep learning without having to go to school, to meet and talk with people to whom one would otherwise have no access.

It was then that I got a chance opportunity to visit China as a tour-group tourist. My mother received the offer, but as a reluctant traveller, she wasn't keen to go. Only after I expressed enthusiasm did we decide to go together.

After two and a half weeks of the Great Wall, the Forbidden City, karst limestone hills, huge crowds on the street in Shanghai and more bicycles than I could count, I knew that was the future, both mine and probably the world's. If I go to China, I thought, I will never run out of things to write about. Almost forty years later, it's still true. I hung up my diving mask (temporarily) and focused on learning all things China, including culture, history and language.

In 1996, I moved to Beijing to start my so-called journalism career with the underground newspaper *Beijing Scene*. Then in 2003, after becoming a PADI scuba instructor following my father's death, I started SinoScuba, Beijing's first professional dive operation, as a side hustle to relieve the boredom of freelance writing about IT. At last my hair was wet, and I had plenty to write about. The story of HMS *Poseidon* was something I stumbled on while looking for new places to dive around China. Maybe I would get to do some Cousteau after all.

Shanghai Shipwreck

On the night of 3 December 1948, anyone stepping out onto one of the numerous terraces along Shanghai's famous Bund riverfront might have caught a glimpse of a ship sailing toward destiny. SS *Kiangya* (pronounced and today spelled *Jiangya*) didn't have four funnels or a swept-up stern; in fact, it looked more like *Annetta* than *Titanic*. A coastal passenger ship, *Kiangya* had none of *Titanic*'s beauty or glamour. It was hauling thousands of people from Shanghai to nearby Ningbo on an overnight run, as most of its passengers were heading home, and China's civil war was heading toward its end.

Near where the Yangtze River empties into the East China Sea, an explosion struck the ship. Immediately, the lights went off and frigid water began pouring in. Panicked passengers, swaddled in winter clothes and unable to swim, jumped overboard to certain death. The crew grabbed an available lifeboat and made for the riverbank, which was close but beyond visibility in the pitch dark. Hundreds clung to the highest parts of the superstructure, forestalling the inevitable.

The ship descended deeper and deeper into the chocolate-milk swirl of the muddy river until, finally, it stopped. *Kiangya*'s hull hit the bottom, halting her disappearance. About 700 people – eerily reminiscent of the number of survivors on *Titanic* – survived. But thousands died in the mysterious sinking.

What caused the blast? A bomb dropped by a fighter plane lightening its load? A boiler explosion? An assassination attempt on Chiang Kai-shek's son, who had planned to but ultimately did not sail?

Kiangya was an obvious choice as a next project. Here was one of the world's worst maritime disasters, with greater loss of life than *Titanic* – a mystery to be solved and a death toll to be determined. Survivors were still alive and available for interview. And all the relevant sites were an easy train ride or even a few subway sites away from the director's base.

We agreed on the new topic and got to work. The *Poseidon* materials went into a box, clearing bookshelf space for the new project.

Civil War

Filming a documentary and writing a book in English about an obscure shipwreck that took place during the Chinese Civil War wasn't going to be easy. It would require quite a bit of scene-setting to provide context for the reader. How would the reader understand the circumstances of the sinking and the magnitude of the loss? Easy: compare it to *Titanic*.

Trips to Shanghai and nearby Ningbo, in Zhejiang Province, *Kiangya*'s home port and the site of its only extant artefact (its helm, the ship's steering wheel, dusty and forgotten in a local museum) followed to conduct interviews with local survivors. Many had been teenagers, some even younger, when *Kiangya* sank. They recalled it like it was yesterday, before the war ended, before their children and grandchildren were born.

I went back to my *Titanic* shelf. No self-respecting amateur maritime historian is without a *Titanic* shelf – except for hipster amateur maritime historians, who declare it too commercial, overdone and uninteresting, and wouldn't be caught with *Unsinkable* as bathroom reading. My bookcase contained paperbacks of *A Night to Remember* and *The Night Lives On*, and a few others I had picked up or inherited over the years.

Of course, the internet provided the greatest wealth of more recent *Titanic* scholarship. Since 2012, the 100th anniversary of *Titanic*'s sinking, new books were still being written about aspects of the ship's history (ahem), but much of the best new material was published online.

One such repository is Encyclopedia Titanica.[1] It is what it claims to be: a compendium of all things *Titanic*. I clicked around to see if it had any references to *Kiangya*, maybe as part of some 'all-time worst' disaster comparison.

I know that I had seen the article 'Chinese Sailors on the *Titanic*' before. I'm sure that I read it, thought, 'wow, interesting', and then did what just about every other reader did: I moved on to the next page. There wasn't much there. A wisp of a mention, almost an apparition that passed in and out of the *Titanic* story, and that was it. Click. Next.

But when I returned to the page and the topic in the middle of the *Kiangya* research, it was different. There wasn't any more information than there had been previously, but this time, it seemed incongruous.

The 100th anniversary of *Titanic*'s sinking had come and gone, and yet despite that fanfare, not one descendant of a Chinese sailor had come forward. No one had raised their hand and said, 'My grandfather survived *Titanic*. This is his story.'

That wasn't possible. Eight Chinese men had boarded *Titanic* and six survived. Not one of them had had a family and related his tale to a daughter or son? I just couldn't accept that. Impossible, no, but unlikely? Yes.

The histories of so many of the ethnic groups aboard *Titanic* are extremely well documented, literal cradle-to-grave accounts of the lives of otherwise ordinary people who survived the world's most famous shipwreck. But the Chinese were almost singularly unknown. Suddenly, here was an opportunity to bring together the world's most famous shipwreck and the world's most populous nation, a country where James Cameron's film was such a massive hit.

Titanic came to film screens in China at a time when desire outstripped technology. The average Chinese cinema in 1997 was like seeing a movie in a school auditorium, but less comfortable, and probably with some of the patrons smoking. Signs for movies were still hand painted, not printed.

The first time I saw *Titanic*, at a theatre on Dongdan Avenue, near the city centre, it was slightly out of focus for the entire two-hour-plus runtime. The projectionist just never came back to adjust it. But its classic love story against the backdrop of impending disaster hit a nerve with Chinese audiences, many of whom went to see it again and again and again. Celine Dion's 'My Heart Will Go On' was in heavy rotation well into the new century. Dion, surprisingly, never cashed in on her popularity by performing in China. Either that or her asking price was too rich for the nation's blood.

China as a nation now suddenly had a consciousness of this shipwreck story about which it had previously known or cared little. While sharp-eyed observers would have noticed a Chinese passenger flashing through the background at key moments during the film – including when Jack and Fabrizio first board *Titanic* and are searching for their cabin, and as Bruce Ismay ponders whether he will enter Collapsible C – most moviegoers walked out not knowing their countrymen's connection to the great ship and its story.

I don't stare at the ceiling in the small hours and ponder the existence of God or the mysteries of the universe. I stare at the ceiling and wonder about the location of shipwrecks and how they got there. But instead of being kept awake by the spectre of a steel hulk at the bottom of a Shanghai river, visions of Chinese men on *Titanic* danced through my head.

Why didn't we know more about the Chinese passengers? Why hadn't they left behind their stories, at least ones that we knew about? It seemed like every Irish villager (relax – my grandmother's maiden name was Donahue) who boarded *Titanic* had their story recorded in full.

It was more than that. Even with limited information, their stories were compelling. Of the eight, four of them got off in the same boat as Bruce Ismay. Another one was rescued from the water, and may have been the last person rescued from *Titanic*. What? A Chinese man was the last person rescued from *Titanic*? I don't remember reading that in *A Night to Remember*.

Later, I told Amy Wang of *The Washington Post* that the Chinese passengers were like *Hamlet*'s Rosencrantz and Gildenstern on the *Titanic*: they weren't major characters, but they popped up at key moments in the ship sinking saga to illuminate the main players and bring more of the story to life. It seemed like a reference *WaPo* readers could handle.

But it was clear that if we could learn more about the Chinese men and their journey across the *Titanic* stage, we would understand better the entire story. Was Ismay truthful in his testimony about the 'four Chinamen or Filipinos' in his boat? What did Harold Lowe's rescue of the passenger known as Fang Lang tell us about him and the rescue effort overall?

I knew very little about these men except for a list of names and some information that they may have been from Hong Kong. But I knew that as gripping as the *Kiangya* story was, it wasn't as good as the story of the Chinese passengers on *Titanic*. After seven months of mining silver, this story was gold. Now I had to convince another miner to change veins.

16

CHANGING COURSE

It's one thing to convince your creative partner to do another maritime history story when he had no particular interest in the topic. It's another to unconvince and then reconvince him and stay focused on big floating bits of steel and the people who live and die on board them.

Arthur's reaction was not positive. 'Could you pick something more mainstream and overdone?'

'Ok, no problem, we'll stay the course,' I said. 'But in the meantime, let me give you some books about how these big wreck stories are handled.'

Of course, the first one I pushed across was *A Night to Remember*. We might be sticking with *Kiangya*, which was fine, but maybe we could slowly migrate to *Titanic*. Or maybe they could be done in parallel.

We were far from focusing on either shipwreck full time. Arthur was still in Shanghai with the production company that he co-founded, Lost Pensivos, or LP Films. I was in Beijing working with my college classmate Mike Wester as the editor of *The Beijinger*, the leading Beijing expatriate magazine of the post-Olympic period. We worked on 'the new project' when we could and when there was time and money for a weekend in Ningbo.

I still poked around on *Titanic* material, but it was clear that it would need focus, not just from me, but from both of us, to make meaningful progress. Arthur was coming to Beijing. It was time to change course.

Over beers at Great Leap Brewing, Beijing's first craft brewery, I made my case. 'You know this is the story. You know I wouldn't lead you into some dog and pony show,' I said.

We hadn't invested much in *Kiangya*. It would be there if we went away and came back to it. The same wouldn't be true with *Titanic*, and if someone did something with it, we would take turns kicking each other in the ass 100 times because we had it in our hands and didn't do anything with it.

Arthur agreed, with certain strictures. We would spend ninety days trying to disprove the story to ourselves. That is, we wanted to make sure we discovered enough material to demonstrate that this would be worthwhile spending months, or ultimately years, investigating and crafting into a story. As with *Poseidon*, Arthur would make a documentary and I would write a book.

We started working separately, meeting as schedules allowed, sharing materials electronically as much as possible. We kept each other posted through regular messages and the occasional call.

We also agreed on one guiding principle that would steer our research: if we were going to question conclusions and narratives that had endured for over 100 years, we would examine the evidence objectively and let that evidence speak for itself. If the evidence left the Chinese men in an unflattering historical light, then so be it. But if the sum total of the historical record, tested against the limitations of physics and human physiology, told a neutral or positive story, then that would be the story we told. What we weren't going to do was traffic in and regurgitate century-old rumours without thorough examination of any factual basis for those statements.

Our respective end products – a documentary and a book – led to a quirk in our process. Because so much of Arthur's planned film would focus on conducting the research, he asked that I not look at some material unless he was present to shoot it. While slightly frustrating, it made sense. It led to some moments of suspense later, as Arthur conducted first interviews with some subjects and knew about discoveries before I did.

The Names

From the beginning, we sought to answer a few critical questions: Who were these men? Where did they come from? How did they survive? Where did they go and what happened to them?

We hit an almost immediate wall: the names of the men. Looking at the passenger list, we saw eight names, each with an apparent given name and surname. But were they written the way Chinese people presented them, with the surname first, or the Western way, starting with the given name? Also, most Chinese names, especially in 1912, had three components: a surname, a generational name and a given name. What names were these, then?

Additionally, what was the source of these names? Did they come from a passport or some seaman's identity card that could be traced? Did their employer provide the names? Or did each man present himself at the White Star Line ticket counter, state his name, and this list was what the clerk thought he heard and wrote down?

We also hoped that the names might reveal what dialect they spoke, and therefore where they came from in China. In 1912, they probably weren't from the north; most Chinese going abroad for work were from the south. But even then, they could speak Cantonese, Hakka, Teochow or another dialect altogether. We put the names aside and looked at other questions we could answer more readily.

The names were largely opaque, but a closer examination of the White Star passenger list led to an early find. For more than a century, the first Chinese passenger's name – which is handwritten on the original manifest – was later typed as 'Ali Lam', like Muhammad Ali. However, the handwriting, which is legible to the average reader, reveals it to be 'Ah Lam'. As this is an informal nickname, immediately we realised that the names likely were not official, and finding these men based on the manifest names alone was going to be difficult. Arthur and I began to look at other areas of the story where we could make quick progress and start to see where the story would take us.

Science and Speculation

Much of what we knew about the men came from official testimony, specifically as given by J. Bruce Ismay, Quartermaster George Rowe and Fifth Officer Harold Lowe. Ismay and Rowe talked about the Chinese men seemingly coming up from underneath or in between seats after hiding there for hours. This could be recreated and tested, something that had not been done in the over a century since *Titanic* sank. The Chinese men were accused of myriad ignoble acts, but simple physics could be the final arbiter. It was clear that we would need to build a model of Collapsible C and find out once and for all what was physically possible and what was not.

The experiment would put Ismay's testimony under the microscope. Senator William Alden Smith and the other senators tried to make political hay by painting him as a coward for not going down with the ship — his ship. *Titanic's* owner walked a fine line, attempting to differentiate his and fellow First-Class passenger William Ernest Carter's survival from that of the 'Chinamen' discovered at the break of dawn.

First Officer Murdoch, who stood by C as it was being loaded, and whom Ismay said suggested he enter the boat, did not live to give an account. A collapsible lifeboat, of which there was no extant example, could be built, and real *Titanic* passenger-sized people put into it to demonstrate once and for all if the four Chinese men could have hidden underneath its thwarts or seats.

There was also the rescue of Fang Lang. Again, the scientific method could help confirm a timeline of events after *Titanic's* sinking. If she sank at 2.20 a.m., that starts the clock on the survival of anyone in the water. Fang Lang would have only had a certain amount of time to find the piece of wood that saved him, haul himself onto it and perhaps tie himself to it. One might live much longer, but motor control would become more limited. Both could be tested.

Also subject to physical scrutiny were the men's potential routes to the Boat Deck. The twenty Third-Class passenger routes to the Boat Deck suggested by David Gleicher in his book *The Rescue of the Third Class on Titanic*[1] could be narrowed down, based on their starting location and the boats they boarded. Even if we couldn't prove exactly which man had got into which boat, the presence of the men was well documented. Knowing when they reached the Boat Deck could suggest why they ended up in Collapsible C – or in the water.

As we planned for the various physical demonstrations, voices echoed in the back of my head, those of the larger *Titanic* community. Our initial requests for information regarding the Chinese passengers were cautious. We didn't want to reveal the nature or size of our project, but we needed to know what was out there and what work had already been done on the topic. We poked around on Encyclopedia Titanica and made a discreet enquiry or two with people that seemed to know what they were talking about.

The *Titanic* community is intense. Almost none of the historians who have done the best work on the ship are able to do it full time. Experts have emerged in different areas, such as model making, technical details, passenger histories, even the history of expeditions to the wreck. Wade into a message board or Facebook page without doing the requisite homework and one will likely get nipped by someone who knows a lot more about the topic.

Early in our information-gathering process, a well-known *Titanic* writer told us 'not to sugarcoat' the Chinese men's story just because we were based in China. It was sentiment like that which put the voices in my head: if we were going to put forward new research and new conclusions regarding the Chinese passengers on *Titanic*, then we had better be sure that we could prove anything we claimed.

For that reason, I knew we had to build a full-size replica of a collapsible lifeboat. Of course, it would have been much easier and cheaper to build a 1 or 2m model and then stuff Kens and Barbies under the lollystick seats to see if men could have concealed themselves. But we needed a real boat with real people.

'What do you know about building boats?' Arthur asked me.

'Nothing. I don't need to know anything about it. I just need to find somebody who is going to do it with us,' I said.

What Did Cameron Know and When Did He Know It?

Had I watched the deleted scenes of the two-DVD collector set of *Titanic* that sat on my shelf for years, I might have considered the fate of *Titanic*'s Chinese passengers much earlier. Cameron certainly had. He filmed an entire scene of a Chinese survivor being rescued from the water, although it didn't make the film's final cut.

In the scene, which chronologically would have appeared after *Titanic*'s final plunge but before Jack Dawson's death and Rose DeWitt Bukater's rescue, Fifth Officer Harold Lowe returns to the area in Lifeboat 14. 'Can anyone hear me? Is anyone alive out there?' he shouts.

A man floating on a piece of wooden wreckage calls out in Cantonese, 'I am here! I am here!'

Lowe responds to the call and the boat pulls up next to the man. 'Bring him in! Help him out! Bring him in quickly,' Lowe says, telling the men to keep him warm and cover him in blankets.

When I first saw the scene, I was shocked. Cameron clearly knew the story of the Chinese passengers — one of whom pops up in the background of several scenes in the film — and specifically about the rescue of Fang Lang. How much research had he and his crew done on the subject?

Something else struck me. A man in the water floating on a large piece of wooden wreckage sounds similar to a heroine floating on wooden wreckage who lets go of her frozen lover, blows a whistle on officer's neck and is saved, also by Officer Lowe. Was it possible that the real-life rescue of Fang Lang inspired one of the most iconic scenes in cinema history?

Aside from being one of the most successful and lauded film directors ever, Cameron is also one of the greatest living underwater explorers and a *Titanic* expert in his own right. Clearly, he had some knowledge of the Chinese passengers and their story. Suddenly, it seemed like interviewing Cameron was something we should try to do.

17

TACKLING *TITANIC*

It's kind of in the name. *Titanic* – it's going to be big. Everything about it – it's going to be large, superlative. And yet Arthur and I overlooked that, thinking that somehow our research work would be something we could bootstrap, putting the story together over time.

We could not have been more wrong. Despite our experience as journalists, we realised early that tracking down six individual stories as they spread out over the globe was beyond us. It wasn't just the amount of work, which was overwhelming; it was specific expertise that we lacked, knowledge about genealogy and records management in different countries, including Canada and the UK.

In the United States, census records are available seventy-two years after the day they were taken; in Canada, it's ninety-five; in the UK, one hundred. That made tracing the movements of *Titanic* survivors entering the latter two countries more challenging. It's also just one example of the kinds of records kept in each place that, while similar, would be unfamiliar to the non-citizen.

None of that begins to address the differences in genealogy between the West and China. Someone researching their history in the West can go two or three centuries back via public records, including church files such as baptisms, weddings and burials, census information and more. In China and the Chinese diaspora around the world, it is the families themselves, or family associations, that maintain records. While a *zupu*, or ancestor book, will often go back centuries, until the latter part of the twentieth century they only contained listings of males; the names of women in the family have only been included recently. Not every family has been diligent maintaining its *zupu* either, and even if it has, they are not necessarily keen on sharing it with non-family members.

After three years of toil as a duo, Arthur and I got a break when Luo Tong, co-founder and producer of Shanghai-based LP films, agreed to produce the documentary. With that support came a budget for an expanded research team.

LP Films already had staff members who were working on aspects of the story. Matthew Baren, from the UK, split his time between the production and research teams and brought valuable perspective to the work. Grace Zhang was a Shanghai native who kept her own counsel but brought a sharp eye for detail to the team. Her purple hair telegraphed that there was more going on under the surface than she let on. Paul Wade came to China from Texas, a guitar player and soccer fan with a knack for following information threads across disparate records.

I moved into the role of lead researcher, but with the same slight strictures that had been in place before. Namely, I got to ask the questions, but often I wouldn't hear the answers until I visited the LP office to meet with the team and could react to them in person. It was frustrating to know that work was going on but not knowing the result.

Over time, we added expertise in different geographic areas. At its most expansive, the research team included sixteen people. New York-based Cynthia Lee pulled out the relevant records for the Chinese men's insurance claims against the White Star Line. She later worked with our chief UK researcher, Clotilde Yap of My China Roots, to trace the movements of Fong Wing Sun back and forth across the Atlantic Ocean. Yap worked The National Archives for material relating to the involuntary repatriation of Chinese diaspora back to China after the Second World War.

Grant Din was a genealogist based in the Bay Area of California. He specialised in the family history of Chinese Americans like himself. Din knew the ins and outs of US Government documents, especially Alien Files, or A-files, a category of document still used for immigrants today.

In Canada, Julie Hamilton responded to a newspaper article about the search for Lee Bing and began working on the story, pinpointing the various members of the Lee family in Galt (later Cambridge), Ontario, and the location of the White Rose Café, Lee's restaurant.

David Lee, who owned a restaurant in Beijing, had met LP Films' Luo Tong socially and became involved because he was from Taishan and had an interest in learning more about this aspect of the region's history. Lee was the best man to have around with a group of strangers; he put everyone immediately at ease, and gently teased out bits of their family history without ever getting their guard up.

Ends, But Not Necessarily Dead

In at least two instances, we had leads on possible relatives of Chinese *Titanic* passengers that ultimately did not pan out. David Lee had been in touch with a Chinese-American man who said that his wife's family had connections to Chang Chip. At first, he seemed enthusiastic to share the story. However, when a visit to the Taishan area was planned and there was the possibility of a meeting, the man said he wasn't available to get together, maybe another time. Eventually, he stopped answering David's calls. He did not contact the team again.

In Shanghai, we were approached by an American teacher who said his mother-in-law believed that she was connected to Lee Bing. The man explained to us the possible link between his wife's mother and Lee. However, there was one significant problem with the story: their own family wasn't sure they believed it. He was never able to convince his wife's family to meet with us.

Some leads on other aspects of the story didn't pan out but were no less intriguing. Early on a November morning, just before Thanksgiving in 2018, Cynthia Lee, Arthur, Luo Tong, the documentary crew and I took the first boat ferrying National Park Service rangers to Ellis Island in New York Harbour. The hour was ungodly, but anticipation ran high.

Professor Judy Yung, who was a pioneer of Chinese-American studies at the University of California in Santa Cruz, had done extensive research on poetry carved into the walls of Angel Island's dormitories in San Francisco Bay, finding about 200 poems. Yung pointed us toward similar examples of poems scratched onto walls at Ellis Island. They were fewer and fainter, but still significant.

As the only Americans in the group, the visit to Ellis Island was perhaps a bit more exciting for Lee and me than for the others. Here we were at this famous landmark, with no other visitors and no one else there except a Park Service ranger to chaperone us. Walking upstairs toward the Great Hall, the arrival building that welcomed the ancestors of millions of Americans, Lee and I almost ran to the rail, gazing down at the orange tile floor, imagining throngs of new arrivals sitting on benches long removed, long lines of people getting off ships, being processed and admitted to the United States.

Only about 5,000 of them were ever Chinese. They must have felt so out of place among all the European immigrants, not to mention being singled out during the years of the Chinese Exclusion Act when they would have been detained and questioned.

In search of poetry, we burst into a men's room not far from the Great Hall. Sadly, for us, the bathroom was newly remodelled, with new marble everywhere. If any scrawled poems had been there, they were now gone.

In the documentary, the only shot used from that morning's visit was a wide shot of lower Manhattan taken from the ferry. For me, the images from that day are as clear and vivid as anything that made the final cut. Those are the moments that make a project like this mentally radiant. It isn't about the results, not always.

18

FINDING
FONG WING SUN

It's easier to find someone when that person is also looking for you. Tom Fong didn't know that a China-based team working on the history of the Chinese *Titanic* passengers was searching for him, but he was reaching out for more information about his father in the *Titanic* community.

During an early 2000s casual stroll through The House on the Rock Museum in Iowa County, Wisconsin, Henry Chiu, whose family Fong Wing Sun had sponsored for immigration to the United States, saw a model of *Titanic* among the house's many artefacts. 'Your dad was on that ship,' Chiu told Tom Fong, Fong Wing Sun's younger and only surviving son.

Fong had never heard this before. He knew that his father had survived a shipwreck, but he thought that had happened in China. For the first time, he connected his father as possibly being a passenger on *Titanic*. He went home and asked his son, Steven, to hop on the computer and do some searching. Yes, there were Chinese passengers on *Titanic*. One of them had the name Fang Lang. But that wasn't his father's name, nor a name Tom had ever associated with him.

Tom then turned to the Encyclopedia Titanica website, registered for a free account and posted to one of its message boards. As early as December 1999, the website's message board had a topic dedicated to discussion of the Chinese passengers. On 28 May 2004, Tom posted, 'To all of you regarding Mr. Fang Lang, (Chinese rescue in lifeboat #14). I have most of the answers to your questions because he was my father.'[1]

Tom, posting via his son Steven, provided more information, but eventually the posts ended, and the briefly lukewarm trail went cold again.

In 2013, the research team sent a message to the registered user who made the post. Although it now shows Tom's name, at the time he used a more obscure username. The message to the poster received no response. Here was someone claiming that a Chinese passenger was their father, but there was no other obvious way to reach them.

It was time for a shotgun approach. Taking the username, we added '@' to a number of the most popular mail program domain names and prepared to email those addresses. We wrote a standard email that asked if the person had posted to Encyclopedia Titanica with information about Fang Lang and provided Arthur's contacts.

Some bounced immediately. Others went out into the void, never to be replied to. I wonder what anyone who received it and was not related to a *Titanic* passenger thought.

'Mr. Jones, I received your email ...' read the beginning of a response from Tom Fong, the man who had posted to the message board. We had our first lead.

Janesville Jaunt

September was a good time to go to Janesville as I was already in the United States for a job. Arthur flew in from Shanghai and we met at O'Hare Airport, picked up a rental car and blazed the two hours west on flat I-94 to the south-east part of Wisconsin, a state I had never visited previously.

These are the best times of a project like this. Visiting places that otherwise would never be on the itinerary, slices of pizza served by friendly people, glasses of bourbon in bars that looked like they'd be a good place for a glass of bourbon, and digging into a mystery that at this point is little more than some scribbles in a notebook and air miles bet against the likelihood that someone has a *Titanic* story that's never been told before.

Janesville is a pleasant green, small town that's about an hour from the state capital in Madison, also home to the University of Wisconsin, and of course, two hours from one of the busiest airports in the United States. Former Speaker of the United States House of Representatives Paul Ryan is from there.

The city of Janesville – not to be confused with the neighbouring town of Janesville, an administrative distinction – is also home to Cozy Inn, the oldest Chinese restaurant in Wisconsin, and one of the oldest in the United States. It happens to be owned by Tom and Amanda Fong, son and daughter-in-law of the man who may be Fang Lang.

We met at Tom and Amanda's lovely home. I couldn't stop thinking that his two children, Steven and Samantha, could be the world's youngest *Titanic* grandchildren.

As Tom and I had not spoken before, he started from the top, beginning with his cousin Henry's mention of the ship, his own research and his interaction with Encyclopedia Titanica. He had been told a few things by family friend and Chicago watercolour artist Grace Lai, who said Fong Wing Sun had survived a shipwreck by using a corpse as floatation or had perhaps lashed himself to a door with a belt. We showed Tom and the kids, who had joined us, the deleted rescue scene from *Titanic*, which they had not seen before.

Tom showed us several photos over decades of his father, who appears in a suit and tie in every one. From his earliest pictures in Chicago, taken at a photo studio, to those shot near the end of his life, his basic attire never changes.

In one photo, believed to have been taken during the Chicago World's Fair in 1933, Fong appears with three other men, all Chinese, all also wearing suits and ties. Each man is identified by Chinese characters written on the photo's cardboard frame. Standing next to Fong is Chang Fa-kuei (Zhang Fakui), whom we would later learn was a top Kuomintang (KMT) general during first the Second World War and then China's Civil War. Tom identified him as a friend of his mother's, and said it was possible that Chang had introduced his parents.

Tom had two identical copies of this photo. One identified his father as Fong Wing Sun. But the other identified him as Fong Sen, a name for him that we had not seen or heard before. Tom had not heard it either.

After seeing some more photographs, we said our goodbyes. We would meet Tom and Amanda again in a few days in Chicago's Chinatown, where Tom would show us his father's former home and some other sites of note.

Despite the Fongs' hospitality and sincerity, after this initial meeting, I was sceptical. Fong Wing Sun had never mentioned being on *Titanic* to his sons. Tom knew about his father surviving a shipwreck only from a family friend and the *Titanic* connection only because of an offhand remark by his cousin. Fang Lang, Fong Wing Sun – the names were close, but not that close. The elder Fong's age was about right and he had served on ships.

Tom said that his father always carried a notebook and regularly wrote in it. Fong told his sons that if they wanted to know his story, they should read the notebook after he was gone. Unfortunately, the notebook was lost, perhaps thrown away when Fong's personal effects were sorted after his death. It all felt like evidence, but it wasn't yet a case.

One thing that impressed me about Tom and his story was his lack of guile. Clearly, he believed it. This affable man just wanted to know more about his father's life, and now he found he had possibly survived *Titanic*, of all shipwrecks.

A few days later, Tom pointed out the last place his father had lived before he went into a hospice, an apartment on the top floor of a building near the Chinatown branch of the Chicago Public Library. In the office of the local Fong Family Association, Tom identified his father in several group photos and saw for the first time pictures of him with Chinese-American political leaders who visited Chicago.

That first trip to meet the Fongs ended with a poignant moment: a visit to Fong Wing Sun's final resting place in Mount Auburn Cemetery. His grave marker has his name in both Chinese and English, the dates of his birth and death, and in Chinese, 'Shui Yang Village, Taishan'.

Arthur and I visited the Fongs on a few more occasions, together and separately. We shared updates with them and eventually interviewed Tom's mother. She said Fong Wing Sun never mentioned anything about *Titanic*. 'He was a very secretive man,' she said.

We also spoke at length with Henry Chiu, Tom's cousin, whom Fong had told about surviving a shipwreck after a collision with an iceberg. A nuclear physicist who had built a home for his relatives in Taishan, Chiu's clear mind lent great credence to his story. The circumstantial evidence was there, but we needed more.

Fang becomes Fong

Over time, the body of evidence about Fong grew, and we believed that he was the *Titanic* survivor known as Fang Lang. But now we had to prove it.

As researcher Cynthia Lee later said in an interview for the documentary, the task was to place Fang Lang, seaman and would-be merchant, in the same place and the same time as Fong Wing Sun. Like a multiverse character, the two had to meet to become one, to prove that this was the same man we had followed from *Titanic* to a ship in New York, where Fang Lang ceased to exist and Fong Wing Sun moved forward into the future.

Grant Din succeeded in obtaining Fong's Alien File, with permission from his son. That gave us his arrival date: September 1920 in New York, aboard the *SS Unknown* (obviously not a real ship). From there, he quickly moved to Chicago, then Milwaukee, and later back to Chicago. He worked mostly as a waiter or cook at Chinese restaurants, briefly operating a laundry at two different times. But the A-File established the date of Fong's permanent arrival in the United States.

It was Cynthia Lee and Clotilde Yap who solved the mystery. In a feat of maritime detective work, the two traced his movements back and forth across the Atlantic for years on multiple ships, still working as a fireman or ship's cook and based for part of that time in Le Havre, France. The France component also confirmed something Tom had said: that he remembered seeing a photo of his father taken on the Champs-Élysées with the Arc de Triomphe in the background.

In August 1920, Fong arrived in New York on SS *Rondo*. It later departed New York in September 1920, but without Fong. He was finally himself – his pursuit of his American dream delayed by eight years.

We had been lucky. Luck is an enormous part of any search, and we had more than our share of it. From a response to a shotgun email to a government file that filled in numerous blanks, to a chain of shipping records that connected the dots of a man's journey to the United States, we had followed Fong on his journey. At last, we had a complete story of a Chinese *Titanic* survivor, from his origins in the South China Sea to his end in the American Midwest.

19

A TALE OF TWO TALES

There were two key interviews that both Arthur and I wanted: James Cameron and Fifth Officer Harold Lowe's grandson, John Lowe. Our interest in Cameron was early and obvious. We also knew it might be the most time-consuming to arrange.

While we were interested in meeting and talking with Lowe, it was equally important that Tom Fong met him. This man's grandfather had saved Fong's father. There was a debt of gratitude that Tom wanted to express. For him, it was a pilgrimage more than an interview.

For me, meeting John Lowe would be my first brush with *Titanic* royalty. I loved our story for its elements, China meets world-famous shipwreck. But this was Fifth Officer Lowe's grandson. He would have photographs, maybe more, maybe a *Titanic* relic of some kind. Like the finger joint of a saint displayed in a French monastery, perhaps this man from Wales might have something that had been there on the night, in Lifeboat 14. Maybe some part of his uniform had even brushed Fang Lang after his rescue.

An Afternoon in Conwy

Tom, the documentary crew and I went together to meet John Lowe. John lived in Harold's former home in Conwy, about as far north and east in Wales as one can get before crossing into England. The modest home stood in a row of houses next to the River Clwyd, which flows majestically north into Conwy Bay. Across the river to the southwest is an imposing eleventh-century Norman castle.

The Lowe home was easy to find, marked with a historical marker that Harold Lowe formerly lived there. Tom stood at the door and introduced himself to John Lowe. 'You're a big boy,' John said, referring to Tom's size, inviting all of us inside.

John went into the kitchen to get some refreshments. I looked around the living room and spotted a distinguished and familiar photo of Harold Lowe in a gleaming silver frame. Although I had got to know perhaps the youngest living son and grandchildren of a *Titanic* survivor over the previous years, suddenly in the Lowe parlour, *Titanic* felt very close.

Lowe is unique among the surviving *Titanic* officers. He was a hero for going back to rescue passengers, but he rubbed Senator William Alden Smith the wrong way during his testimony. 'I am not having a very easy time with you, because you do not seem to be willing to answer my questions,' he said to Lowe.[1] The officer had also ascribed so many misdeeds to 'Italians' in his account to the US Inquiry that he was required to apologise.

Tom and John talked amiably. Harold Lowe was not known for his sense of humour, and didn't find it funny when, after falling into the river one day stepping from his boat to a dinghy, the local newspaper ran a headline to the effect of '*Titanic* Survivor Survives Again', John said. There were photos of Harold holding John, but the grandson had no specific memory of the grandfather.

John showed Tom and me several photos, including Harold with large fish he had caught. In a frame, he had two buttons from Harold's uniform, worn on the night. Relics, I thought.

He then presented Tom with the photo of Harold in the silver frame. 'You can have that,' he said.

Tom stopped short of shedding a tear, but his emotion was palpable. He thanked John profusely for the gift, which he later placed opposite a photo of his father on the Fong family mantelpiece.

'The circle is complete. We found each other,' John told Tom as they said their goodbyes. I had felt like a third wheel during what seemed like a reunion of long-lost family members. But it was an unforgettable experience and, well, a titanic moment.

Tom Fong, the youngest son of *Titanic* survivor Fong Wing Sun, at his home in Wisconsin in November 2018. (Photo courtesy of LP Films)

Author Steven Schwankert inspects a life-size reconstruction of *Titanic*'s Collapsible Lifeboat C in April 2019, built by students of the Western Academy of Beijing (WAB). (Photo courtesy of LP Films)

Members of the extended Fong family, relatives of *Titanic* survivor Fong Wing Sun, enjoy a pre-Thanksgiving dinner in Wisconsin, November 2018. From left: Henry Chiu, nephew of Fong Wing Sun; Julian Chiu, Henry's son; Steve Fong, Fong Wing Sun's grandson; Amanda Fong, wife of Tom Fong (with back to camera); Stacey Fong, wife of Steve Fong; Samantha Fong, Fong Wing Sun's granddaughter; Tom Fong, Fong Wing Sun's son; Marie Shum, Fong Wing Sun's former wife. (Photo courtesy of LP Films)

Author Steven Schwankert visits Fairview Lawn Cemetery in Halifax, Nova Scotia, Canada, where the body of one of the Chinese victims of *Titanic*, Lee Ling or Len Lam, may lie in burial plot 233. (Photo courtesy of LP Films)

An aerial view of a bay on Xiachuan Island, off the coast of the Taishan region of China's Guangdong province. Fong Wing Sun, and perhaps other eventual Chinese *Titanic* passengers, may have departed Xiachuan Island from this bay on their way to Hong Kong to seek employment. (Photo courtesy of LP Films)

Author Steven Schwankert (right) visits the childhood home of *Titanic* survivor Fong Wing Sun on Xiachuan Island, Guangdong Province, China, in May 2018. (Photo courtesy of LP Films)

Author Steven Schwankert (left) inspects shipping records relating to *Titanic*'s Chinese passengers at the Bristol Archives, Bristol, United Kingdom, in July 2018. (Photo courtesy of LP Films)

Author Steven Schwankert (second left, in blue) examines a glass plate containing a photographic image believed to be of *Titanic* survivor Lee Bing, in November 2018 at the Cambridge City Archives, Cambridge, Ontario, Canada. The City of Cambridge Information and Archives Analyst is on the left; Arthur Jones, co-creator and director of the documentary film *The Six* is on the right (with back to camera). (Photo courtesy of LP Films)

A photo of *Titanic* survivor Fong Wing Sun (right), identified in this photo in Chinese as Fong Sen, taken during the Chicago World's Fair in 1933. To his immediate left is Chang Fa-kuei (Zhang Fakui), a Kuomintang (KMT) general who may have introduced Fong and his wife in the 1950s. (Photo courtesy of the Fong family)

Fong Wing Sun (right) is shown with friend Grace Lai, a Chicago artist known for sketches and watercolours of Chicago's skyline and industrial sites, in the late 1970s or early 1980s. (Photo courtesy of the Fong family)

Fong Wing Sun (left, in suit) poses with his son, Tom (second left, sitting) and members of the Chiu family, whom Fong sponsored to immigrate to the United States. They arrived on 13 September 1971. Fong told Henry Chiu (second right, in yellow) that he had survived a shipwreck in which his large ship had crashed into 'an ice mountain' and sank. (Photo courtesy of the Fong family)

The Fong family in the 1960s. From left: A-Fon Tom (Marie Shum); Tom Fong; Fong Wing Sun; John Fong. (Photo courtesy of the Fong family)

Fong Wing Sun (centre) is shown with his sons John (left) and Tom. (Photo courtesy of the Fong family)

A CR 10 seaman's identity card for Lam Choi, believed to be the *Titanic* survivor Ah Lam. (The National Archives, Photo No. 356009)

A CR 10 seaman's identity card for Yum Hee/Hui, believed to be the *Titanic* survivor Ling Hee. (The National Archives, Photo No. 261023)

A photo of Fong Wing Sun, believed to be *Titanic* survivor Fang Lang, around 1920. (Courtesy of the Fong family)

Possible images of *Titanic* survivor Lee Bing, reproduced from a glass plate. The image was taken around 1920. (Courtesy of the Cambridge City Archives, Cambridge, Ontario)

Titanic under construction at Harland & Wolff in Belfast, just before its launch in 1911. (Library of Congress)

Titanic just after its launch on 31 May 1911. Its funnels and other equipment would be installed once the hull was afloat and free of its slipway at Harland & Wolff. (Library of Congress)

All's Well that Ends in Wellington

I had met James Cameron once before, in 2011 in Beijing, along with his business partner Maria Wilhelm and members of his team. I saved all the email addresses collected from that event for a rainy day.

That day arrived in 2019. Knowing that it would take some time to schedule an interview with Cameron, who was deep in the production of the second *Avatar* film, *Avatar: The Way of Water*, Arthur and I began reaching through our respective networks, he in film and I in exploration.

We were surprised at both the speed of the response and the level of enthusiasm: Cameron had heard about our project and was interested in participating. We moved to schedule an appropriate time and location.

By June 2019, filming for the documentary had wrapped and the research was completed. Originally, we were set for the Fourth of July weekend in Los Angeles. That plan was scuttled by an earthquake in southern California. So the date and destination shifted: 7 July in Wellington, New Zealand, where Cameron calls home and where he was doing some shooting on the first *Avatar* sequel.

For Arthur and me, it was a milestone: the story of *Titanic*'s Chinese passengers had now taken us to a fourth continent.

We booked a suite at a Wellington hotel recommended by Cameron's staff where the interview would take place. Thanks to Cameron and his friend and neighbour Peter Jackson (the director of Lord of the Rings), Wellington film crews get more work than perhaps those in a similar-sized city elsewhere might. The camera operator and sound man hired for the interview had both worked with Cameron before, shooting behind-the-scenes material for *Avatar*.

The tall *Titanic* director arrived for the interview and greeted us warmly. After some quick lighting and focus adjustments, we began shooting.

Yes, he knew about the Chinese passengers when he wrote *Titanic* and he particularly admired the 'grit' that Fang Lang had demonstrated by swimming through the frigid water and saving himself on wooden wreckage. Yes, Fang Lang's rescue was the inspiration for the

Jack and Rose ending. As Arthur asked our questions, I paced quietly in the suite's kitchen, a clenched fist affirming each of the director's responses. The real-life rescue of Tom Fong's father had given rise to one of cinema's eternal moments.

With the interview wrapped, Cameron asked if was there any other part of the project with which he could help – a generous offer that eventually led to both Cameron and Wilhelm executive-producing the documentary and helping to transform the filmed side of the project.

A key creative challenge was how to show the *Titanic* itself in the film. Obviously, re-enactment wouldn't work well, especially given the existing great films about the *Titanic*. Animation was chosen to depict the Chinese passengers during moments of their struggle to survive. We chose a relatively crude style of animation to convey that, while the escape scenario we were suggesting was possible, some uncertainty remained.

For other scenes, using footage from the Cameron film seemed like the only viable option. Using footage from feature films is prohibitively expensive, costing thousands if not tens of thousands of dollars per minute, especially from an all-time classic like *Titanic*. With their assistance, we were able to use footage from the 1997 film at no cost.

Including footage from *Titanic* presented an additional challenge: we would need special permission from the actors appearing in those scenes. Actors have the right to payment when their scenes are reused, called residuals. We would need the assent of every speaking actor in the featured scenes – with Cameron and Wilhelm's help, we cleared all the necessary authorisations, including from the stars Leonardo DiCaprio and Kate Winslet.

Cameron and Wilhelm did more than just broad strokes. They saw many of the trailers cut for the documentary and provided valuable feedback. Although Covid delayed the documentary's theatrical release in China by a year, Cameron made videos promoting the film that were played before screenings.

Although our interest had always been in Cameron's expert knowledge of the Chinese passengers and the *Titanic* story overall, his credibility in China meant having his involvement with the documentary was an incredible advantage. Because Cameron was associated with it, audiences that were not accustomed to watching factual films in cinemas were willing to give it a try. *The Six* opened in 10,000 cinemas across China, playing for a full month, before eventually being released on all major streaming platforms there.

20

WATERTIGHT

From the outset, we were determined to take a fresh look at the circumstances of the Chinese passengers leaving *Titanic*, either in lifeboats or into the water. Starting from their quarters on G Deck, we wanted to know their route out of the ship to the Boat Deck, to the lifeboats and then Fang Lang's circumstances once in the ocean. To do so, it was important to strip away speculation and apply science, or at least the limitations of physics, wherever possible.

Looking at *Titanic* deck plans, passengers emerging from their rooms on G Deck in the bow could go in several directions. In this case, the map is not the territory. During the research, we stumbled on a man named Tom Lynskey, who with a business partner was developing a virtual reality model of *Titanic*. This offered us the opportunity to walk through *Titanic* as passengers (or crew) would have to see their options in almost the original context.

Meeting in New York, we began looking at possible paths for the Chinese passengers. One thing became immediately clear: on G Deck, the watertight doors would have dropped into place by the time the Chinese men noticed water seeping into their cabin. That significantly limited their choices of where they could go. Aside from other staterooms, their only real choice was to go up a staircase that would lead them to Scotland Road.

As shown during the walkthrough, likely the men first went to the Third-Class sitting room in *Titanic*'s stern. But as the sinking continued, that room offered no solution. Walking out of the sitting room, they would have encountered the aft staircase and, following the stairs up, they would have emerged near the aft lifeboats, specifically Lifeboat 10. This creates the opportunity for the passenger traditionally identified as Cheong Foo to enter and escape in that lifeboat. It might have been virtual, but the ability to walk through *Titanic*'s decks in a similar way to the Chinese passengers gave us a sense of their reality on the night.

Author as Test Subject

Understanding Fang Lang's time in the water and the circumstances that led up to his rescue was important to confirm the timeline of his survival and the return of Lifeboat 14 to the area in search of survivors. To determine how long Fang would have been in the water and how long he could have survived, your author participated in an experiment supervised by the University of Portsmouth's Professor Tipton at the Extreme Environments Laboratory.[1]

The experiment involved thirty-five minutes of motionless immersion up to the neck, in 12°C (54°F) water. Although the water on the night of *Titanic*'s sinking was 0–2°C (32–35.6°F), Professor Tipton refused to lower the temperature beyond 12°C (53.6°F), as he believed it to be unethical and unnecessary for the purposes of the experiment.

During the experiment, your fully clothed writer shivered for most of the first and last ten minutes, as my body temperature dropped consistently. That temperature was monitored using a thermometer inserted internally. By remaining still, the body can build up a thin layer of warmer water around itself, delaying the loss of heat. But Fang would have had no such option, not until he found the board and hauled himself out. The water around him was a sea of writhing bodies, and he swam to find safety for himself and perhaps protect himself from others who might use him as floatation.

Most revealing from the Portsmouth experiment, two manual tasks – screwing a nut onto a bolt and tying a knot around a piece of wood – each took two to three times longer after immersion than before. Despite understanding the task and wanting to complete each more quickly, it simply felt physically impossible to finish more swiftly than cold fingers and hands would allow. Tipton estimated that Fang would not have had more than fifteen to twenty minutes in the water before he would start to lose motor function and be unable to rescue himself.

Rebuilding the Lifeboat

I didn't know anything about building boats, but I also didn't need to. I just needed to find someone who could, and more specifically, someone who understood it as a unique opportunity.

Beijing is blessed with more than sixty international schools. Among their top ranks are a few schools that want to command the big bucks of the diplomats and international businesspeople who will send their children there. Through my scuba business, I had come to learn that the most innovative was Western Academy of Beijing (WAB). Although its stuffy and uptight competitor, International School of Beijing, was, strictly speaking, better academically, WAB was the most open-minded and amenable to projects like, well, building *Titanic* lifeboats. Through my scuba network, I put out a call to international schoolteachers who were also instructors and divemasters, and asked if anyone's school had a design shop or wood shop. My prayers were answered when Chris Clark, a member of WAB staff, said that his school did.

I emailed him a proposal to share with his school administration: the materials would be covered via the documentary's budget. With our supervision, WAB students would build a lifesize replica of a *Titanic* collapsible lifeboat, using original Engelhardt plans available online. Upon completion, we would use their students as stand-ins for *Titanic* passengers and recreate the loading of Collapsible C. Once and for all, we would know if the Chinese men could have hidden in the boat, and why they may not have been immediately noticed by Quartermaster George Rowe or J. Bruce Ismay.

I met with Mark Trumpold, WAB's design teacher to discuss the plan. Did the boat need to float? Did it need to be seaworthy, the Australian asked? No. He said that they might try to make it float anyway.

What about the boat's sides? Did they need to be canvas? It might be a cost issue. Could they be plywood instead, as long as the dimensions were correct? I agreed.

Trumpold wasn't a shipwright, but he was an experienced builder of sets for school plays. Armed with a set of plans and a team of students, they set to work, a unique after-school activity.

Because the boat did not need to be seaworthy or even float, Trumpold and his students used lighter, less-costly plywood to build the hull, but retained its original dimensions. The cork and kapok bottom was not included. Again, to reduce costs, the canvas sides were replaced with plywood and permanently fixed in place. Construction took the students approximately ten months, including cold winter afternoons, at the sacrifice of other activities.

After the boat was assembled and painted, the school gathered forty interested students, some of whom were part of the construction crew. Of particular interest were students who were about the size of the six Chinese survivors, in the range of 5ft 6in–5ft 8in (168–73cm). The demonstration took place on a sunny April afternoon – far more favourable conditions than the cold, dark night on which the real Collapsible C put to sea.

Four of the students, representing the Chinese men, entered the boat and attempted to squeeze underneath the thwarts (wooden bench seats). While this was physically possible, they were clearly visible and would have been felt or stepped on by anyone else getting into the lifeboat, as well as pressed by passengers sitting on the benches. There were neither enough thwarts for each man to hide underneath, nor would they have fitted underneath them sufficiently to conceal themselves entirely. Assuming any of that had been possible, any attempt to hide would have had to take place once the boat was assembled and ready for loading, which means they would have been spotted trying to enter it by others nearby.

During the lifeboat demonstration, your author, in the role of Ismay, sat at an oar, as *Titanic*'s owner claimed he had. Teacher Trumpold stood as Rowe would have at the boat's stern. From these vantage points, if the Chinese men were crouching near the boat's bow or simply sitting on the boat's bottom, not on a thwart, they would not have been visible either to Ismay or to the quartermaster.

Without attempting to conceal themselves at all, the men could not be seen by Rowe, who would have been looking in their direction, nor by Ismay. Even today, crouching is a common repose for people in some parts of China, especially men, if seating is not available. It makes perfect sense that if there was no bench upon which the men could sit, they would assume this posture in the lifeboat or have sat directly on the deck.

All this was revealed in the moment – none of it was apparent until the boat was loaded and observers placed in the correct locations. Neither Ismay nor Rowe's observations were driven by malice. They simply could not see the Chinese men, hence their 'surprise' when lighting and other conditions allowed them to be noticed. In a few minutes, what had been seen for more than a century as a shameful act was disproven. Building a full-sized model had been the right decision.

THE SIX

For more than 110 years, the *Titanic* story has been buoyed by an obsession with technical detail, stories of its passengers' wealth or relative destitution, and heroism or ignominy side by side. *Titanic* captivated us because we could always see ourselves in someone on board, imagining that we would have done the same thing if that had been us on the ship instead of them.

Titanic also left us with enough missing pieces, misinformation and mystery to continue fascinating us. What song did the band play as the ship sank, if it played any song at all? What was the light that so many *Titanic* officers and passengers saw in the distance that night? Could it have saved more lives? And of course, everyone's favourite game: who is to blame for the deaths of almost 1,500 people?

We are now in a new era of *Titanic* research. All the survivors, and many of their children, are now dead, so there are no first-hand memories left to mine. Our technology gets better and better, allowing us to create new models of *Titanic*, including virtual-reality walkthroughs and complete photo mosaics of the ship's entire wreck site, lying on the bottom of the Atlantic Ocean. Thanks to the internet, we can search entire databases in hours or even minutes, a feat that once took researchers days to accomplish after physically travelling to the site of those archives.

But time remains against us. After more than 100 years at the bottom under crushing water pressure, *Titanic* itself is disappearing.

Every shipwreck is destined to become a rust stain on the sand, and the beautiful ship one day will be no different. Similarly, existing paper records, old photographs and family heirlooms are at risk of deteriorating unless we make efforts now to preserve them.

Similar stories of the search for employment, enduring discrimination and settling in the West could have been told by grouping any eight Chinese migrant workers from the first part of the twentieth century together. But the eight Chinese men travelling aboard *Titanic*, and especially the six survivors, create a focal point at one of the best-known and best-documented events before the First World War.

From there, it is possible to follow them as they are pushed back and forth by large forces such as war, demand for labour and discriminatory immigration policies. At very few points in their lives did they seem in control of their own destinies.

Some of the stories are genuinely sad, such as the loss of Lee Ling and Len Lam on *Titanic*, the untimely death of Chang Chip, and how Ah Lam seemed resigned to a life on ships with no foreseeable end. Lee Bing and Fong Wing Sun both found relative success, but one wonders whether they viewed their own lives as successes or failures. It's impossible to know what their lives would have been like if they had chosen to stay close to where they grew up, whether in the long term they had earned more and had better lives than if they had never gone to sea.

Certainly, enough men, and later women, went overseas between 1850 and 1950 that it not only had an impact on culture and society in China, but also on the countries where they settled in the largest numbers, namely Canada, the United Kingdom and the United States. That influence continues today, in both positive ways, such as the rising number of elected officials of Chinese heritage in those countries, along with successful entrepreneurs and scientists and professional athletes; and negative, like the anti-Asian violence that occurred in the United States in the spring of 2021. What the story of the Six shows is that the roots of both these personal successes and societal failures are more than a century old and are not likely to be resolved quickly.

History gives us a chance to examine past events objectively and in greater detail. The story of the Six set out to do just that, including the accusations levelled at the men more than 100 years ago, besmirching their names and those of Chinese people in general ever since. They may not have been heroes, but they certainly were not villains. They faced whatever challenges presented themselves, whenever they arose. But they kept going to the best of their ability.

Whether it was lack of employment opportunity, sinking ships, exclusion laws or unseen misfortune, the Six moved forward. They never gave up.

That is deserving of our attention and our respect, no matter the time period or the people. The story of *Titanic* is now passing into legend and myth. At last, the story of her Chinese passengers will endure alongside her.

ACKNOWLEDGEMENTS

Without Arthur Jones, my creative partner on a China shipwreck story for now the second time, I could not have written this book. Arthur's initial scepticism about doing a *Titanic* story was the crucible that *The Six* needed to get under way, to prove that the concept held water. After finishing this book, please see his beautiful and moving documentary of the same title.

Jo Lusby and I first met at a meeting of scuba divers in Beijing. About ten years later, she and I found ourselves trapped underwater in the Philippines. Thank you, Jo, for being a source of emergency air – then and now.

As of writing this, I have not met Marysia Juszczakiewicz of Peony Literary Agency in person, yet without her this book would not exist. Thank you for bringing it to life.

Luo Tong of LP Films made much of this work possible. Thanks, LT. I hope we make at least one more film together.

I hope that someday there will be a CSI-style show focusing on genealogists named Grant Din, Julie Hamilton, Cynthia Lee, Paul Wade, Clotilde Yap and Grace Zhang. Without their determination and skill with public records, I'm not sure we would have ever known the full story of the Six, particularly of Fong Wing Sun and Lee Bing.

Special thanks to James Cameron and Maria Wilhelm for all they did to help bring *The Six* to life, and for the kind foreword to this book.

Thanks to all the authors who provided encouragement and advance praise: Amy Tan, Eric Jay Dolin, James Zimmerman, Paul French, Tad Fitch and Nelson Aspen. Thank you to Duncan Clark – we've come a long way from Café Café. Gratitude to L.A. Beadles of the *Unsinkable* podcast, for her constant support.

At The History Press, I am grateful to Amy Rigg and Jezz Palmer for their editorial work and timeliness. At Pegasus Books, Jessica Case's and Julia Romero's enthusiasm helped take this book to places I only dreamed possible.

David Concannon very kindly opened a door for us, and the late, great Capt. Don Walsh held that door so that we could walk through it. I am indebted to both. Cathy Ye Guozhi's early poster design inspired the cover for the U.S. edition of this book. Thank you, Cathy.

Much more than with my previous book *Poseidon*, there are those who did not live to see its publication. I'm sad that I cannot present signed copies to A-Fong Tom/Marie Shum, Tom Fong's mother and Fong Wing Sun's former wife; Henry Chiu, whose comment about *Titanic* first brought Tom face to face with his father's role in the great ship's history; Professor Judy Yung, the pioneer of Chinese American studies; and John Lowe, who kept and honoured his grandfather Harold Lowe's *Titanic* artefacts throughout his life.

My mother, Ginger Schwankert, saw the beginning of this work but not its end – something I regret deeply. She did an excellent edit on my first book. And my friend David Wolf, the third hand on my keyboard for *Poseidon*, left this world so suddenly. If the wages of sin is death, then the wages of procrastination is heartache.

Thank you, QX, for bringing the Chinese edition of this book to life, and for everything else, always.

And He who should be first I mention last: thank you to Our Lord and Saviour Jesus Christ, from whom all good things come.

BIBLIOGRAPHY AND
SOURCES

Books

Anderson, Roy Claude, *White Star* (Prescot: T. Stephenson & Sons Ltd, 1964).

Bartlett, W.B., *Titanic, 9 Hours to Hell: The Survivors' Story* (Gloucestershire: Amberley Publishing, 2010).

Behe, George, *Voices from the Carpathia* (Stroud: The History Press, 2015).

Butler, Daniel Allen, *Unsinkable: The Full Story* (London: Pen & Sword Books Ltd, 2012).

Davenport-Hines, Richard, *Voyagers of the Titanic: Passengers, Sailors, Shipbuilders, Aristocrats, and the Worlds They Came From* (New York: William Morrow Books, 2013).

Cheng, Lucie, & Edna Bonacich, *Labor Immigration under Capitalism: Asian Workers in the United States before World War II* (University of California Press, 2021).

Cho, Lily, *Mass Capture: Chinese Head Tax and the Making of Non-Citizens* (Montreal: McGill-Queen's University Press, 2021).

Collyer, Charlotte, 'How I Was Saved From the Titanic', *San Francisco Call, The Semi-Monthly Magazine Section*, May 1912, 'A Survivor of the Most Dramatic Maritime Disaster in the World's History ... Exclusively to Readers of the Semi-Monthly' (Spitfire Publishers Ltd, 2019).

Eaton, John P., & Charles A. Haas, *Titanic, Destination Disaster: The Legends and the Reality* (New York: W.W. Norton & Co., 1996).

Gleicher, David, *The Rescue of The Third Class on the Titanic: A Revisionist History* (Liverpool: Liverpool University Press, 2006).

Green, Bob, *Eavesdroppings: Stories From Small Towns When Sin Was Fun* (Cambridge, Ontario: Dumdum Press, 2006).

Lee, Erika, & Judy Yung, *Angel Island: Immigrant Gateway to America* (Oxford: Oxford University Press, 2012).

Lopez, Kathleen, *Chinese Cubans: A Transnational History* (Chapel Hill, North Carolina: University of North Carolina Press, 2013).

Lord, Walter, *The Night Lives on: Thoughts, Theories and Revelations about the Titanic* (Penguin Books, 1998).

Lord, Walter, *A Night to Remember* (Henry, Holt, and Company, 2005).

McCutcheon, Janette, *White Star Line: A Photographic History*, (Gloucestershire: Amberley Publishing, 2013).

Matsen, Brad, *Titanic's Last Secrets: The Further Adventures of Shadow Divers John Chatterton and Richie Kohler* (New York: Hachette, 2008).

Maxtone-Graham, John, *The Only Way to Cross* (New York: The Macmillan Company, 1972).

Menary, David, *Gordie Howe: A Year in Galt* (Lulu.com, 2014).

Oldham, Wilton J., *The Ismay Line*, E-book edition (Chaplin Books, 2013).

Saloum Elias, Leila, *The Dream and Then the Nightmare: The Syrians Who Boarded the Titanic, the Story of the Arabic-Speaking Passengers* (Damascus, Syria: Atlas for Publishing and Distribution, 2011).

Spence, Jonathan D., *God's Chinese Son: The Taiping Heavenly Kingdom of Hong Xiuquan* (New York: W.W. Norton & Company, 1996).

Wilson, Frances, *How to Survive the Titanic, or the Sinking of J. Bruce Ismay* (New York: Harper Perennial, 2012).

Websites

Atlantic Liners: www.atlanticliners.com/white_star_home/titanic_home/

Bill Wormstedt's *Titanic*: www.wormstedt.com/Titanic/index.html

Bristol Archives Register of Ships Registered at the Port of Bristol, 1824–1994: archives.bristol.gov.uk/records/37908

Encyclopedia Titanica: www.encyclopedia-titanica.org

Titanic Inquiry Project: www.titanicinquiry.org

NOTES

Chapter 1

1 Fong Wing Sun, personal correspondence. Courtesy of the Fong family.

Chapter 2

1 'Yacht Nourmahal Beached: Accident to John Jacob Astor's Handsome Craft', *The New York Times*, 29 September 1893, p. 1.

Chapter 3

1 The materials relating to the early life of Fong Wing Sun are imagined by the author, based on research and conversations with his descendants.

2 'Statistical Communiqué on the National Economic and Social Development of Jiangmen City in 2022' ('2022年江门市国民经济和社会发展统计公报') www.jiangmen.gov.cn/home/tzgg/content/post_2852650.html (accessed 4 March 2024).

3 Spence, Jonathan D., *God's Chinese Son: The Taiping Heavenly Kingdom of Hong Xiuquan* (W.W. Norton & Company, 1996) p. 88.

4 Cheng, Lucie, & Edna Bonacich, *Labor Immigration under Capitalism: Asian Workers in the United States before World War II* (University of California Press, 2021) p. 237.

5 'Chinese Exclusion Act (1882)', www.archives.gov/milestone-documents/chinese-exclusion-act (accessed 19 May 2024).

6 'The Burlingame-Seward Treaty, 1868, history.state.gov/milestones/1866-1898/burlingame-seward-treaty (accessed 4 March 2024).

7 Chinese Exclusion Act (1882).

8 *Ibid.*

Chapter 4

1 Maxtone-Graham, John, *The Only Way to Cross* (New York: Macmillan, 1972) p. 5.

2 Oldham, Wilton J., *The Ismay Line* (Chaplin Books, 2013) Chapter 4.

3 McCutcheon, Janette, *White Star Line: A Photographic History* (Gloucestershire: Amberley Publishing, 2013) Chapter 2.

4 Anderson, Roy Claude, *White Star* (Prescot: T. Stephenson & Sons Ltd, 1964.) p. 182.

5 'SS *Atlantic*: A Captain's Fateful Decision', *The Maritime Executive*, 31 March 2016, maritime-executive.com/article/ss-atlantic-a-captains-fateful-decision (accessed 4 July 2024).

6 *Ibid.*

7 Wilson, Frances, *How to Survive the Titanic, or The Sinking of J. Bruce Ismay* (New York: Harper Perennial, 2012).

8 *Ibid.*

9 Gilkes, Paul, 'Recovery Efforts Planned for Cargo Lost in RMS 'republic' Wreckage', CoinWorld, www.coinworld.com/news/us-coins/recovery-efforts-planned-for-cargo-lost-in-rms-republic-wreckage (accessed 7 January 2024).

10 Matsen, Brad, *Titanic's Last Secrets: The Further Adventures of Shadow Divers John Chatterton and Richie Kohler* (New York: Hachette, 2008) p. 131.

Chapter 5

1 Butler, Daniel Allen, *Unsinkable: The Full Story* (Pen & Sword Books Ltd, 2012) p. 37.

2 Lord, Walter, *A Night to Remember* (Henry, Holt, and Company, 2005) p. 21.

3 'Overview + History: Ellis Island', Statue of Liberty & Ellis Island, 26 September 2022, www.statueofliberty.org/ellis-island/overview-history/ (accessed 13 March 2024).

4 Bristol Archives, 30182/53: SS *Annetta* Agreements and Crew Lists, 1909–13.

5 Louden-Brown, Paul, 'Titanic – Food for All Classes', Titanic Belfast, www.titanicbelfast.com/history-of-titanic/titanic-stories/titanic-food-for-all-classes/ (accessed 23 May 2024).

6 'Chinese Maid Wants to Die', *The Akron Beacon Journal* (18 April 1912) p. 2.

7 *Ibid.*

8 'Claim of Yong Lang', US National Archives, NAID: 6210878, Local ID: B176, 19 April 1913.

9 Lord, Walter, *The Night Lives On: Thoughts, Theories and Revelations about the Titanic* (Penguin Books, 1998) p. 175.

Chapter 6

1 Eaton, John P., & Charles A. Haas, *Titanic, Destination Disaster: The Legends and the Reality* (New York: W.W. Norton & Co., 1996) p. 12.

2 *Ibid.*

3 *Ibid.*

4 United States Senate Inquiry, Day 7, Testimony of George T. Rowe (Quartermaster, SS *Titanic*), www.titanicinquiry.org/USInq/AmInq07Rowe01.php (accessed 4 March 2024).

5 Butler, Daniel Allen, *Unsinkable: The Full Story*, p. 110.

6 United States Senate Inquiry, Day 1, Testimony of Charles Lightoller, Cont., www.titanicinquiry.org/USInq/AmInq01Lightoller04.php (accessed 4 March 2024).

7 United States Senate Inquiry, Day 13, Testimony of Daniel Buckley (Third-Class passenger, SS *Titanic*), www.titanicinquiry.org/USInq/AmInq13Buckley01.php (accessed 4 March 2024).

8 Gleicher, David, *The Rescue of the Third Class on the Titanic: A Revisionist History* (Liverpool: Liverpool University Press, 2006).

9 Encyclopedia Titanica (2018), 'Fahīm Rūḥānā al-Zaʾinnī' (ref: #965, last updated: 19 October 2018, www.encyclopedia-titanica.org/titanic-survivor/fahim-philip-zenni-leeni.html (accessed 5 March 2024).

10 'Lifeboat Launching Sequence Re-Examined', Bill Wormstedt's Titanic, wormstedt.com/Titanic/lifeboats/lifeboats.htm (accessed 5 March 2024).

11 United States Senate Inquiry, Day 7, Testimony of Frank O. Evans (Able Bodied Seaman, SS *Titanic*), www.titanicinquiry.org/USInq/AmInq07Evans01.php (accessed 5 March 2024).

12 British Wreck Commissioner's Inquiry, Day 6, Testimony of Charles Joughin (Chief Baker, SS *Titanic*), www.titanicinquiry.org/BOTInq/BOTInq06Joughin01.php (accessed 5 March 2024).

13 Beesley, Lawrence, *The Loss of the Titanic: Written by One of the Survivors* (Auckland: The Floating Press, 2009) p. 136.

14 United States Senate Inquiry, Day 7, Testimony of Frank O. Evans (Able Bodied Seaman, SS *Titanic*).

15 United States Senate Inquiry, Day 9, Testimony of William Burke (Dining Room Steward, SS *Titanic*), www.titanicinquiry.org/USInq/AmInq09Burke01.php (accessed 5 March 2024).

16 'Women Revealed as Heroines by Wreck; Mrs. J.J. Brown of Denver Tells Story of Her Seven Hours in Lifeboat', *The New York Times*, 20 April 1912, p. 4.

17 'Names of 27 Recovered Dead', *Rutland Daily Herald*, 23 April 1912, p. 1.

18 'Chinese Maid Wants to Die', *The Akron Beacon Journal*, 18 April 1912, p. 2.

19 *Ibid.*

20 *Ibid.*

21 Tipton, Dr Mike, 'Cold water immersion: sudden death and prolonged survival', *The Lancet*, Vol. 362, December 2003, pp. S12–S13.

22 Collyer, Charlotte, 'How I Was Saved From the Titanic', The Semi-Monthly Magazine Section, May 1912, A Survivor of the Most Dramatic Maritime Disaster in the World's History … Exclusively to Readers of the Semi-Monthly (Spitfire Publishers Ltd, 2019).

23 *The Six*, directed by Arthur Jones (LP Films, 2021).

24 British Wreck Commissioner's Inquiry, Day 6, Testimony of Charles Joughin (Chief Baker, SS *Titanic*).

25 Behe, George, *Voices from the Carpathia* (Stroud: The History Press, 2015) p. 145.

26 Lord, Walter, *The Night Lives On*, p. 81.

27 Bristol Archives (UK), 30182/53: SS *Annetta* Agreements and Crew Lists, 1909–13.

Chapter 7

1 'Chinamen in Lifeboats', *The Brooklyn Daily Eagle*, 19 April 1912, p. 3.

2 'Chinese Stowaways', *The Daily Telegraph*, 20 April 1912, p. 15.

3 'Names of 27 Recovered Dead', *Rutland Daily Herald*, 23 April 1912, p. 1.

Chapter 8

1 Lord, Walter, *The Night Lives On*.

2 Cheng, Wei, *Titanic's 'Chinamen'* [*Tai Tan Ni Ke Hao Shang de 'Zhong Guo Lao'*] (Lijiang Publishing House, 2013).

3 United States Senate Inquiry, Day 4, Testimony of George T. Rowe (Quartermaster, SS *Titanic*).

4   United States Senate Inquiry, Day 11, Testimony of Joseph B. Ismay, Recalled, www.titanicinquiry.org/USInq/AmInq11Ismay01.php (accessed 5 March 2024).

5   British Wreck Commissioner's Inquiry, Day 15, Testimony of George T. Rowe (Quartermaster, SS *Titanic*), www.titanicinquiry.org/BOTInq/BOTInq15Rowe01. php (accessed 18 March 2024).

6   United States Senate Inquiry, Day 11, Testimony of Joseph B. Ismay.

7   British Wreck Commissioner's Enquiry, Day 9, Testimony of Albert V. Pearcey (Third Class Pantryman, SS *Titanic*), www.titanicinquiry.org/BOTInq/ BOTInq09Pearcey01.php (accessed 18 March 2024).

8   United States Senate Inquiry, Day 5, Testimony of Harold G. Lowe (Fifth Officer, SS *Titanic*), www.titanicinquiry.org/USInq/AmInq05Lowe01.php (accessed 16 March 2024).

9   United States Senate, Day 7, Testimony of George F. Crowe (Saloon Steward, SS *Titanic*), www.titanicinquiry.org/USInq/AmInq07Crowe01.php (accessed 16 March 2024).

10 Collyer, Charlotte, 'How I Was Saved From the Titanic'.

11 *Ibid.*

12 Sheil, Inger, *Titanic Valour: The Life of Fifth Officer Harold Lowe* (Stroud: The History Press, 2012) p. 107.

13 United States Senate Inquiry, Day 7, Testimony of Edward J. Buley (Able Bodied Seaman, SS *Titanic*), www.titanicinquiry.org/USInq/AmInq07Buley01.php (accessed 17 March 2024).

14 United States Senate Inquiry, Day 9, Testimony of Frederick D. Ray (Saloon Steward, SS *Titanic*), www.titanicinquiry.org/USInq/AmInq09Ray01.php (accessed 22 March 2024).

15 United States Senate Inquiry, Day 18, Testimony of Frederick Barrett (Leading Fireman, SS *Titanic*), www.titanicinquiry.org/USInq/AmInq18Barrett01.php (accessed 22 March 2024).

16 United States Senate Inquiry, Day 13, Testimony of Daniel Buckley (Third-Class passenger, SS *Titanic*).

17 Beesley, Lawrence, *The Loss of the Titanic: Written by One of the Survivors* (Auckland: The Floating Press, 2009) p. 136.

18 J. Hedgepeth Williams, personal communication, 17 March 2018.

19 'Titanic Survivor Relates Tale of Agonizing Terror', *The Dayton Herald*, 13 June 1912, p. 1.

20 *Ibid.*

21 United States Senate Inquiry, Day 4, Testimony of George T. Rowe (Quartermaster, SS *Titanic*).

22 *Goldsmith Dayton Daily News* interview 1943.

23 United States Senate Inquiry, Day 4, Testimony of George T. Rowe (Quartermaster, SS *Titanic*).

24 *Ibid.*

25 United States Senate Inquiry, Day 13, Testimony of Daniel Buckley (Third-Class passenger, SS *Titanic*).

26 'Titanic: Who Was the Man in Drag Who Survived?', BelfastTelegraph.co.uk,

24 March 2012, www.belfasttelegraph.co.uk/archive/titanic/titanic-who-was-the-man-in-drag-who-survived/28730106.html (accessed 24 April 2024).

27   United States Senate Inquiry, Day 5, Testimony of Harold G. Lowe (Fifth Officer, SS *Titanic*).

28   'Perils End in Meeting', *Detroit Free Press*, 24 April 1912, p. 1.

29   Chapman, Earl J., 'Gunshots on the Titanic', www.encyclopedia-titanica.org/gunshots-on-titanic.html. Accessed 17 March 2024.

30   United States Senate Inquiry, Day 10, Testimony of Hugh Woolner (First-Class passenger, SS *Titanic*), www.titanicinquiry.org/USInq/AmInq10Woolner01.php. Accessed 17 March 2024.

31   *Ibid.*

32   *Ibid.*

33   *Ibid.*

34   Davenport-Hines, Richard, *Voyagers of the Titanic: Passengers, Sailors, Shipbuilders, Aristocrats, and the Worlds They Came From* (New York: William Morrow Books, 2013), p. 243.

35   *Ibid.*, p. 244.

36   Gleicher, David, *The Rescue of The Third Class on the Titanic*, p. 200.

37   *Ibid.*

38   *Ibid.*, p. 201

39   Saloum Elias, Leila, *The Dream and Then the Nightmare: The Syrians Who Boarded the Titanic, the Story of the Arabic-Speaking Passengers* (Damascus, Syria: Atlas for Publishing and Distribution, 2011).

Chapter 9

1   'Survivor Tells of Titanic Wreck', *Bureau County Tribune*, 2 May 1912, p. 1.

2   'Chinese Stowaways', *The Daily Telegraph*, 20 April 1912, p. 15.

3   'Heroism of the Anglo-Saxon Sailors Stands Out in Disaster', *Brooklyn Daily Eagle*, 19 April 1912, p. 2.

4   'Harrowing Tales of Scenes on Titanic By Miss Dowdell', *Hudson Chronicle*, 20 April 1912.

5   Behe, George, *Voices from the Carpathia*, p. 106.

6   O'Neil, Tim, 'When Titanic sank in 1912, P-D reporter Carlos Hurd landed the story of a lifetime', *St. Louis Post-Dispatch*, 15 April 2024, www.stltoday.com/news/archives/when-titanic-sank-in-1912-p-d-reporter-carlos-hurd-landed-the-story-of-a/article_d9c85a14-ffef-5b71-924f-c3b2e32bff95.html (accessed 15 April 2024).

7   'Survivors Add to Disaster Tales', *The New York Times*, 20 April 1912, p. 3.

8   'Claim of Yum Hee', US National Archives, NAID: 6210878, Local ID: B176, 19 March 1913.

9   'Claim of Yong Lang', US National Archives, NAID: 6210878, Local ID: B176, 19 March 1913.

10   'Limitation of Liability Hearings', Final Decree, www.titanicinquiry.org/lol/finaldecree.php. Accessed 17 May 2024.

Chapter 10

1   Urban, Andrew, 'People-Works', *International Association for the History of Transport Traffic and Mobility*, 29 October 2018, t2m.org/restricted-cargo-chinese-sailors-shore-leave-and-the-evolution-of-u-s-immigration-policies-1882-1942/ (accessed 23 March 2021).

2   *Ibid.*

3   Lopez, Kathleen, *Chinese Cubans: A Transnational History* (Chapel Hill, North Carolina: University of North Carolina Press, 2013). p. 22.

4   *Ibid.*, p. 1.

5   *Ibid.*, p. 4.

6   'Passenger Search – The Statue of Liberty and Ellis Island', heritage.statueofliberty.org/passenger-details/czoxMjoiMTAwMjI3MTIwMTg4Ijs=/czo5OiJwYXNz-ZW5nZXIiOw== (accessed 14 April 2024).

7   US Constitution 14th Amendment, constitution.congress.gov/constitution/amendment-14/ (accessed 23 April 2024).

8   'Departure Statement of Wong Kim Ark, 1894', National Archives and Records Administration, www.archives.gov/san-francisco/highlights/wong-kim-ark. Accessed 23 April 2024.

9   'Immigrant Voices: Discover Immigrant Stories from Angel Island', www.immigrant-voices.aiisf.org/737-my-father-was-a-paper-son/. Accessed 14 January 2024.

10 'Chinese Exclusion Delegates' Reports', *The Pomona Progress*, 12 December 1901.

11 Lee, Erika, & Judy Yung, *Angel Island: Immigrant Gateway to America*, p. 4.

12 *Ibid.*, p. 39.

13 *Ibid.*, p. xviii.

14 'U.S. Immigration Station, Angel Island', US National Park Service, US Department of the Interior, www.nps.gov/places/u-s-immigration-station-angel-island.htm. Accessed 23 March 2021.

15 'California State Parks', www.parks.ca.gov/?page_id=1309. Accessed 17 April 2024.

16 Bristol Archives, 30182/53: SS *Annetta* Agreements and Crew Lists, 1909–13.

17 *Ibid.*

18 *Ibid.*

19 *Ibid.*

20 Certified copy of an Entry of Death, No. 9415507-7, CHONG Chip, 3 July 1914. Poplar, London.

21 uslaw.link/citation/stat/38/1164. Accessed 14 January 2024.

22 *Ibid.*

23 'Europe's oldest Chinatown fights for survival', *The Economist*, 31 May 2018, www.economist.com/britain/2018/05/31/europes-oldest-chinatown-fights-for-survival. Accessed 3 June 2018.

Chapter 11

1   *The Six*, directed by Arthur Jones. LP Films, 2021.

2   *Ibid.*

3   *Ibid.*

4   'It Is All Lies', *Hartlepool Northern Daily Mail*, 23 June 1936, p. 8.

5   'On This Day (19 December) WW1 Shipwreckollections', shipwreckedmariners.
     org.uk/shipwreckollections/day-19th-december-ww1-shipwreckollections/.

6   Seed, John, 'Limehouse Blues: Looking for Chinatown in the London Docks,
     1900–40', *History Workshop Journal*, Issue 62, Summer 2006, p. 58–85.

7   'Exit Chinatown', *Leicester Evening Mail*, 15 December 1920, p. 6.

8   Hancox, Dan, 'The secret deportations: how Britain betrayed the Chinese men
     who served the country in war', *The Guardian*, 25 May 2021, www.theguardian.
     com/news/2021/may/25/chinese-merchant-seamen-liverpool-deportations.
     Accessed 17 May 2022.

Chapter 12

1   'LEE COON', *The Galt Daily Reporter*, 2 June 1943, p. 10, col. 5.

2   Bristol Archives, 30182/53: SS *Annetta* Agreements and Crew Lists, 1909–13.

3   Cho, Lily, *Mass Capture: Chinese Head Tax and the Making of Non-Citizens*, p. xii.

4   Green, Bob, *Eavesdroppings*, p. 17.

5   *Ibid.*, p. 18.

6   '1929 Galt Flood', Grand River Conservation Authority, 4 September 2018,
     www.youtube.com/watch?v=uueaGUul9W0

7   Bartholomew, Marjorie, personal interview, 26 November 2018.

8   'Cops Rue the Day Lee Bing Ran Away', *Waterloo Region Record*, 10 June 1938, p. 3.

9   Bartholomew, Marjorie, personal interview, 26 November 2018.

10   Menary, David, *Gordie Howe: A Year in Galt*, p. 20.

Chapter 13

1   National Archives, Kew: BT 165/917.

2   'Claim of Yong Lang', US National Archives, NAID: 6210878, Local ID: B176.
     19 March 1913.

3   Tom Fong, personal interview, 21 November 2018.

4   Fong Wing Sun, Alien Registration File 7556981, 29 June 1956.

5   *Ibid.*

6   *Ibid.*

7   *Ibid.*

8   'It's This Way in America', *Tucson Daily Citizen*, 4 July 1966, p. 30.

9   Tom Fong, personal interview, 21 November 2018.

10   Fong Wing Sun, personal correspondence, 26 November 1979.

Chapter 14

1   Encyclopedia Titanica (2009), 'AN ECHO OF A PAST TRAGEDY' (ref: #10051,
     published 22 April 2009, generated 5 August 2024): www.encyclopedia-titanica.
     org/diary-of-frederick-hamilton-cable-engineer-mackay-bennett.html

2   Bartlett, W.B., *Titanic, 9 Hours to Hell: The Survivors' Story* (Gloucestershire:
     Amberley Publishing, 2010) p. 271.

3   *Ibid.*

4   Encyclopedia Titanica (2009), 'AN ECHO OF A PAST TRAGEDY' (ref: #10051, published 22 April 2009, generated 5 August 2024): www.encyclopedia-titanica. org/diary-of-frederick-hamilton-cable-engineer-mackay-bennett.html
5   Bartlett, Titanic, *9 Hours*, p. 273.
6   *Secrets of the Dead: Titanic's Ghosts* (Episode 103, first aired 2002) www.pbs.org/ wnet/secrets/titanics-ghosts-breaking-news-dna-names-unknown-child/1529/. Accessed 31 July 2024.
7   Encyclopedia Titanica, 2 June 2024, Anon, et al., 'Description of Recovered Bodies (1875)', www.encyclopedia-titanica.org/description-of-recovered-titanic-bodies.html. Accessed 16 June 2024.

Chapter 15

1   www.encyclopedia-titanica.org

Chapter 16

1   Gleicher, David. *The Rescue of the Third Class on the Titanic.*

Chapter 18

1   Tom Fong, 'Chinese passengers', Encyclopedia Titanica, 28 May 2004, www.encyclopedia-titanica.org/community/threads/chinese-passengers.6061/ page-2. Retrieved 13 August 2024.

Chapter 19

1   www.titanicinquiry.org/USInq/AmInq05Lowe04.php

Chapter 20

1   *The Six*, directed by Arthur Jones. LP Films, 2021.

INDEX